THE FREEDOM REVOLUTION

THE FREEDOM REVOLUTION

The New Republican House Majority
Leader Tells Why Big Government
Failed, Why Freedom Works, and How
We Will Rebuild America

Representative Dick Armey

Regnery Publishing, Inc.
Washington, D.C.

Library of Congress Cataloging-in-Publication Data

Armey, Richard K., 1940-
    Freedom revolution : the new Republican house majority leader tells why big government failed, why freedom works, and how we will rebuild America / by Richard K. Armey.
       p. cm.
    ISBN 0-89526-469-2
    1. Republican Party (U.S. : 1854-) 2. United States. Congress—Elections, 1994. 3. United States—Politics and government—1993- 4. United States—Economic policy—1993- 5. United States—Social policy—1993-
I. Title
JK2356.A75   1995   95-9254
320.973'09'049—dc20   CIP

Published in the United States by
Regnery Publishing, Inc.
An Eagle Publishing Company
422 First Street, SE, Suite 300
Washington, DC 20003

Distributed to the trade by
National Book Network
4720-A Boston Way
Lanham, MD 20706

Printed on acid-free paper.
Manufactured in the United States of America

10 9 8 7 6 5 4 3 2 1

Books are available in quantity for promotional or premium use. Write to Director of Special Sales, Regnery Publishing, Inc., 422 First Street, SE, Suite 300, Washington, DC 20003, for information on discounts and terms or call (202) 546-5005.

To Susan, with love.

CONTENTS

PREFACE

In January 1994 I decided it was necessary for someone to write a conservative Republican public policy agenda that could reaffirm the overreaching principles of individual freedom and responsibility. In a world without President Reagan, Republicans seemed to have lost their understanding of that "vision thing." The result was a nation backsliding from the freedom lessons of the eighties into the New Deal–New Frontier–Great Society pretensions of modern-day liberal Democrats. Our world looked dark and scary at the time. Following my father's advice, "if you want something done, do it yourself," I decided to write this book under the working title, "Freedom Works."

While working on the manuscript throughout 1994, most often on a laptop computer on airplanes between campaign stops for House Republican candidates, it became clear that the Freedom

Revolution was once again at hand. On November 8, Republicans won the House majority, the Senate majority, and just about everything else in sight. I felt the same sense of hope and "revolution" I felt in 1980 when Ronald Reagan won the presidency. It soon became clear that this book, which had been intended to foment this new beginning, had been overtaken by events. Instead of fomenting the Freedom Revolution, what was needed was an agenda for these revolutionary times. The Contract with America offered a solid blueprint on which House Republicans could begin, but the Freedom Revolution needs to be extended much further as we enter this new era.

While much of this manuscript was written before the November election, it needed to be completed during our Contract's first 100 days. Thanks to a lot of help and support, I was able to balance the heavy legislative schedule with the attention required to finish this book. For better or worse, this book could not have been written without the extraordinary support of many people.

Chief among those I want to thank is Brian Gunderson, who spent countless hours of his personal time editing this manuscript. Brian was my constant sounding board and advisor as the book developed.

Many thanks are also due to Matthew Scully, who helped shape the manuscript into a finished book.

I would also like to thank Dean Clancy, Peter Davidson, Andy Laperriere, and Ed Hudgens for giving up some evenings and weekends researching some of the chapters. Lee Kessler supplied valuable research. Greg Hamm also provided some fine advice.

The folks at Regnery were very generous and patient in their understanding that I was already trying to manage the revolution while writing about it at the same time.

Needless to say, my role during this time of great change would have been far more difficult without the help and contribution of a very able staff, led by Kerry Knott, who has for years been the key strategist in my organization and who oversaw the Contract, and Ed Gillespie, who has handled press relations for me since I came to Congress (for which he deserves combat pay) and has always been a key policy advisor, along with Gayland Barksdale, Jean Campbell, Tiffany Carper, Horace Cooper, Michele Davis, Martin Fox, Kimberly Frambach, Brenna Hapes, Cindy Herrle, Betsy Hirsch, Shelby Hiser, David Hobbs, Doug Koopman, Leah Levy, Kristin Lewandowski, Kris Mackey, Siobhan McGill, April McKinney, Julie Nichols, Maria Nirschl, John Sampson, Valerie Shank, Pat Shortridge, Raena Smith, Carie Stephens, Virginia Thomas, and Jim Wilkinson.

I also want to thank all House Republican members. Not a day goes by that I don't learn something new from one of our members. The teamwork displayed over the past year and particularly these past one hundred days was tremendous. I want to particularly thank Newt Gingrich, our new Speaker, for his vision and never-ending enthusiasm while leading the Freedom Revolution.

One works with ideas for the sake of those he loves the most. If these ideas have merit, they are dedicated to the ones I love: my parents, Marion and Glenn Armey; my other parents, Ted and Alyne Byrd; my children, Kathy, David, and Scott Armey, and Chip and Scott Oxendine; my daughters-in-law Lori Armey and Christine Oxendine; and my grandchildren yet to be born. Most of all, this work is dedicated to my wife, Susan Darlene Armey, without whom I could not work. I love you honey.

Dick Armey
April 7, 1995

THE FREEDOM REVOLUTION

Introduction

FREEDOM REVOLUTION

Recently, a journalist came to my office to interview me for a book she was writing about the new Republican Congress. Mostly we talked about big events—the upheaval of November 8th, 1994; the great debate over the Contract with America; the grave miscalculations by the Democrats. But I also directed her, as I would any historian, to some of the smaller, nearly forgotten moments that signaled an end to the old regime.

There was, for example, that remarkable day in 1991 when Senate Majority Leader George Mitchell took to the floor in a state of deep moral outrage, as we'd seen him do many times before. This time the issue before us was a bill to require that the Occupational Health and Safety Act, one of a long series of laws Congress had imposed on businesses across America, be applied to Congress. Senator Mitchell, like most Democrats, was dead set

against the idea. "This," said Senator Mitchell, "is the most bla-
tantly, flagrantly, obviously unconstitutional proposal I've seen
since I've been in the Senate." He went on in this vein for a while
and finally directed his eloquence at what he saw as the bill's central flaw—"this phony argument that we ought to be treated like
everybody else."

None of us on the Republican side were as surprised by the sen-
timent as we were by the senator's unguarded expression of it. The
reasoning was familiar around the Capitol by the time I had
arrived in 1985. But there was something different here. The
words were taking on an indignant, haughty edge. Even though
the next year would bring us Bill Clinton, it was right about that
time that I began to sense something big in the air. Liberals, I
knew, always attacked with greatest indignation when they most
feared that the public understood what was going on.

It was Senator Jay Rockefeller III of West Virginia who finally
convinced me a revolution was on the way. "We're going to push
through health care reform," he vowed one day, "regardless of the
views of the American people." As I watched him rush to the
microphone to place this remark "in context," I almost feared for
his party. Leaders loved by their fellow citizens generally do not
talk like this in any context. But the senator had been an ardent
advocate of nationalized health care for years. Now it seemed the
big day was drawing near, and he wasn't about to let a little thing
like public "views" get in the way. One of Armey's Axioms had
been demonstrated yet again—"There's nothing so arrogant as a
self-righteous income redistributor." As the health care debate
moved on, it looked to me as if the Democrats were standing with
feet of clay on sands that had long since shifted in another direction.

THE RULES OF THE GAME

Senator Mitchell could say such a thing only against the backdrop of the three bedrock assumptions that defined Congress in the eyes of Democrats after nearly three generations of one-party rule.

First, the argument that members of Congress should be treated like any other American citizen was phony to them because when you got right down to it, senators and congressmen really were not like everyone else. So enough of this guff about equal treatment. They were law *givers*. To compel their own observance of these laws was an affront and a distraction from their Olympian labors. Senators did not need the rule of law. They were ruled quite adequately by their own moral and ethical superiority. I'm caricaturing their position, but not by much. The touching thing about Senator Mitchell's quote was that, after a relatively brief eleven years on Capitol Hill, he believed it. A typical citizen visiting the Senate gallery that day might well have wondered, how could this have come about? Was that really the majority leader of the United States Senate standing there acting like an aggrieved spokesman for some persecuted minority? Having watched privileged classes all my working life—first tenured professors and now the Washington elite—I was not surprised. Another Armey Axiom: "It is always the most privileged who complain the loudest."

Second, not only were congressional Democrats a special class and therefore exempt from mundane rules and regulations, they were *the* ruling class. As the seasons follow each other at their preordained time, as the Earth revolves on its axis, so Democrats run Congress. They might make mistakes, but none could ever be grave enough to disturb this natural order. God reigns in Heaven, and Democrats reign in the House.

The third assumption explains why. The Democrats thought

they would always run Congress because their party—not without the help of Republicans—had spent the past sixty years constructing a state of public dependency. The folks out there might be restless at times. They might be disillusioned, frustrated, impatient. Troubling signs of this distemper popped up in 1992. Here and there a Wright, Coelho, or St. Germain were picked off, dying for the sins of all congressmen (one to rise again as party co-chairman). But in the end, the old coalition would come through. Whatever doubts the people might have, they would in the end vote for Democrats and like it. Trouble would pass, and all would go on as before.

I remember in October 1993, during a leadership shakeup on the Republican side of the aisle, riding in a car with Richard Gephardt, the Democrat House majority leader. "Dick," he said, "I notice you haven't thrown your hat in for the minority whip race. Why not?"

"Well," I replied, "I really have my eyes on the majority leader spot." He looked at me as if I'd just told him I was angling to be tapped as successor to the Pope—and I'm a Baptist. At the time, Majority Leader Gephardt thought it was a great joke.

Strangely, the nation believed it, too. Before November 8, 1994, your typical political analyst might have put it this way: Yes, people are very frustrated, angry, uneasy. The Perot vote in 1992 indicated just such frustrations with government and thus an eroding loyalty to both parties. Incumbents in general had better watch out. The voters have had it. Had it with profligate federal spending. Had it with the endless array of federal regulations. Had it even with the entitlement programs that account for most of the federal budget.

But—so ran the standard analysis—these same people by and large are the beneficiaries of one or another Democrat-created federal program, subsidy, grant, or tax break. Their congressmen know that. So we in Washington should play along with the populist rhetoric but not get carried away and actually do anything. After all, Democrat rule survived the Reagan years. However conservative the country might be, in congressional elections people can be counted on to "vote local." As I heard it put on the pundit shows maybe a hundred times: Voters may oppose the welfare state in the abstract, "but no one wants to give up *their* benefits."

The trouble with that whole outlook is that it offers a pretty depressing vision of the American people. What all these analysts were really saying was that enough people had been bought off. The most independent people on earth, we were led to believe, had contracted out on the future; grown weary of relying on themselves and just plain quit, leaving more and more of their affairs in the hands of politicians and bureaucrats. And liberals were not alone in suggesting this. I recall one conservative columnist arguing a few years ago that fellow conservatives should snap out of their "taxophobia" and embrace the welfare state. For all the expense in dollars and freedom, he said it represented "an ethic of common provision" with which "conservatism, properly understood" was entirely consistent. (He has since returned to the fold.)

A tone of futility bordering on cynicism marked the whole debate: America had long ago embarked on the road to statism, there was no going back. Along with two-thirds of the federal budget, almost our whole economic future had become "nondiscretionary." The problems were "structural," therefore insoluble, because only Congress could address such problems. Real change would take one of two things: a giant act of resolve from Congress, or else a new Congress altogether. Realistic people should not expect either one. Taking the world as we find it, about the best we could hope for was better Big Government, "reinvented" in a new, more efficient, friendlier incarnation. Democrats counted on an American people who wanted peace and security more than Freedom and personal responsibility.

And then one beautiful fall day in 1994, the people went to the polls and decided to change the world. What Alexander Hamilton used to call the political "lines of force" had shifted, and shifted dramatically. The people who had been overtaxing the voters had, it turned out, seriously underrated them. It was not a good day for the "realists."

BREAKING THE RULES

I decided to write this book for two reasons. One reason is very practical, the other more philosophical. The first reason doesn't need much explanation. America will never again have an opportunity like this one. Ronald Reagan used to talk about our "rendezvous with destiny." But that destiny wasn't fully met on January 20, 1981. This is it right now, and we have his example to guide us. Above all the moment requires clarity: What is it exactly that we aim to accomplish? Which reforms are essential, and which are simply "undoable"? Unhumbled by their recent record, the "realists" are again pressing and pulling and pushing on every side, urging compromise. How do we steer the straight course? How do we stay true to the ideas that got us this far, true to our world-changing mandate? The answer: Follow those who demand Freedom. Ignore the warnings of those who would settle for peace.

Most of the warnings about being too confrontational in advancing our agenda come from the same folks who told us Republicans would never even be the majority. We heard the same voices during the great health care debate of 1993 and 1994. We were told we had better get with the Clinton program—or else! So, not to put too fine a point on it, I don't place much stock in their current advice either. It sounds a little too familiar. Theirs are only survival instincts—they bring a minority-party mindset to a majority-party mandate. Life itself, let alone one congressional term, is too short for a timid response to the challenge. We may at times step on the toes of Democrats and their publicists in the major media. But I don't recall, in my oath of office, swearing not to offend the liberal establishment.

There are other dangers, too. You hear people, even Republicans, talking about the electoral "tidal wave" or "earthquake" of November 8th, 1994, as if our ascension to power were of some mysterious origin. This too has been a theme of the media—the sheer "unpredictability" of the electorate. Here I want to bring the debate back down to earth. Quite simply, we were given our responsibility to pursue very specific objectives. Failure to pursue them with all our ability will bring about a very abrupt turn in the auguries. We'll be tossed out just as readily, and just as deservedly, as the Democrats were in November 1994. In that sense the electorate really is nonpartisan: The people want Big Government reigned in. Whoever proves most able—Democrat, Republican, Independent—will get the job.

I began my involvement in politics when Reagan was elected in 1980. Until then, I believed that no one with Reagan's vision could be elected. After all, look what happened to Barry Goldwater in 1964. But when Reagan won, I became a "born-again freedom fighter." All of a sudden I had fewer reasons to quit than to go on. And I've discovered something wonderful about the American people during these past fifteen years: They are decisive.

Americans give you a little time to prove your worth, in which case they hire you back. If you prove to be a bitter disappointment, you are unceremoniously fired. Reagan set the standard.

Ronald Reagan is loved in America because he personifies America. In a word, he is us. What we learned about politics after Reagan is that when politicians act like us, they get elected. When they act like them (liberals, that is), they get fired. If liberals want to get elected, they have to act like us. President Clinton and the New Democrats managed to sound more like us than George Bush did. But soon after they took office they proved that a New Democrat was a counterfeit conservative looking for work.

We now have a new chance with a Republican majority in Congress. We can be timid and appease the Left. We can have peace. We can be a bitter disappointment. Or we can rise to meet the challenge as true Americans, confront the ruling class elite, fight for freedom, break the old rules of the game, and get rehired. That's what I intend to do.

In short, people want principled leadership. They want to look to Washington and see us doing what we promised to do. Only then—only if we do this, trying our level best against all pressures—will they say in 1996, "Things really are different now. Let the Republicans finish what they started." Whenever the debate turns to how confrontational we are, we're playing the liberal Democrats' game—to ensnare us in the same confusion and inertia that rendered *them* irrelevant. Further into these pages I'll offer a specific program of action, along with a few of my own notions about carrying the Republican Freedom Revolution beyond the Contract with America. I'll try to be clear about when I speak for the Republican majority and when I speak for Dick Armey. But I know I can speak for all of us when I say: This is a serious business, and for the sake of our children and their children, we must see it through.

WE HOLD THESE TRUTHS...

My philosophical reason for writing this book begins with the simple conviction that what happened last November really was, in every sense, a Freedom Revolution—a revolution in the bold sense of scrapping an entrenched, arrogant political order, of tossing out the moneychangers. But even more, a revolution in the humbler, Jeffersonian sense of revolving back to our points of origin. A revolution not so much in power as in faith—the faith of our fathers.

America, unique in the world, began with faith. Philosophically, we were born of humble origins. We had no grand new ideology for remaking mankind as had other revolutions—just one simple principle: all were born equal in the image of their Creator, and thus all were born to Freedom. These were America's first words. They're right there in our country's birth certificate, the Declaration of Independence. From this principle emerged our founding vision of government as the quiet guardian of Freedom. Today it sounds like a civics-lesson platitude (who isn't for freedom?), but in the maelstrom of day-to-day politics we often forget it. One cannot overstate the depth of its place in the hearts of Americans. As our Constitution says, the reason for the political order is to "secure the blessings of liberty for ourselves and our posterity."

One of the saddest facts about our national condition today is that we must pause and reaffirm our understanding of Freedom. Freedom is the ability and responsibility to control one's own destiny. It is not freedom from responsibility; it is acceptance of it; it is a personal, not a social responsibility. It is, as Milton Friedman says, "to be free to choose," not to be free from choice. As my father put it, it means that you must travel on your own hoof if you expect to be your own man. We must understand what we are asking for if we want Freedom. It is no policy for the faint of heart. And understand that when someone says, "Put your life in my hands and I'll make you free," he or she is lying.

Think back on our great historic debates—Jefferson's clash with the central bank, Lincoln debating Douglas, the Depression and the New Deal. These debates were about the greatest of political questions—what it means to be free. Few of us ever have a central role in these debates, but it's a uniquely American experience in which just about every one of us chooses a side, and declares for a true vision of freedom or a false promise.

Freedom was our faith. Lincoln called it our "political religion." Our whole history has been an extended quarrel, punctuated by one Civil War, over its exact meaning. And the debate has always been joined by more than a fair share of charlatans, camouflaging their lust for power in the language of love.

At the heart of this book is a reminder that however complex our modern debates might be—amid all the jargon of programs and flow charts and policy options—the issue remains quite simple: Freedom. If one phrase sums up the returns of November 8, 1994, it is this: dependence was rejected in favor of Freedom.

Liberal analysts have cast the election in terms such as "anger," "resentment," and "volatility." Peter Jennings of ABC scolded Americans for acting like "two-year-olds," evidently an embarrassment to liberal grown-ups like himself. You wonder how he would have described the first blow of the colonial revolution: "childish bostonians destroy tea."

Apparently these pundits had never experienced the discovery of Freedom and the joy it brings. They had never experienced or did not understand an event such as I had with my daughter Kathy some years ago. When Kathy was four years old, I explained to her that she would soon have a new brother and that she would have to be less dependent on Mom and Dad and accept responsibility. Kathy innocently asked, "What are responsibilities?" I explained that she would have to start taking care of herself a bit. She said that she did not want responsibilities and she was going to push them away. I implored her to give it a try. Soon after, she would say to me, "I can do it myself, Daddy." Today she is a healthy, happy, self-sufficient adult because she had what Peter Jennings would have called "a temper tantrum."

But the idea that we throw tantrums and object to things is an old problem for conservatives. As a practical matter, the conservative way of seeing the world tends to be defined in the negative. Liberals keep coming up with their schemes for collective progress, which makes them seem positive and hopeful. In our view these plans are generally hare-brained, which makes us seem negative. But if they did work they would insult the dignity of a free people. Sure, there was a lot of anger among those Americans who voted November 8th. There should have been. People should get a little worked up when their leaders treat them like helpless children. But anger and frustration were secondary to the real point of this deeply idealistic election. Those who write it off as one big tantrum don't display a very high opinion of their fellow Americans.

THE SECULAR PRIESTHOOD

All along, I have believed that faith in government is only a substitute for faith lost in people. The 1994 election wasn't so much a rejection as a recovery. As the metaphysicians would say, our negation of one thing was an affirmation of something greater— an affirmation of Freedom. The voters didn't want government friendlier, they wanted it far away. They weren't demanding more efficiency in government, they were demanding more humility in it. They were telling George Mitchell, Tom Foley, and all the others that, as a matter of fact, members of Congress really are just people, and, like other people, they should have the decency to let their neighbor run his or her own life. That to my mind is a very positive and hopeful development.

In America faith in government began with the New Deal and all its grand theories of government. The New Deal came to us during the Depression when our country was vulnerable. Among its adherents were men and women with the best interests of America at heart. It was embraced when there seemed little else to hold on to. In a sense the New Deal never really ended until November 1994.

Theories of government, after all, matter a lot less than the sort of people who carry out those theories, the people who man the offices and administer the programs and judge the results. And the New Deal brought to Washington a kind of person who bore little resemblance to the average citizen. And I don't mean to be too harsh here. Mostly we're just talking about well-meaning, often highly intelligent people who are caught up in the attitudes of their time.

So who were the people who carried out these theories? The list must begin with all the leftist intellectuals who, on leave from their universities and schools of public policy, and seldom taking the trouble to get elected, have been trekking to Washington for half a century, full of bold new ideas for reordering our lives. Universities, in my experience, have never been a breeding ground for modest people. Other eras, though, had sense enough not to entrust important work to men of theory. When you wanted a secretary of commerce, you hired a successful businessman. When you needed a secretary of labor, you looked for a guy who'd done some laboring in his day and had a callus to show for it. Over at the Interior Department you'd want maybe a farmer or rancher. But our New Deal heritage is different, and you can trace a direct line from it to the Clinton cabinet, most of whom are professional politicians, academics, lawyers, or a strange hybrid of the three.

Next on the list are the ever-present professional activists, all those secular missionaries for whom one or another social "crisis" always promises a job opportunity. Then, to fine-tune all these reforms, there is legion after legion of lawyers. We can thank them for our 6,435 pages of tax regulations and the endless multiplication of laws—what National Review's John O'Sullivan calls modern Washington's "Innumerable Commandments," which replace the ten we used to work with. And then there are those less complicated folks, the precinct politicians who never cared much for theory or higher meanings, but with childlike faith have always held to Harold Ickes's New Deal credo: "Tax, tax. Spend, spend. Elect, elect."

Reasonable people may point to a better side of the New Deal. But I leave it to them to explain how an activist state that began with the Four Freedoms ended in forty volumes of government regulations. It began as a plan to help the American worker. But how is he or she helped today by regulations that force employers to eliminate jobs, or not create new jobs at all, or to back off from starting a new business in the first place? Congressman John Kasich tells a story about a friend of his back in his district who hangs wallpaper.

"So how are things going?" John asked.

"Well," the man said, "I was recently offered a contract to paper twenty new houses."

"That's great," said John. "When do you start?"

"Didn't take it," he said.

"Didn't take it?"

"Hell, no," the man replied. "I'd have to hire a dozen guys to help me, and the taxes and paperwork would be too much of a pain in the rear."

Imagine that one incident, a perfectly rational economic decision, played out daily all across our $7 trillion economy, and you have a sense of the terrible waste of it all. Theories of government aside, this is exactly what you'd expect to happen when the fates of productive citizens are put into the hands of an unproductive managerial elite. The arrogance was there from the start, the arrogance of a secular priesthood. Behind our New Deals and New Frontiers and Great Societies you find, with a difference only in power and nerve, the same sort of person who gave the world its Five-Year Plans and Great Leaps Forward—the Soviet and Chinese counterparts. Both, when they look at their neighbor, see a revenue resource. The more theoretical types share the same level-thy-neighbor impulse, the same self-serving illusion that complexity mandates a centrality of power, and the same amazing knack for redoubling their efforts when the first effort fails.

THE ECONOMICS OF LIBERTY

The saddest part is that we were warned. To leaders before the New Deal, the terms "human liberty" and "limited government" meant roughly the same thing. The words are all familiar. Jefferson: "That government which governs best, governs least"; "Government can do something for the people only in proportion as it can do something to the people." Lincoln: "I go for a government doing for the people that which they cannot do for themselves." Even Woodrow Wilson: "The history of liberty is the history of resistance... a history of the limitation of governmental power." Government's job was neither to favor particular economic interests nor to hinder them, but simply to secure the rights of both in competition. Political and economic freedom, they understood, work toward the same end; neither can survive without the other.

Nor is this the free market idealism of another, less complex era. Ted Forstmann, a New York entrepreneur, put his creed this way in a June 1994 speech: "Take all the endless warnings of our past leaders against unchecked political power, and what we have is the enduring moral case for the free market." Forstmann continues:

> For all its rough edges, one cannot pay the free market a great enough tribute. It is hardly a system to be apologetic

about.... It is rooted in a belief in the ultimate worth of the individual. And, although supremely practical, it functions well fundamentally because of giving, not taking; of investing and producing, not consuming and destroying. Unlike modern government, it does not try to palm itself off as the answer to all human problems.... Unlike the socialist world we have seen dying around us, it does not promise a blueprint for blissful equality and freedom from failure. It promises only freedom, with all the risks that entails, all the endless possibilities for success or failure. It simply acknowledges that God made our individual lives to be meaningful enough without us all being herded into vast collective endeavors.... It declares that our lives are our own to live; our decisions, within reasonable bounds, our own to make; our property our own to use as we think best.

Is this a crass, selfish vision of life? Not to me. To me, it has always seemed a profoundly optimistic vision. Where socialist schemes arise from a deep wariness of people, capitalism regards the ordinary person as a moral actor, flawed yet competent to work out his or her own fate.... It may not be perfect, but the free market is so far the world's only workable vision of men without masters. It understands that life's great dramas are private ones, that goodness and compassion work better as personal virtues than federal mandates. It is a system based on trust of the ordinary person. It is not a license for rapacity: It's a pact of self-discipline, above all on the part of government.

The difference, in other words, between the free market advocate and the liberal is not that one believes in helping his neighbor and one does not. The difference is that one regards it as a commandment to individuals and the other as a function of the IRS. To our forefathers, as Forstmann points out, this was all so basic that in President Wilson's day Americans paid no more than

10 percent of their earnings to all levels of government to sustain it in its minimal role. He goes on: "When the income tax was first proposed in 1909, one senator rose to suggest a constitutional limit of 10 percent. And it's staggering to reflect how this idea was greeted. After further heated debate, the proposal was rejected on the grounds that if a 10 percent maximum were set, the income tax would inevitably rise to that 10 percent level."

But economic hardships came and, little by little, we forgot those warnings. The results, fifty years later, are everywhere around us. When in 1994 the voters finally called for an end to that great social experiment, 40 percent of everything the average American family earned was being spent by politicians and bureaucrats rather than by the family itself. That is more than the ordinary family spends on basic necessities—on food, clothing, and shelter combined. And like so much else that government touches, the dollars grow fruitless and multiply. Where is the money (counting property, sales, local, state, and federal taxes) going? To a public sector larger today than the entire economy of any nation in the world except Japan and the United States itself. To a public sector employing more people today than who work in our manufacturing sector, where things are actually produced. To a federal government now spending 23 percent of our entire gross national product, or about $16,000 per family. You've probably heard this other statistic: All the money the average taxpayer earns from January 1 to May 5 each year goes to the government. Forget the 1994 election results and ask yourself this: would Americans even in the desperation of 1932 have endorsed the New Deal philosophy of government knowing it would lead to this?

Part One
THE WORLD TURNED RIGHT SIDE UP

We have only begun to grasp the meaning of the great events of recent years. We speak of the revolution that brought down communism, the free-market revolution, the computer revolution. But really they are just episodes in the Freedom Revolution, now changing our world forever. At the heart of this drama is Freedom, the simple idea that people should be trusted to spend their own earnings and decide their own futures. The most just and compassionate societies, it turns out, are also the most free.

Chapter 1

WHAT HAPPENED?

What really happened last November 8th? In a certain sense not very much. That election, now dubbed by so many the Republican Revolution, was really the culmination of a struggle that has consumed American politics for more than three decades, and world politics for much of this century. It was simply the latest, but not the last, victory in the Freedom Revolution, a knock down drag out struggle between the forces of bureaucracy (at best) or tyranny (at worst) and free people in free societies. November 8th was a substantial victory, but the truth is we have been winning a whole string of victories lately.

"Men can be made blind to anything," G.K. Chesterton once observed, "so long as it is big enough." Perhaps this explains the failure of most people, including some fellow conservatives, to grasp fully what's going on everywhere around us: the stunning triumph of Freedom as one of the most troubled centuries in history comes to a close.

In the Introduction I spoke of errors that have marked our recent history. But what I really want to convey in this book is a way of seeing the future. To me the really astonishing thing—the point that cries out to be made—is how, despite all its trials the world has joined at last in such breathtaking demands for individual Freedom.

During the era of government expansion, many conservatives spoke with a certain air of tragedy. Our literature is beautiful reading, but mighty depressing. There was Bill Buckley's famous first editorial in the *National Review* in 1955, declaring that conservatives would "stand athwart history, yelling Stop!" A few years ago we heard Allen Bloom in *The Closing of the American Mind* eulogize the passing, more or less, of all things good and noble in American life. You can even find Thomas Paine fearing at the very beginning of our history that America would go the way of Europe, becoming "the fair cause of freedom that rose and fell." But, for me, the literary culmination of this spirit was Whittaker Chambers' advice— that we gather up whatever few "tokens of hope and truth" remained of Western civilization and recall what it once was.

As an author, I don't expect to rank with any of those men. They are truly giants. Buckley in particular, I believe, has shaped this country as few others have. But as the first conservative majority leader of the House of Representatives in at least two generations, maybe I can point up a few ways in which these much more important conservative thinkers got things wrong.

FIFTY YEARS OF FEAR

Like most of us who are not philosophers, I tend to look at history less in the abstract than in terms of my own life experience.

Take, for example, the world as it looked in 1940, the year I was born. Try to see it as my parents and their neighbors in Cando, North Dakota, saw it at the time, think of the problems and prospects America and the world faced.

In 1940 the United States was still in the depths of the Depression and would be until the jolt of converting to a wartime economy. Europe already was at war. Across that continent there was a sprawl of vast armies, booming weapons factories to supply them, and concentration camps just opening. When I was born the news of the day was that Nazi forces had taken France and Holland in under two weeks. Great Britain was beset by raids on its major cities, sirens, and blackouts. And on the minds of all was one question, would the Americans save us?

I doubt my parents would often pause in their workday to ponder the world's future. But when they did, they saw another even worse threat emerging—way off in the distance, the Soviet empire. Stalin and Hitler had shaken hands, throwing leftist intellectuals into turmoil. To the rest of humanity it seemed a natural, though ominous union. Together these dictators seemed ready to make light work of Europe and from there progress to even bigger conquests. Although a second "great betrayal" set them at odds, these two monumentally evil powers were nevertheless loose in the world. It is astounding to recall today that in the forties people as smart as George Orwell were debating not whether state tyranny was good or evil, but whether Socialist tyranny was preferable to Fascist tyranny. Things at the time were that bad.

Now flash forward to 1950, when I was ten years old. Hitler and Mussolini were gone, one a suicide in a battered bunker, the other shot and put on display in a town marketplace. Many brave people had suffered and died to be rid of both. And yet, for all the sacrifice, only five years after we'd fought and won a world war, the best the world could hope for was "containment" of a vicious imperialist power. Soviet liberation forces became armies of occupation, with puppet governments to lend them an air of legitimacy. The Soviet shroud stretched darkly across Eastern Europe. Other countries just barely escaped, such as Greece and Turkey, where the Communists were trying to spread the revolution by going from town to town executing people. Perhaps the most revealing picture from the era is the one of a dying FDR sitting next to Stalin in a lawn chair at Yalta, surrounded by a coterie of bright young aides, including the traitor Alger Hiss, as the West gave over half of Europe to Communist tyranny.

On the other side of the world, China had also fallen to the Communists. Soon America's young men would be in Korea, fighting to contain Communism. Many would die at Pusan as Douglas MacArthur's men were driven back almost to the Sea of Japan. About the same time Soviet scientists, with help from American and British spies—the products of our best universities—were putting final touches on the atomic bomb. This was the world in which Whittaker Chambers could say, with deep resignation, that believers in freedom were simply "on the wrong side of history."

Next, 1960. The Soviets had the hydrogen bomb. Now they had missiles. For the first time since the War of 1812, Americans were vulnerable to attack by foreign forces. Schoolchildren were being taught to "duck and cover" when they saw a nuclear flash. Fathers were bruising their thumbs building backyard bomb shelters. Mothers were storing canned goods and first-aid kits for the inevitable attack. Then with Sputnik the Cold War was well under way, and we were losing. Some of our best minds, surveying the future, agreed that Communist central planners would in time overtake us in producing goods and services. In theory, that's how it would work. They alone had an organized labor force. They alone had unrestricted access to vast material resources. Their system alone seemed to have that drive, that uniformity of purpose the intellectual is always yearning for. When Nikita Khrushchev said, "We will bury you," millions of Americans believed him. Our libraries are full of learned discourses from the era detailing the superiority of a planned economy over our own disorderly way of producing and selling things.

Now it's 1970. Earlier predictions, it turned out, could be disregarded. We were not facing imminent nuclear ruin. There might, after all, be something to deterrence. And probably we would not be buried by the Soviet economic juggernaut, either. But a new wolf was clawing at the door: industrial suicide.

Like most manias, this one is hard to recall now that it's spent itself, but for a while it gave us an entire genre of hysterical literature. The planet was dying! We were killing it! How? Well, mostly by inhabiting it. *There were too many people.* We still hear such doleful predictions from the Left. In the seventies, a few of these doomsayers got the idea of loading up a computer with all known data about population growth, pollution, and natural resources—everything. The computer's prediction: Apocalypse Soon—the destruction of civilization before the end of the twenty-first century. Then there was Professor Paul Erlich and his "population bomb." By 1985, said this prophet, the developing world would become a cesspool of poverty. He even recommended "a powerful government agency" to tax diapers and babycribs so as to discourage new births. And then there was the fashionable economist Robert Heilbroner, another guy you want close by in a national emergency. "If, then, by the question, is there any hope for man?" he wrote in *The Human Prospect*, "we ask whether it is possible to meet the challenges of the future without the payment of a fearful price, the answer must be, 'No, there is no such hope.'"

By 1980, all the fears of fifty years seemed to converge into a general malaise. Americans, once the world's foremost suppliers of oil and gas, were standing in long lines like beggars holding out their hands to a foreign cartel. Our economy seemed spent, with inflation and interest rates in the double digits. Our president's response was to load up Marine One with even more academics and fly them all to Camp David for further discussion of the problem. Meanwhile our embassies were blanketed by mobs, swarming like ants at picnic tables. Flags were burned. Americans abroad feared kidnapping or worse. Red Army tanks rumbled into Kabul, a short trip from our Persian Gulf oil supplies. Sandinista revolutionaries burned churches and shut down newspapers in Nicaragua, winning congressional favor along the way.

These are just snapshots from memory; I don't mean to oversimplify. But they do capture, I think, the general sense Americans and certainly intellectuals had back then of where the world stood. But what actually happened?

THE RIGHT SIDE OF HISTORY

The "human prospect" turned out a lot better than the professors and just about everyone else expected. Most of us cannot look back on all our fears for the world without feeling a little humbled. A lot of things happened that we didn't think could ever happen. Who, in 1980, expected to see over the next ten years the greatest peacetime period of economic growth in history? When the tanks moved into Warsaw in 1981, who envisioned the day when Lech Walesa would be president of Poland, or Vaclav Havel the president of a Czech Republic, or Boris Yeltsin the president of a nation called Russia? Who would ever have imagined Nelson Mandela the president of a relatively peaceful, integrated South Africa? Twenty years ago during its last purge, who would have thought that China would become, however haltingly, a capitalist giant?

As for the swamps and food wars and nuclear winters the environmentalists envisioned for us, as of this morning the sky was still up in its heaven. We still have the usual problems of nature to contend with, but so far, no sign of global conflagration. And, economically, it turns out America and other Western nations were doing quite well all along in comparison to the Socialist world that was in the hands of state planners.

To the same list we might add the arrival of the personal computer, which has revolutionized the way the world works; the explosion of telecommunications; the great wave of automation that has transformed office work as well as factory labor from numbing drudgery to largely creative activity.

The one astounding fact of our time, crying out for a satisfactory explanation, is that everything that so many people feared about the future was wrong. The world of the year 2000 will not be some Soylent Green hothouse, nor will it resemble something out of George Orwell. It will actually be a cleaner, richer, more dynamic world than the world of today. Indeed, considering what we thought might go wrong, the future has never looked this good. Why?

The answer, as we survey all this from the world's only remaining superpower, is of course Freedom. We triumphed over all these challenges because, it happily turns out, Freedom works—works in the sense that societies that are fully free (both economically and politically) tend to become far more powerful than their unfree competitors and far more capable of dealing with even the seemingly most intractable material problems. That is the great and undeniable lesson of the twentieth century.

I believe that a sudden deliverance of this magnitude is bound to cause a truly seismic political shift in this country. The November 1994 election, I think, was only the first tremor of the major quake to come. All the big events in recent years that have marked our great reversal of fortune—the vast economic growth in the 1980s, the collapse of communism, the success of once-basket case Third World economies, even the rise of the personal computer—are causing Americans to look at the world in a whole new way. They are now demanding a radical transfer of power away from bureaucracies of all kinds and back to individuals and families. We are living in a Freedom Revolution.

The two people who, more than any others, personified and illuminated this great lesson of our times were Ronald Reagan and, in his own way, Jimmy Carter. Together, their administrations provided a back-to-back demonstration of the effectiveness of central planning by a government elite versus returning power to the people. You can guess which came out ahead.

Chapter 2

A TALE OF TWO PRESIDENTS

Cultural historians will not point to America in the seventies as a high-water mark of civilization. Walk into a thrift store today and you can still see surviving remnants of the era: leisure suits, those low-buttoned silk shirts John Travolta sported, mood rings, lava lamps, a few Bee-Gees records, and, in the way of political memorabilia, maybe a WIN (Whip Inflation Now) button. In general the decade is for most of us a source of unsettling memories, a period we prefer to pass over quickly in our family albums, memorialized forever by Jimmy Carter as the time of the Great Malaise.

Malaise, however, didn't capture what was going on. I leave it for deeper minds to explain the cultural developments, but the economic condition of the country then is easily understood. To put it simply, in 1979 it made more sense to run out and charge a stereo to your VISA card than to put that money in the bank or invest it in a new enterprise. And that's because America in that year had an inflation rate of 11 percent and a "bracket creep" that sent people into higher and higher tax brackets. Investing under these conditions was futile. Everything was losing value. Figuratively speaking, the entire American economy was walking around in a cheap leisure suit with our government ready to set a match to it.

Inflation

The 13 percent inflation rate in 1980, combined with the 11.3 percent rate the year before, meant that prices had risen 25 percent in only two years.

Interest rates

These were in the double digits, hitting 21.5 percent in 1980. Why is this important? Well, who's going to invest in anything when you must pay such high rates just to take out a loan? Maybe you wanted to buy new equipment for a factory, open a retail outlet, or buy a new home. Profit margins are seldom in double digits, so why bother? The one incentive that makes our economy run—investing now in expectation of a brighter tomorrow—came to seem almost pointless.

Hidden tax increases

If incentive is the "hidden hand" of a free economy, here we had the hand of Big Government working its own inner logic. Inflation, caused by government policies, raises your income. Suddenly you are in a higher tax bracket. You must pay higher taxes, your "fair share," even though the value of your income has actually declined. The next election comes around and, adding insult to injury, the big thinkers behind this charade smile winningly and claim, "We didn't raise taxes."

All of this bred a healthy cynicism about Big Government. But again malaise—meaning you the people have lost confidence in yourselves—was far from the cause. What had happened was that we had quite rightly lost faith in the integrity of our government. We didn't lack faith in ourselves, we lacked the material incentives to act on that faith.

Government's response only made matters worse. President Carter tried six separate anti-inflation policies, a bewildering series of "wars" on inflation. Often these were contradictory. One was called "voluntary wage and price controls." He installed a man—aptly designated our new Inflation Czar—whose job it was to watch how quickly companies raised their prices and then browbeat them into lowering them. "Voluntary" meant if you didn't do what the government was suggesting, of your own accord, the government would have no choice but to impose mandatory wage and price controls. Government, in essence, was commanding the nation to be prosperous again. It was a little like the king in that old fable, who with a wave of the hand ordered the tide not to rise.

Meanwhile, a strategy for economic growth was being carefully prepared by a team of experts. With just the right combination of pressures and incentives, they would solve all our problems. The most memorable inspiration was Carter's $50 tax rebates to every American. "Here's fifty bucks," the government was saying grandly. "Now go out and save the economy." Skeptics at the time said we might as well load up a few Air Force planes with freshly printed money and scatter it to the winds. This was how the best and brightest in Washington were going to turn things around and salvage a multitrillion dollar economy fifty big ones at a time.

To his credit, Jimmy Carter did see the need for a simplified tax system. The system we had, said Carter, was a "disgrace to the human race." As usual, though, the accusation was off the mark. It was not a fallen humanity that had come up with the tax code, but only a few humans, most of whom belonged to his own party. And maybe because he never got more specific, nothing happened. Under Jimmy Carter our taxes got higher and our tax code remained complex.

As chaotic as President Carter's economic ideas were, they were in their own way consistent. For all his folksy moralizing, Jimmy Carter had pretty much accepted the basic premise of his party—that the government can and should manage the economy. The intellectual roots of his undoing could be found in books like *The Affluent Society* by John Kenneth Galbraith, Harvard professor and longtime critic of free enterprise. Galbraith argued that if money were left in private hands—that is, yours—it would be put to self-indulgent use and wasted; to create a proper "social balance," excessive money should be taxed and spent by government decision makers who would, after all, spend it more wisely by spreading it among all people.

Keynesian economic advisors had easily convinced Democrat presidents like Kennedy, Johnson, and Carter that they could "fine-tune" the economy by manipulating taxes and spending. The most important book for the Democrats during Carter's presidency came from MIT's Lester Thurow, who argued in *Zero Sum Society* that America had reached the end of rapid economic growth and that therefore it was imperative that government effect a proper distribution of a fixed economic pie.

These ideas entranced Big Government during the late seventies. As the country slid deeper into its economic morass, Galbraith and others actually proposed tax increases. The thinking—guaranteed to keep Big Government at the center of events—was that ordinary people have a fixed idea of how much money they need to have a good life. Once they have that amount of money, they will stop working hard to earn more. Therefore, higher taxes will force them to work harder to reach that desired level of income. Government controls the carrot and stick. Guess who's the mule?

A more patronizing economic theory is hard to imagine. It's the sort of theory a man dreams up in the comfy office of a lavishly endowed university (there wouldn't be a Harvard but for surplus income). But no matter how wild the theories, the Democrat party under Carter could not, no matter how bad things got, surrender control of the economy. In their terms it would have seemed "irresponsible." Running the economy was what government did. It was said of Jimmy Carter that he personally supervised the log book for staff use of the White House tennis court. Whether it's true or not, the same fastidiousness was apparent in his view of the entire economy: Everything must be carefully supervised lest anyone abuse his own money. Nobody should play without the president and his experts knowing about it. Everything must be carefully monitored.

Take the great "oil shortage," for example. President Carter had come to office after the Arab's oil cartel, OPEC, had sent shock waves throughout the world. It prompted him to announce in 1977, "We could use up all of the proven resources of oil in the entire world by the end of the next decade" (meaning five years ago). We faced, he added, "the moral equivalent of war." And he proposed a Pentagon-size bureaucracy to manage our dwindling supplies. Soon plans sprang up for a massive government program to make synthetic fuel (it never worked); bureaucrats testifying on the Hill demanded the power to regulate blenders and hair dryers; talk was in the air of filling up salt mines with oil for the coming final days. Americans were called upon to turn down their thermostats, and the brilliant lights that bathed our national monuments were dimmed. There was almost a religious aura to the whole affair—as if we were paying for the sin of our society's success.

The truly comical aspect of it all was this: the whole "crisis" the government was trying to solve was itself caused by the government. Throughout the 1970s, Washington had slapped stiff price controls on domestic oil production, with the result that U.S. production dropped from eleven million barrels a day in 1971 to nine million in 1980. These controls, which held the price of oil unnaturally low, not only made it unprofitable to produce oil, they also encouraged industry to use more of it. As the government-induced crisis deepened, gas lines at service stations spread across the nation. It was absurd. Here was the government demanding stern austerity measures from its citizens and increased power for itself, all to meet a crisis of its own making.

TRUSTING THE PEOPLE

So along came Ronald Reagan. And the world would change forever. Yet there was nothing particularly complicated about what Reagan did. The big thinkers departed. No more macroeconomic meddling. No more talk of aggregates this and aggregates that. Above all, no more reliance upon "experts," but instead a reliance on real men and women.

Ronald Reagan, his critics used to say, had a simple, "anecdotal" vision of America. They were right. And it was one of his best traits as a leader. If you showed him a chart with the lines heading down, he saw people—the store owner, the hard-working employee, the parents with higher bills and less income. If these people were failing, something must be wrong. Something was interfering in the natural sequence of work, sacrifice, and attainment.

That simple, gut instinct brought about the greatest peacetime growth any economy had ever seen. For starters, President Reagan cut the top income tax rate from 70 to 28 percent. That top rate is crucial: It's the rate that applies to our last dollar earned—meaning the extra dollars we get by working overtime or making a new investment. Obviously, there's not much incentive to make a new investment if the government's going to seize 70 percent of it.

Next, inflation. Jimmy Carter's explanation of inflation, which rose during his tenure to 13.5 percent, was that it was caused by greedy companies charging more for their products. Therefore they must be supervised by high-minded men like himself. In real life it works a little differently. If a company charges more for its product than people are willing to pay, it will either lower its prices or go out of business. Reagan traced the problem to another source, the government printing presses. Government in its desperation was printing bad money, thereby devaluing good money—that is, money bearing some relation to real production. Reagan understood that inflation was caused by too much money chasing too few goods. For this reason, unlike Big Government Democrats, he ordered the government to stop printing bad money. In the space of about eighteen months, Americans ceased to think of inflation as a mysterious, inescapable affliction of modern life. By 1982 inflation had been cut in half, to 6.2 percent. It would hover around 3 to 4 percent for the rest of his years in office. To this day we have not again seen double-digit inflation.

Then, regulations. President Reagan fired 14.2 percent of the federal regulatory "work" force and reduced the number of regulations (measured in pages in the Federal Register) by 38.7 percent. Just as cutting taxes makes people more free to spend their own money, cutting regulations makes people more free to conduct their own affairs, and in both cases Reagan was led by his understanding that Freedom works.

As for the "oil crisis," in his first official act, Reagan decontrolled the price of oil with a simple stroke of a pen, allowing it to rise to its natural level. Production increased, consumption dropped, and the crisis just went away. By 1985, we were awash in an oil glut, prices dropped again, and to this day we are paying far less for energy than before.

And most crucial, he lowered tax rates so the American people could keep a little more of what they earned from working hard. Reagan's policies liberated the venture capital needed to invest in often risky new enterprises. Venture capital outlays rose by a factor of two hundred; new public share issues on the stock market rose tenfold; small business starts nearly tripled, from an anemic 270,000 in 1978 to 750,000 in 1988.

These are Wall Street terms most of us don't deal with every day. But think of it in terms of people trying to get enough money to start a business and thereby create a living for themselves and jobs for others. In the Carter years, they faced a capital gains tax of between 35 and 49 percent, plus state and local taxes. Add that to inflation, and the government was actually confiscating more than 100 percent of all real gains in the economy. Why bother building a business when on top of all your other costs, the government wants maybe 70 percent of your (in most cases) minimal profit? Most Americans didn't bother.

From 1978 to 1981, the capital gains tax went down to 20 percent, still fairly high but enough to restart the economy. Back in 1977 the venture capital industry raised just $39 million in new venture capital. In 1983, when the Reagan taxes had taken full effect, the industry raised $4.5 billion. "High-yield bonds," the riskier variety, had raised $5.4 billion in 1980. In 1986 the figure was $46 billion. This set off an explosion of entrepreneurial activity.

The essence of Reagan's policies was always the same: trust the American people. Rather than trying to plan, fine-tune, manage, order, or cajole Americans out of the doldrums, he turned the job over to them. He restored an environment in which people could build better lives for themselves—low inflation so they could count on the money they earned being there in the future, and fewer regulations so they could make decisions based on what the economy really needed, rather than on what some bureaucrat in Washington decided it needed.

THE BOOM

We've had many periods of rapid growth since the eighteenth century—but none was sustained for as long or produced as many jobs or as much wealth as did Reagan's during the eighties. Moreover, since ours is the largest economy in the history of the world, this expansion was unique. Consider the statistical evidence.

The entire economy grew by 31 percent in real terms. The same result would have eventuated if the entire economy of West Germany, or two-thirds of Japan's, had been grafted on to ours. And West Germany was easily the most economically successful nation in Europe.

The expansion during the 1980s occurred even as America's population rose by 28 million. Yet per person the gross national product still rose by 18 percent. Living standards are best measured by real median family income. Under Reagan, that income rose from $34,390 to $38,710, meaning that the typical family had 13 percent more money to spend as it saw fit.

All income groups gained. The statisticians break our population into five income groups, called quintiles. During the eighties they gained in average real income as follows:

- Lowest-quintile—up 12.2 percent.
- Second-lowest—up 10.1 percent.
- Middle—up 10.7 percent.
- Second-highest—up 11.6 percent.
- Highest—up 18.8 percent.

You hear it said that middle-class people were making less during the Reagan years. That's simply not true. Ronald Reagan proved, as John Kennedy said, that a rising tide lifts all boats. From 1979 to 1988, 85.8 percent of the folks in the lowest quintile moved into a higher group. Meanwhile, 60 percent of those in the second quintile moved up. About 47 percent who began the eighties at the middle moved into a higher quintile. As for fifth, richest quintile, 35 percent moved *downward*. Among the richest 1 percent of the population, over half moved down. All told, a person in the poorest income group in 1979 was more likely to end the decade in the richest quintile than to remain at the bottom.

The American people created over four million new businesses and 18.6 million new jobs, increasing total employment by 20 percent. This fact alone—a solid, empirical fact—discredits the claim that the middle class and the poor were hurt by Reagan policies. The 1980s were a gigantic job fair to which all Americans were invited. Every class of people, every segment of society, gained from this unprecedented growth.

For instance, almost 23 percent—4.2 million jobs—went to black Americans. By 1989, unemployment had fallen to 5.4 percent, the lowest since 1973 and down from 7.1 percent in 1980. As for the "McJobs" argument—that these were low-paying service jobs offering no future—82 percent of the jobs created in the Reagan years were higher-paying, high-skilled occupations. Service jobs (which shouldn't be disparaged too glibly) accounted for just 12 percent of new employment. And if you were in one of those service jobs, you saw an average 6.8 percent raise in hourly pay.

Interest rates, especially for new home buyers, fell dramatically. New home mortgage rates fell from 14.7 percent in 1982 to 8.07 percent in 1992. The prime rate fell from a peak of 21.5 percent in 1981 to 6.5 percent in 1992.

Our manufacturing productivity—the surest gauge of competitiveness in the world marketplace—grew by 3.4 percent per year. The eighties gave American workers new confidence in their ability to match and surpass the achievements of a foreign work force that, for a while, seemed to be gaining the upper hand.

America resumed its place as the world's leading exporter. The goods we shipped abroad nearly doubled from $213 billion in 1985 to $394 billion by the decade's end, further proof that both the American economy and the American worker were again operating efficiently and competitively.

Investments in new plants and equipment grew 41 percent during the first year of the boom and 27 percent during the first two years, twice as fast as typical recoveries. This creative use of capital was unthinkable under the high Carter interest rates. But with interest rates down and a freer market, corporations and independent investors could spend money to create new enterprises and revitalize established ones.

Manufacturers in particular became leaner and more competitive. The *New York Times* in an unguarded moment described the "almost unbelievable productivity revival" in manufacturing. Our total output rose by 38 percent (in real dollars) between 1981 and 1989—the biggest surge in manufacturing since World War II.

Discount stores altered the face of our entire economy. Think of the growing discount chains we see everywhere today: Circuit City, CompUSA, Best Buy, Price Club, Sam's Membership Warehouses. In the late seventies these were good ideas waiting to happen, but they needed the financial incentives. In most cases the idea was simply to cut out the retailing middleman by inviting the buyer straight to the warehouse. Result: A wider selection of goods at lower prices; therefore more sales, more production, and more jobs. In Japan they still buy things from a small retailer 60 percent of the time; in America it's now only 3 percent of the time. This explains why consumer prices in Japan are, on average, 41 percent higher than in the United States. By inaugurating such innovations, rich people like Sam Walton, founder of WalMart, did indeed get richer in the eighties, because he provided consumers greater choice and lower prices.

These statistics contain nothing less than the complete and utter destruction of the idea that Washington should take away our Freedom in an attempt to manage the national economy. Throughout my career, and particularly when I suffered as the lone conservative in a university economics department during the Carter years, I have never been able to get over the sheer arrogance of Washington politicians who felt they could do that. For decades, they confidently expounded the dictums of Lord Keynes—pump priming this, fine-tuning that, all the while taxing and spending our money. When their theory lay in a giant smoking ruin in the late 1970s, they actually asked for even more power to do even more of the same. When Ronald Reagan took over and returned a measure of economic freedom to the people, instantly the economy took off. That, my friends, is case closed. Freedom works. Central planning does not.

THE FEDERAL TRUST DEFICIT

The Carter era, such as it was, began in New York City at the Democratic National Convention when he vowed to America, "I'll never lie to you." This was an allusion to Watergate, but on a deeper level it was Carter's profession of faith in government. After Watergate, so his catechism went, we "lost our faith in government," "we were lied to." This was a timed disillusion. Our faith needed to be restored, and here, in the candidate from Plains, was just the man to do it.

This always struck me as a shallow interpretation of the times. Watergate consisted of one incident of breaking and entering and one lie. It was bad enough—and showed how arrogant government can become—but hardly the sort of event to rock the central faith of a people in their government. Most people run a little deeper than that. If anything, Watergate provided a theater for endless liberal posturing, and a nice opportunity to undo the results of the previous election—an election in which liberalism had not fared too well.

Long before the media melodrama of Watergate Americans had begun to lose whatever faith they had in Big Government. The people detected not one lying president, but a whole pack of lies. Big Government itself was one giant fraud.

Even so, President Reagan understood that what most bothered average citizens was *not* the sense that they could not trust government—distrusting government is the American way and the bedrock of the Constitution—but the sense that the government doesn't trust the average American.

Indeed, the real crisis arose when we *tried* trusting government and it failed—monumentally. As government grew in arrogance, it declined in moral authority. The paradoxical effect was to make government that much more sure of itself and lay the blame for its failures on us. We didn't give all the planners and politicians enough support, enough money, enough power to carry out their mission. They failed, not because government itself was too incompetent or irresponsible, but because we were too "greedy."

In other words, whatever trust and good faith we did extend to the government was not returned. Ronald Reagan was the first president in fifty years to understand all this, and the people rewarded him with two landslide victories. His success called upon the liberals' deepest analytical reserves: How to explain the Reagan phenomenon?

A DECADE OF GREED?

During the 1980s the standard line went something like this: Well, of course, he has that winning personality. After all he was an actor. People liked him personally, but it was all a veneer covering a Decade of Greed. This tautology—Reagan was popular because Reagan was popular—was their way of dismissing his real achievement, which was to connect with the American people as few presidents have ever done.

What they really meant by the Decade of Greed charge was that we were a Nation of Greed, that people in all economic sectors became greedy at the first opportunity. Ronald Reagan in a sense did nothing but withdraw government influence from people's private economic decisions. They could then make their own choices, choices tending toward material gain. They invested, reinvested, retooled, produced, spent, acquired, invented, sold, competed, and in general tried and succeeded in making more money. Whatever happened in the 1980s, happened not because of one person but because of some 200 million people. Reagan only gave them the opportunity. Reagan was only the occasion for the liberals' resentment toward free enterprise—that is, toward the choices free people tend to make—and their general dissatisfaction with the way the universe operates without government supervision.

When we talk about "trust" and "power," after all, what we are mostly talking about is money. Liberals don't like the sound of that. When they talk about all their solemn pledges and "New Covenants" with the people, they want us to ponder the noble ends and not add up the practical means, like a used car salesman going on and on about the wonders of modern transportation and skirting the exact price of the car. But the practical means are always money—our money. The one VIP you will never see posing in a photo-op with any president is the most indispensable official in government—the director of the IRS. Taxation is the business end of government. It is first and foremost what government does: it takes and distributes the people's money, under threat of force.

Nor should we be in the least ashamed of this down-to-earth outlook. You and I go out every day and earn money. Most need to work pretty hard for it, sometimes doing things we'd rather not be doing. Always when we speak of money, we're talking about labor. When we talk about labor, we're dealing with people's deepest hopes. As government takes more and more of our money—no matter under what high-flown rhetorical banner—it takes away more and more of our hopes.

Under today's tax rates government is saying to the average citizen every January 1: "For the next five months you'll be working for us, for goals we shall determine. Is that clear? After May 5th you may look after your own needs and ambitions, but report back to us next January. Now move along." Even the citizen who happens to share the officially proclaimed goals, let alone the one who disagrees, ought to resent being treated this way. It insults the dignity of free men and women.

I illustrated this difference on the House floor with one of my liberal colleagues—a good friend of mine—when we were considering a giant spending bill. "Dellums," I said to his amazement, "we're exactly the same, you and I. I spend that money like it's my money—and you spend that money like it's my money."

A NEW COUNTRY

Let's look at what exactly free enterprise produced in the 1980s, when in the liberal construction, Ronald Reagan set off this madcap race for material acquisition. Just what was it that made up all those numbers I cited a moment ago?

Computers are now everywhere. Here's how economist George Gilder described what happened: "Software is chiefly a product of individuals working alone or in small teams with minimum capital. Between 1975 and 1985, some 14,000 new software firms rose up in the United States, lifting [our] share of the world software market from under two-thirds to more than three-quarters... created mostly since 1981, the new US software firms transformed the computer from an esoteric technology into a desktop appliance found in 20 percent or more of American homes and ubiquitous in corporate workplaces."

The central planners in the government never would have anticipated this development. Indeed, the very people who invented the first computers in the 1950s and 1960s didn't imagine it. Back then, computers were huge, taking up entire floors of office buildings. If you wanted to use one, you had to take your information to white-frocked computer technicians and then go back to your desk and wait hours, days, or weeks for the results. As the inventors looked to the future, they imagined the machines becoming ever larger, until eventually, one huge computer might serve the computing needs of an entire city.

Free people were wiser than that. Working on their own with no central direction, free Americans discovered a way to greatly miniaturize computers, build them cheaply, and put them into virtually every home, office, or shop floor that wanted or needed one. A couple of decades ago, millions of American office workers slaved away in drudgery, performing routine tasks of filing and typing and categorizing, filling out forms in triplicate.

Today these same people are working hard, but they are working at creative tasks, using their brains and creativity while the little machine on their desk does the rote work for them. Even in factories—indeed especially in factories—a manufacturing worker today generally does not simply turn bolts and hammer in rivets until his mind is numb. He oversees high-tech devices and automated manufacturing processes, using his human ingenuity to solve problems and find an even more efficient way to produce his products.

At the same time, Americans in ever larger numbers were moving away from the often decaying, polluted cities to new and much more pleasant communities on the cities' edge. Again, no government bureaucrats would have predicted this, much less done much to help. Back in the central planning 1970s, mass transit was all the rage, as government departments, environmental activists, and politicians all assumed that the great masses of Americans would continue to live in precisely planned suburbs and pack themselves into the 7:45 each morning to hang on to a ceiling strap on the way to work. But, it turns out, free people, allowed to make their own decisions and given the economic freedom to do so, did not want to do that. Instead, they began living in so-called edge cities, with their workplaces, the all-American shopping mall, and other amenities only a mile or two from their homes. And they continued to drive to work in their own cars.

Then there was the communications explosion. While still hampered by the government, investors pumped billions into telecommunications firms like MCI and Sprint and McGraw. Fax machines and E-mail and cellular telephones became indispensable to millions of us. The cost of long-distance service dropped dramatically. In 1980 nearly every household had to watch whatever the programmers of the big three networks chose to offer. Before the decades' end, 60 percent of households had a VCR and today over half the homes in America have cable.

In sum, thanks in part to the economic expansion of the Decade of Greed, we are living in a different kind of society than before. With the new information age economy now emerging, the labor of most Americans will be more stimulating and creative. They will enjoy a far richer variety of education and entertainment. Millions will work close to their homes and possibly—thanks to modern communications—from their homes. It will be a society, in short, in which individuals have more power over their lives, more choices, and in which they use more of their unique qualities. It will be a society much more appropriate for human beings than the society of the past or present.

This was the Decade of Greed, the period about which one liberal would write: "Wake me up when it's over." What she really meant, I suspect, was wake me up when people are again ready to embrace Big Government, wake me up when liberalism is again relevant, wake me up when it's time for new taxes and regulations. And that's one alarm that will never sound. In the eighties, one man reminded 200 million people what each could do by him- or herself. They rose to their own call, pursued their own ambitions, and began to look to their own responsibilities. The results bear witness not to human greed, but to the infinite superiority of Freedom over any program ever devised by the grasping hand of government.

Chapter 3

HOW TYRANNY PERISHED

Ronald Reagan and Margaret Thatcher's successes and their intransigent defense of Freedom carried forward a worldwide revolution on a much higher plane, involving our entire outlook on the world. All the fears that had darkened our world throughout this century—from totalitarian terror, to miserable poverty and mass famine, to global nuclear war—began to look a lot less likely as the Freedom Revolution took hold.

The rebirth of Freedom in the West apparently so demoralized the totalitarians in the Kremlin that their vast empire of fear collapsed with barely a shot being fired.

THE LAST PAGES OF A BIZARRE CHAPTER

To gauge the speed of this reversal, consider the following. As recently as 1983 a widely respected French philosopher wrote a book that opened with this incredible sentence: "Democracy may, after all, turn out to have been an historical accident, a brief parenthesis that is closing before our eyes."

I remember reading Francois Revel's *How Democracies Perish* with a certain sense of alarm. About the time I arrived in Washington it was the in book in conservative circles. It offered the sweeping vision, the air of finality, so appealing to political types who every day contend with the unresolved. So this was how it was going to work out. So we're all doomed after all. This impulse to know what lies ahead—just to know, even if it's bad news—has accounted for similar political palm reading on the Left, with all their nuclear countdowns and "population bombs" and the like. For a while it looked as if we might succumb to it as well.

Appealing as it was to many, it must rank as one of the most spectacularly wrong prophecies in history. Only five years later, in 1989, the Soviet empire in Europe simply melted away like a bad dream, with an ease and suddenness predicted by no one and astonishing to everyone. With little warning, the workers and writers of Eastern Europe spontaneously rose to throw off the yoke of their oppressors who, to everyone's great surprise, simply turned and fled. It was a leftist's fantasy, except the heroes and villains were reversed. The frightened oppressors were leftists themselves, and the revolutionaries sung not the "Internationale," but their own traditional national anthems. Bourgeois, American-style liberal democracy and capitalism were the subversive creed.

A couple of years later, when the rest of the Soviet empire collapsed, an American army officer visiting the former Soviet Union looked at the shabbiness and poverty of the place and wondered, "This was supposed to be the wave of the future?" Coming from his high-tech country, in which a free teenager could revolutionize the world economy by inventing a small computer in his garage, he could not see how the rigid Soviets could ever hope to compete with us economically. They had actually put mimeograph machines under lock and key.

Much has been made of the role of the United States military build-up in the 1980s causing the communist implosion—and to be sure, it was critical. The great Russian writer Aleksandr Solzhenitsyn himself said, "The Cold War was essentially won when Ronald Reagan embarked on the 'Star Wars' program and the Soviet Union understood that it could not take the next step. Ending the Cold War had nothing to do with Gorbachev's generosity; he was compelled to end it. He had no choice but to disarm." When Ronald Reagan announced the Strategic Defense Initiative program, the hysterically reviled "Star Wars" plan, the Soviets clearly believed that their entire beloved ICBM fleet was about to be rendered obsolete, and they knew that their decrepit Socialist economy could never compete with such exotic new weapons as particle beams and X-ray lasers. In fact, while liberals in the United States scoffed at the feasibility of the plan (one of their many characteristics is a strain of Luddism in which they consistently underestimate the powers of capitalist-produced technology), to the Soviets, Freedom's technology was as mysterious and unattainable as black magic. As far as they were concerned, we could do anything if we only had the will to try—which in Ronald Reagan, we certainly did. Not a happy prospect for a country whose sole claim to superpower status was measured in the number of American civilians it could theoretically incinerate.

But if it was only overwhelming military force outside the empire that frightened the Soviets, that hardly explains why they gave up power within their borders so bloodlessly. The Soviet government, remember, was quite simply the most murderous regime that had ever existed in human history. (One of my projects at the moment, incidentally, is to organize a Washington memorial to the many victims of communism. The new Holo-caust museum is useful in reminding people of the Nazi horrors, but the Nazis never even pretended to be humane, even going so far as to wear death's head insignias. It's just as important, I think, to remind future generations of crimes committed in the name of building paradise on earth.) To give one grisly illustration, Joseph Stalin on average killed roughly two thousand people *each day* of the thirty-one years he reigned. And yet for all this mass murder, Stalin's successors throughout Eastern Europe and the Soviet Union surrendered their power in the end almost without once firing on their rebellious subjects (the few exceptions, which high-light my point, include three weeks of street fighting in Romania, a dozen people shot in Lithuania, and three people killed in the final 1991 Kremlin coup attempt).

The answer lies in the devastating effect of an American pres-ident simply asserting, loudly and self-confidently, the moral and practical virtues of Freedom—something the Soviets had not heard in a very long time. Ronald Reagan simply said what almost all Americans outside the looney Left and the liberal establish-ment believed.

Understand that the Soviets had always been militarily and eco-nomically inferior to us. But they faced a string of U.S. leaders who seemed to treat them as permanent and even legitimate play-ers on the world scene. Henry Kissinger's détente, of course, was based on the idea that the Soviets would be around for a long time and that we must learn to "manage the competition" with them (sort of like Elliot Ness managing his competition with Al Capone). Jimmy Carter was far worse. It's time, he said, for Amer-icans to get over their supposedly "inordinate fear of commu-nism." He had a secretary of state who actually said (months before the Soviets sent 100,000 troops into Afghanistan) that the United States and Soviet Union shared "similar dreams and aspirations" for peace and stability in the world. His spokesman to the world, United Nations Ambassador Andrew Young, said that Soviet proxy troops in Africa were "a force for stability," and if the Soviets had political prisoners, well, so did the United States—tens of thousands of them.

One can hardly fault the Soviets for believing they might outlast the free world after all, when confronted by such supine, visionless American leaders.

But Reagan took a different tack. "I believe that communism is another sad, bizarre chapter in human history," he said in a 1983 address, "whose last pages even now are being written. I believe this because the source of our strength in the quest for human freedom is not material but spiritual. And because it knows no limitation, it must terrify and ultimately triumph over those who would enslave their fellow man."

All this had a powerful effect. As late as 1981, the Communists in Poland had no trouble finding 50,000 Polish policemen to impose martial law and try to extinguish the Solidarity movement. By the time the Socialists reached their terminal crisis ten years later, they apparently could find no one willing to pull the trigger on their countrymen.

Faced with a strong and self-confident America, proclaiming the coming triumph of Freedom and the doom of communism, the Communist regimes died, in Jeanne Kirkpatrick's words, "of a broken heart." With no hope of resisting the seditious ideology of Freedom, they hardly even tried. The Evil Empire went away and with it—for the time being anyway—the threat of nuclear incineration.

RISE OF THE "BASKET CASES"

A good deal of liberal hysteria in the early eighties centered on the fear that we would somehow choke on our own economic success. It was a classic leftist argument: the more prosperous we became, the closer we were to the final breakdown. Every success of the free market was only further proof of impending ruin. In the catch phrase of the day, our economic growth was not "sustainable." The world would run out of natural resources to support its "exploding" population, a crisis supposedly hastened by the developed world's tendency to use far more than its "share" of natural resources, resulting in a Hobbesian horror of mass famine, miserable poverty, and a savage struggle of the poor nations against the rich nations.

As is often the case with these apocalyptic scenarios, there was an element of extortion: Redistribute your wealth or else. One could argue that until quite recently trade with the Third World was a negligible part of our economy. We could not "loot" or "exploit" poor nations even if we had wanted to. Or one could argue that during the previous century the chief Western influence in the Third World came from British Socialists. In India or Africa or the Arab world, chances were the leaders of those countries had learned their economics at some British university under the guidance of a Socialist. Or we could note that some of the world's least developed nations—Pakistan, for instance, or Afghanistan—were never even colonized. But, these rational replies miss the point of the liberals' accusations, which arise less from compassion toward poor nations than hostility for the rich, free-market nations. (The liberal, as columnist Joseph Sobran has observed, doesn't rob Peter in order to pay Paul. He pays Paul in order to rob from Peter.)

At any rate, what's happening right now in the Third World eviscerates the leftist critique. Not only are Third World societies far from starvation and ruin, these once-basket case nations have begun to prosper by embracing Freedom. Korea is now richer than Italy, though that happy nation has in recent years been the fastest growing economy in Europe. Thailand's economy routinely grows by 7 percent a year. In India, the public sector still takes half the country's capital, but tariffs are being drastically reduced; corporate tax rates have been cut to 46 percent (not much higher than our own); state-owned businesses are being sold off; and industrial output is rising at an 8 percent clip.

Even Vietnam began market reforms in 1986 and is expected to double its gross national product in a decade; economic growth in 1992 was 8 percent, industrial population rose by 15 percent, Vietnamese exports rose by 19 percent. Sixteen international airlines now fly into Ho Chi Minh City. Singapore and Japan are building steel plants in that country, while Australian companies are installing a phone system.

China is one of the most surprising stories of all. Back in 1975, the state controlled 97 percent of industrial fixed assets, 86 percent of gross industrial output, conducted 92 percent of retail sales in state stores, and commanded 63 percent of all employees. As a result, Chinese industry declined by an average rate of 2 to 3 percent per year between the early 1950s and the late 1970s.

In the past decade, things began to change dramatically. "Collective" fields were given to families. Households were allowed to sell their "excess production" on the open market, paying no taxes at all. Farmers could own tractors and trucks. And peasants could even hire other peasants as laborers.

The result: From 1979 to 1985 China's agricultural output rose at double the rate of that of 1953 to 1978. Rural per capita incomes doubled. China—where millions had died in famines— became a grain exporter for the first time in its history. In 1978 anywhere from 200 million to 270 million people were living in absolute poverty (that is, starving). In the first six years of reform, the number was reduced to 100 million. From 1979 to 1991 grain consumption for the average Chinese rose 20 percent; seafood consumption doubled; pork consumption more than doubled; egg consumption tripled.

In America veterans of the Great Society still boast of their glorious War on Poverty, which in fact brought millions to ruin or near-ruin. In China we are seeing a real war on poverty—100 million people raised up from the depths in just six years of free market reform. It's one of the most amazing economic achievements of modern times. As the *Economist* put it, "China's performance in the [past] 14 years has brought about one of the biggest improvements in human welfare anywhere at anytime." By the next century, Richard Nixon predicted, we will see China rise to become one of the great capitalist powers. The country has been described as one vast construction site, with cranes dotting the skyline from Manchuria to Hong Kong. And yet from the leftists back home, we hear hardly a word about this phenomenon—one of the biggest economic miracles in our lifetimes. And although the Chinese people still suffer from brutal political oppression, these market reforms will likely lead to greater political freedom for the Chinese people, because capitalism usually goes hand in hand with democracy.

In Latin America, we find a similar although less dramatic story. For years, Latin Americans were looked down upon as less productive. Not only was this insulting, it overlooked the real problem—the quasi-Socialist Peronist economies that severed the connection between work and reward. Today the entire region is becoming more democratic, more capitalist, and richer—and the culture is changing with it.

Chile, under its Socialist president in 1973, was the world's largest recipient of foreign aid. Salvadore Allende, having edged into office in a three-way race, promptly invited Soviet and Cuban "advisors" to Chile to help him manage things. As if on cue, massive strikes followed each of his economic decrees. Under his rule

Chile's gross domestic product shrank 5.6 percent annually; by the end of his rule the government controlled 75 percent of the Chilean economy.

What happened after the coup? Chile launched a rapid series of free-market reforms, reducing the government sector to just 25 percent of the economy (even privatizing the country's social security system). The gross domestic product has risen an average of 7.3 percent per year since 1988. Infant mortality is down, life expectancy is up. In 1986 the reviled coup leader, Augusto Pinochet, announced his intention to return the country back to democratic rule, and in 1989 he did so.

According to Freedom House, as of 1993 seventy-five nations could reasonably be described as free, up from fifty-five nations a decade earlier. Thirty-one percent of humanity lived under repressive regimes, down from 44 percent. One of my favorite economists, Alvin Rabushka, gives us the grand sweep:

> What a difference a decade makes! Statism still dominates [the Third World] but it is on the defensive and is increasingly recognized as the cause of many Third World countries' debt crises. Today the Third World throbs with Capitalism. In Buenos Aires, Calcutta, and Chiang Mai, profitable private companies running smaller buses provide better services than heavily-subsidized government-owned or regulated bus companies. In the Ivory Coast, a private water company provides the most reliable urban water service in sub-Saharan Africa. Private firms do a more cost-effective job in maintaining the national road networks in Argentina and Brazil compared with government departments in previous years. In Bangladesh, the government has privatized wholesale distribution of fertilizer. Governments throughout the world are exploring ways of selling state-owned industries to private ownership, loosening trade restrictions, lowering

trade barriers, emphasizing private sector development, and reducing high marginal rates of taxation that discourage work, saving, and investment.

THE PRICE OF TEA IN CHINA

As for the fear of diminishing resources, a line of liberal reasoning that once dominated analyses of less-developed countries, I once did a study on just this question. There is only one sure way to tell whether resources, like anything else, are becoming more scarce: look at their prices. If they really are becoming more rare, the price will invariably rise to reflect their increasing value. If they are becoming more plentiful, the price will just as surely drop. It's basic economics. Before coming to Congress, I was a college professor and made a living dressing up this sort of common sense as "theory."

Thus we at the Institute for Policy Innovation, a foundation I started, surveyed the world's natural resources, fixing the price of each, especially food. The picture that emerged was as follows:

- Of thirty-eight crucial natural resources examined, thirty-four declined in price between 1980 and 1990, as free-market influences spread. Two had no change in price since 1980. And only two, manganese and zinc, had a higher real price than in 1980.

- Many of the commodities studied had substantial real price reductions. Today, for instance, eleven of these resources—antimony, corn, mercury, oats, platinum, rice, silver, sorghum, soybeans, tin, and tungsten—cost only half what they did in 1980. Others—aluminum, barley, carrots, cement, coal, cotton, glass, lead, milk, oil, rubber, wheat, and wool—each declined in real price by at least 30 percent over the 1980s.

- The biggest gains were in agriculture. On average, food prices declined by more than 40 percent in the 1980s to an all-time low in 1990. Meanwhile, a composite index for mineral prices fell by about 25 percent, energy by 20 percent, and forest products by 15 percent. These prices reflect not only current supplies but also the expectation of supplies in the future. If something is thought to be running low, its price will be high even if supplies today are adequate.

Notice in particular the price of food. In Congress, the Agriculture Committee's chief "problem" is our farmer's ability to grow an unimaginably large surplus of agriculture products, which the government deals with by paying farmers not to farm on almost 60 million acres of perfectly arable land—roughly equal to the entire area of Indiana, Ohio, and half of Illinois. Europeans have the same "problem." In other words, just listening to our inane agriculture debates, it's obvious that if we had to we could probably feed a couple of planet Earths. Moreover, new strains of crops developed by our biotech industry—which leads the world—are increasing productivity all the time.

What of the terrible famines we see from time to time on the nightly news? Like all famines of the modern era, they are truly tragic in the classical sense; they came about through the foolishness or malevolence of man, usually in the name of socialism. The Soviets in the late twenties sent armies out to confiscate all grain produced by the kulaks (successful farmers) in order to sell it abroad for Western cash. About five million people were systematically starved to death. The Soviets did it again in the thirties to kill Ukrainian independence. This time an estimated ten million people starved to death. In 1959 Mao Tse-tung decided he'd have a go at reorganizing Chinese agriculture and in so doing he managed to kill nine million people. In 1975, the Khmer Rouge in Cambodia forced people out of the cities into the countryside to be "reeducated" in agriculture. Half the country was starved or beaten to death. And then there were the famines we watched on television, in Ethiopia in the mid-eighties and in Somalia in 1993. The first was caused by a Socialist government that had criminalized any preparations for a drought as "capitalist hoarding." The second was the work of warlords using food as a weapon in their bids to be the baddest guy in Mogadishu.

What all this means is that the world is not running out of anything important to society—except in Socialist or tyrannical nations. Freedom breeds abundance. And this will remain true even as the world's population grows by hundreds of millions. The population control dogma (which I've always felt amounts to the message, "No room at the inn") is quite simply wrong. There is plenty to go around. The problem is not one of redistributing scarce resources. The problem in the Third World is a scarcity of Freedom. Today nation after nation is grasping the solution—capitalism. When the Chinese government finally came around to a modicum of economic freedom, food production in the most populous country on earth doubled in just ten years. When India, once renowned for the cesspool called Calcutta, did the same, it had similar results.

By the end of the 1980s, individual initiative around the world had triumphed over collective fear. Freedom pointed the way out of all these artificial crises. There would be no nuclear holocaust, no mass famine, no war of rich against poor. Just the opposite: Where people are most free today, resources are most abundant and governments are most stable. Where people are not free, resources grow more scarce and governments more desperate.

Finally, as my last bit of evidence that the world has changed, I should note that finally, by the mid-1990s, even our European friends, the inventors of the welfare state, are themselves getting on board the Freedom train.

The European nations, of course, went far further than we ever did toward setting up maternalistic welfare states and inadvertently extinguishing free enterprise. Thanks largely to government regulations and mandated employee benefits, the average hourly labor cost in Europe is around $27 compared with about $16 in America and Japan. While we gained 20 million jobs in the eighties, in Europe the net increase of jobs was exactly zero. The typical French worker gets five weeks of paid vacation; a Christmas bonus equal to a month's pay; nine months paid leave for new mothers; and a mandatory employer contribution to the family's education, medical, and pension costs. The down side of these benefactions—none of which are realistically tied to how hard or productively a worker works—is a stagnant economy, high and persistent unemployment, and little incentive to further achievement.

This, too, is changing. In Europe at this moment, an estimated $100 billion to $150 billion in government-owned assets will likely be sold to private investors, lowering costs, freeing capital, and creating jobs. As the *Washington Post* put it recently: "After decades of sluggish management in state-owned European industry, they now see privatization as the necessary response to the post-Cold War global economy. World markets demand faster, smarter, more flexible, and more ruthless corporate management."

Around the world, for the past decade, about $338 billion in state-owned enterprises have been sold to private hands—or an estimated 8,500 enterprises. Moscow was the sight of a Rock Concert for Privatization. In Greece, bus drivers rioted when the new government pledged to reverse the country's privatization plans, which would repossess buses that had been sold to drivers and management. In Israel, too, where the Socialist bureaucracy requires a huge portion of Israeli income, reform is in the air. Since 1974 per capita gross national product growth in Israel has averaged about 1 percent per year; the country's chief export is people (20,000 per year) in search of economic opportunity; the country is kept afloat by an infusion of $40 billion over the last ten years in foreign aid. But last year Israel passed a bill to create a free trade zone where foreign investors could operate free of the oppressive taxes and regulations that afflict Israelis. And from Libya comes word that even our old friend Mu'ammar Khadafy is privatizing the camel industry, transferring six thousand state-owned camels to private hands. "A transfer of ownership on this scale," concludes the London *Economist*, is "a global revolution."

Further evidence can be seen in tax rates. Recall that before the Reagan presidency the talk among Western leaders was of "a third way"—a middle ground between the "extremes" of communism and the free market, anything to cure what journalists called "Europessimism" or worse, "Eurosclerosis"—their version of "malaise." Then Reagan came to office and promptly cut America's taxes. Nearly every Western nation followed. It was, as one economist later put it, "a tax cut for the world."

By 1988, Canada had cut taxes from 58 percent to 45 percent; France, from 65 to 57 percent; Denmark, from 73 to 68 percent; Italy, from 65 to 60 percent. Even semi-Socialist Sweden cut taxes: down from around 90 to a maximum of 75 percent.

How Tyrannies Perish

Not only in America but throughout the world starting in the 1980s, Freedom got the upper hand against tyranny. As Big Government in all its mutations declined, Freedom took on a dynamic of its own that has rendered a return of statism not only unlikely, but nearly inconceivable. But if that is true, what changed? Why was Revel wrong? Why didn't democracy perish, and why won't it perish?

"The natural progress of things," observed Jefferson, "is for liberty to yield and government to gain ground." Part of the bold adventure of America was that no democracy before it had ever survived. Over in England, at the very moment of America's birth, one historian, Andrew Tyler Fraser, carried the point still further. "A democracy," he wrote, "cannot exist as a permanent form of government.... [Eventually], the majority always votes for the candidates promising the most benefits from the public treasury, with the result that a democracy always collapses over loose fiscal policy."

He then added this prophecy:

> The world's greatest civilizations have progressed through this sequence: From bondage to spiritual faith; from spiritual faith to great courage; from courage to liberty; from liberty to abundance; from abundance to selfishness; from selfishness to complacency; from complacency to apathy; from apathy to dependence; from dependency back again into bondage.

Our founders took such warnings seriously. The *Federalist Papers* is replete with ancient examples of democracies that rose boldly and fell quickly. We've all heard Benjamin Franklin's reply to the fellow who rushed up to him as he left the Constitutional Convention, asking what kind of government America would have: "A Republic—if you can keep it."

So, to give him his due, Revel had reason enough to strike a cautionary tone about human freedom. It brings its own set of familiar dangers, as people in the newly liberated Eastern Bloc are discovering. Nevertheless, he was wrong in supposing that democracy must inevitably submit to the superior will of totalitarian states.

When people are really free, nothing must happen in one way or the other. Out of hand, I reject any and all brands of determinism, whether it declares that "progress" is absolutely inescapable or that civilization must inevitably unravel. Certainly, large cultural influences are always working in one or the other direction. But always, I believe, our destiny is ours to shape. Individuals— not vague historical forces or those "cycles" modern historians talk about—determine the future.

When our forefathers rebelled against British tyranny, they were not puppets guided by the grand design of history. They took history by the horns and mastered their own fate.

The libraries are full of books by Marxists proving scientifically that no such thing could ever happen. But it wasn't a "force of history" that jumped the gates of a Gdansk shipyard in Poland to set in motion the end of the Communist world. It was a small group of people with a great deal of courage. Theoretically, the state held absolute power. But one day some shipyard workers led by an electrician decided, to hell with the millennium, to hell with "power principles" and "dialectics" of history and all that.

THE "END OF HISTORY"

Maybe the deeper problem is the prophets, with their sweeping predictions of doom, were pessimistic about history because they had low opinions of their fellow men. As profoundly as Revel might have understood freedom, he didn't give the ordinary person sufficient credit for the wisdom and courage to use it—or preserve it. In short, he had an elitist outlook not much different from that of the totalitarian elitists. Where the Marxists saw "the masses," the democratic elitists saw a fickless and self-indulgent rabble that would in the end drag democracy down. Both, I suspect, missed the big point: human beings are not in the background, they are the heart of the whole drama.

The democratic elitists, who, like Francois Revel, cherished democracy but did not believe it could survive, wanted men to be free, but feared they could never be equal to their Freedom. But Freedom is a challenge men rise to. And the very experience of Freedom makes men fit to be free. The free market alone entrusts each one of us with a leading role and calculates that, given the chance, the average person is always a little better than average.

Nevertheless, free societies today do have two advantages our ancestors, or even thinkers as recent as Revel, could not have counted on. To begin with we have all had a vivid lesson in what follows when the state assumes control over private life. What's happened these past eighty years has no parallel in history. For decades, even after the worst of Communist rule was well documented, we had Socialists here and elsewhere insisting the evidence was insufficient. We should not rush to judgment. "True socialism," the refrain went, "has never really been tried." Well, most everyone today agrees the jury has returned a verdict. The historical sentence has been passed. Socialism, in all its guises, if it is ever seen again, will not reappear in our lifetimes or the lifetimes of our great-grandchildren. We now know once and for all that the free market is superior in every way to command economies. And it's not a lesson the world is likely to forget.

The second difference is even more profound. The free market has always had human nature on its side, that basic aspiration we all have to better ourselves, run our own race, rise to our own reveille, and meet our individual goals. But in the past fifteen years Freedom has invented the means for its own lasting survival.

Freedom won the Cold War by out-thinking and out-producing a totalitarian state, which competed for the most part by stealing our secrets, commandeering scientists, and financing the effort with help from slave labor. By the same means we have now created safeguards to personal liberty against further intrusion by our own government. Anyone, asked to list the major changes in the world, can rattle them off: the personal computer, E-mail, the Internet, CNN, the fax machine, and all the other outpourings of the information economy, all driven by the development of the microchip.

None of these new marvels are of any use to the would-be dictator. All these technologies shift control of information from government and other large institutions to individuals. Once it seemed the technology revolution would centralize power, culminating in a nightmarish vision of a single giant computer overseeing all society, on the order of Big Brother. Technology has had just the opposite effect. Recall, for instance, the day when calling the folks from college was a big event. Today, parents and their children can be scattered across the country and still chat whenever they want. I know of a French family with one daughter in Holland, one in Germany, one in Virginia, and a son in Texas. The father went out and bought $250 fax machines for each, and so for the start-up price of $1,000 he keeps his family in almost daily contact. Before too long they'll be hooked up to the Internet gabbing at no transmission cost at all; the Internet by then will permit voice telecommunications at a price far smaller than we pay for long-distance phone service today. And far from "depersonalizing" our working lives, technology allows more mothers and fathers to work at home all or part of the time. In the years to come, fewer and fewer kids will land in day care centers because more parents will be right there at home with them.

Information is power. Power is rippling outward to the people, and technology is drawing them closer together. We are becoming more interdependent and more self-reliant all at once. It is the major social event of the era, and government had little to do with it and will be hard pressed to regulate it or slow it down.

Chapter 4

WHY FREEDOM WORKS

So much of our politics today is a competition over words whose great prize is Freedom. No matter what cause you advocate, you must sell it in the language of Freedom. No aspiring tyrant ever declared, "Follow me and I will enslave you!" They all say, "I will make you free!" Freedom is the universal currency. Even proponents of discredited causes like communism and socialism offer it as an all-excusing defense: their "isms" began as visions to make men free. It was, alas, supposed to work out differently. The most sinister symbol of this was the sign greeting prisoners to Auschwitz: "Work Makes Free."

The same goes for people enslaved by one or another false idol. The addict doesn't take his first pill or drink saying to himself, "I'm having this now in the hope that one day it will make me a miserable, dependent wretch respected by no one." He thinks,

"This will help. This will free me from (fill in the blank)." On the label of every poison man ever concocted for himself is the word "Freedom."

The idealism of a truly free society, it seems to me, lies in the belief that we are all called to do certain work that no one else can do for us. This does not mean every man is out for himself and we are trapped in furious competition for goods like rivals in a state of nature, with minimal government providing a veneer of civility. The most important responsibilities we undertake—marriage, parenthood, vocation—are personal. No one else can shoulder the burden for us, and indeed only in Freedom do we come to realize they are not burdens at all.

MORALITY AND THE MARKET

A few remaining critics still regard the free market as an arena for raw, unbridled self-interest. This charge always leaves me a little bewildered. Yes, capitalism declares that we are free to pursue our own interests. And, yes, often those interests are material. We are partly material beings, so what else can you expect? But that seems to be the only side of the idea that the critics ever see, perhaps reflecting their own narrow view of people.

What these critics don't notice is the humility underlying the idea of individual Freedom. We are not free because we stand at the summit of existence, worshipping nothing beyond our own powers and appetites. We are not free because we have willed it so, because we want and demand Freedom. We have been called to Freedom by God. I think the free market arose from that calling. We feel the stirrings of Freedom in our anger when others presume, under whatever pretext, to give us orders or to divvy up our property. Alone among economic systems, the free market answers the protests of our spirit against wrongful power. It's the only available economic meeting ground of the idealistic and practical worlds, the world of duties and the world of opportunities. Adam Smith could be invoked on this point, or George Gilder, or any number of free-market philosophers, but probably no one has ever quite captured it like Clint Eastwood as the preacher in Pale Rider: "The spirit ain't worth spit without a little sweat now and then."

We are, I believe, beginning to feel for the free market the same reverence we moderns have always had for democracy. There has in the past been something a little grudging in our acceptance of capitalism. We accepted its practical superiority: it worked. It was the source of most everything we have, including the time and luxury to sit back and debate the finer points of public policy. But always, off to the side, scoffers pointed to the crudeness and materialism of it all. But every year, as the free market lifts up more people, produces better technology, creates more cures and conveniences, simplifies our lives, and raises our vision—this old criticism rings more and more hollow. The intellectual "vanguard," it turns out, has been outwitted by the "proletariat." Ordinary people relying on their own powers and their own vision decided to lead a little revolution of their own, proving not only that democracy and capitalism work—they work together.

THE WEALTH OF NATIONS

History bears out these intuitions. Not long ago I came across a newly published set of books on the daily life of people in each different age of recorded history. There was a volume about colonial America, another for Victorian England, and so on. And then there was one covering the entire 3,000-year history of ancient Egypt. Given that we know a fair amount about ancient cultures, how could one book capture daily life over such a long period?

Because, the author explained, very little had really changed from the days of the early pharaohs to, well, the days of the pharaohs five millennia later. The human experience was not primarily of innovation and change but of sameness and continuity. The Indians Columbus met in 1492 were living much as long-forgotten tribes had lived maybe some 20,000 years before.

At the beginning of the Middle Ages, economic growth was hardly even conceived. A medieval knight in chainmail, except for a stirrup and bigger horse, had about the same technology as a Roman legionnaire a thousand years before. Europe was in many ways the least advanced of the world's civilizations. The Arabs at least had hot baths. Northwest Europe was the backwater of the world: cold, dark, impoverished, and savage.

And yet within a century or two, this backwater of civilization erupted into a fit of creativity that continues to this day. When Adam Smith wrote his masterpiece he didn't call it *The Wealth of Nations;* he called it *An Inquiry into the Nature and Causes of the Wealth of Nations.* Why the West grew rich is one of the great questions of history.

Ask any public schoolteacher today why, and he or she will tell the class about Francis Bacon inventing the scientific method or Guttenberg building the printing press, or note that Western Europe had access to the sea and many inland rivers. As a National Education Association member in good standing, the teacher might further inform the class that it all happened because the oppressive dogmatism of Christianity gave way to rational enlightenment. But all this would miss the point. Asia, Africa, and North America all had more natural resources than Europe, and plenty of rivers too. The great discoveries of the Renaissance came after the great economic expansion began and were in fact made possible by it.

Other civilizations were as totalitarian as primitive technology allowed. "What pleases the prince, that is the law," read the old Roman code. But in Europe, under the guidance of Christian notions of equality before God, subjects and citizens developed rights under the law that could not be contravened even by kings. Parliaments formed, compacts were made between rulers and the ruled. A few cities gained their Freedom by contract with the surrounding barons. The accumulation of freedoms, allowing shopkeepers, merchants, and tradesmen to pursue their callings and keep the fruits of their own labor, sparked an economic explosion. Instantly, in historical terms, the West began to grow rich. A flatline across the centuries, economic progress took off exponentially. As the medieval cities became centers of manufacturing, the power of the great feudal nobles declined, as did the attractions of the manor. Having a handful of serfs at your disposal, scratching out a subsistence living, and sleeping on rotten straw, could not compare with the unheard-of riches the cities were producing. As workers were freed, the lock that the nobles enjoyed over the land vanished. Populations and life expectancy increased, living standards rose dramatically, and the world was transformed.

Adam Smith had the correct answer: the West prospered because of Freedom—Freedom in the fullest sense, economic as well as political.

This was truly history's own New Deal. No longer was history the monotonous story of the rise and fall of essentially similar states and empires, it now took on a new direction. Soon, in the bustling cities of our own New England, it reached critical mass, producing what we inaccurately call the Industrial Revolution. Inaccurately, because it was less a distinct era than the outpouring of forces building for three hundred years. All the while, this Freedom-driven change was compounding itself, accelerating, until we reached this century, in which the world changes more in one or two generations than in all the previous generations combined.

Societies ruled from above had enjoyed only the benefit of whatever knowledge and common sense the rulers happened to have. But when ordinary people have the right to make decisions for themselves, their knowledge becomes society's capital. Freedom liberates the intellectual capital squandered by tyranny. Far from being a system based upon self-worship, the free market alone takes account of what each person can learn from others.

MATERIAL GOODS AND MORAL GOODS

We did not just stumble upon Freedom. It was not a happy accident that the West "discovered" the merits of rights over rulers.

Political and economic Freedom were born in the West because long before we had either, we inherited spiritual Freedom. Through no particular merit on our part—nor sheer luck either—we inherited the belief in one God. Monotheism alone—for which we can thank Judaism ultimately—brought to man a personal, loving God.

Recall the words of the Declaration of Independence, this nation's founding document: All men are created equal, all men are endowed by their Creator, all have an equal right to life and liberty and the pursuit of happiness. We sure didn't get these moral ideas from any "state of nature." They are the great legacy of the Judaeo-Christian revelation, the source of true Freedom.

The Enlightenment may have full bragging rights over modern science and math. But without one thing, all our feats of genius would have little meaning and no direction. That one thing was a belief in the moral dignity of each person, our calling to a greater cause than any state could ever command. This is the true Freedom our culture discovered. Its lineage traces back well before the Enlightenment, to what many of us still consider the Light of Lights.

THE MANY WARS AGAINST ECONOMIC FREEDOM

History has played a bitter joke on the modern idolaters of Big Government. Suddenly, they're the reactionaries. What seemed only yesterday the new order of the modern state is today a state of shambles. Anytime the world changes, lots of little worlds are overturned. Ruling classes become irrelevant classes. The orders and directives once so swiftly obeyed are stamped "Return to Sender" by the people or else just laughed off and discarded. The people, it turns out, can do without daily supervision, and they can do without the elite's "help."

The more I read of history, the more I view what is happening in just these terms. In all the major events and upheavals of the past half millennium can be found the twin themes of revolutionaries and reactionaries, of change and stability, of Freedom and power. Our Civil War, the rise of fascism, the turbulence in the Third World, the rise and fall of communism—these were not isolated events. They were part of a response to the only really fundamental change of the last five hundred years, the Freedom Revolution. We are living somewhere within a story too big for us to understand, just as medieval men and women did not walk around aware that they were in the Dark Ages.

I wasn't born in the South, but I did have the good sense to move there, and I can't help admiring the ragged and brave soldiers of the Confederacy. But their cause isn't called the Lost Cause for nothing; they never had a chance. In Sam Houston's words, the Southern war was a rich man's war; the aristocrats who engineered the secession were fighting to preserve a world about to be swamped by the Freedom tide. There was no way an agrarian society based on landed hereditary aristocracy and powered by human bondage could hope to compete with an energetic and creative free society. Read a biography of Abraham Lincoln and you will find him to have been a typical young man of the 1820s pursuing a dozen get-rich-quick schemes, like starting a riverboat service with his friends. That's capitalist Freedom at its best, and it built the country.

In the South, the common man was often derided by counterfeit cavaliers who imagined they were descendants of the European aristocracy. As a tragic consequence, although North and South had been economic equals when the Constitution was signed seventy years earlier, by the 1860s the South had been left far behind. To save their dying way of life, the aristocrats took their people to war. It turned out they could fight like the devil—Stonewall Jackson and Robert E. Lee showed that—but in the end they were defeated by railroads and telegraph lines and, finally, the better equipment of the North.

Next to fall was the old order of Europe. World War I was a complex event, but here too you can see desperation in the traditional monarchies trying to shield themselves from capitalist-led change. The emperor of Austria-Hungary sparked the conflict in a futile attempt to preserve his anachronistic empire. The German monarch continued it at the bidding of the landed gentry of Prussia. The Junkers, threatened by Germany's rising commercial (that is, capitalist) class, as well as by the cheap grain grown by liberated European peasants in free America, believed that a successful foreign war might shore up their position. Even if they had won the war, it wouldn't have worked.

Then, of course, came the really extreme attempts to turn back Freedom. Scholars speak of the Nazi "revolution." It's true that Hitler and his cronies hated the landed gentry of traditional Germany, but only because they themselves were far more reactionary, trying to return Germany to the era of pagan tribes complete with torchlight ceremonies. What the Nazis called "Jewish capitalism" wasn't meant kindly either (they hated both.) Modern science, a product of Freedom, was to them "Jewish science." Even if the Nazis had won the war, their Germany would quickly have become an economic basket case.

Communists were always a peculiar breed. They liked to think of themselves as "scientific Socialists," with their impenetrable dialectics and pretensions of moving to more advanced stages of history. But, beginning with Marx, they, like the Nazis, were unnerved by the tremendous changes that Freedom unleashed. Marx saw the Dickensian slums of early industrial Britain and jumped to the conclusion that those slums would become worse and worse until there was a class war pitting rich against poor. By attacking free markets the Communists made themselves reactionaries, working to destroy the only hope of their "worker's paradise."

In the nations that escaped Communist and Nazi reaction there were no class wars. Freedom produced such great wealth that even the lowliest worker could generally buy the products he produced and lead a far better life than the Communists could ever possibly provide.

The same, finally, is true of all the sorry Third World terrorists who continue to buzz around us. Note that the Castros and Khomeinis, the Saddams and Sukarnos, the Ho Chi Mihns and Kim Il Sungs, who rail against "reactionary imperialist America," also call themselves "president" or "prime minister," set up mock elections for their mock Western-style legislatures, and even wear Western-style military uniforms complete with Western-style fruit salad on their chests. They use all the Western science and technology they can get their hands on. Thus they pay unconscious tribute to what they condemn. Far from offering a coherent alternative to the free market, they merely react against the change Freedom has set in motion, often out of pure envy. What angers them most is that we are the true revolutionaries.

At home, the spectacle of a passing order—with the "progressives" furiously digging in—is different only in degree. The odds for their success do not look good. Theirs is another lost cause, waged without even the dignity of an unselfish faith. The direction of events is evident in the occasional breaking of the ranks, as Big Government types pay rhetorical homage to economic Freedom. We didn't used to hear this. Fifty years ago unionists and New Dealers proudly avowed their Socialist creed. During the Great Society we had "Social Democracy"—meaning "capitalism, but...." Then came the managed-decliners of the Carter era. And finally, after Reagan, we got the vague "New Democrat"—the "I'm not like those other folks the public has come to despise" types. But these were verbal equivocations only, new labels for old reactionary nostrums.

In the end the greatest victory for capitalism will be to do all the good works its ambitious critics have left undone. Equality? The free market has left America so militantly egalitarian that teenagers (and many adults) of all social classes wear workers denims, as if to proclaim that under capitalism no man is presumed better than any other. Environmentalism? The capitalists, especially of the 1980s, will one day be hailed for moving America beyond the old smokestack industries and into the age of the computer, which does not pollute and often frees the worker to work at home. Women's rights? The general affluence created by the free market allowed more women to become educated and choose to enter the work force or to stay at home to raise their own children than all the hysteria of the radical feminists. Fairness? Capitalist economic growth, not the dreary welfare state of the Left, is an ever-wider path leading millions out of poverty.

Having come this far, I can't see us ever going back. But there are some who would like us to.

Part Two

THE ROCKY ROAD
TO FREEDOM

People around the world have seen their faith in Freedom vindicated. Yet Washington was slow to catch the direction of history. Under the Bush and Clinton administrations, government continued to expand its powers, demand more in taxes, and operate by regulatory decree instead of democratic trust.

That era is passing quickly. The most revolutionary document of recent times was a simple pledge to trust the people by reducing the power of government—the Contract with America.

Chapter 5

HOW REPUBLICANS ALMOST BLEW IT

One morning in the summer of 1990 I was sitting in the Roosevelt Room, a few steps from the Oval Office in the West Wing of the White House. President Bush was on the verge of giving in to pressures from Congress. He was going to raise taxes after all. I was there with five or six other backbenchers in the House who were strongly against it.

"Mr. President," I said, "if you raise taxes, you will be a one-term president."

Nothing, it seemed to me, could be more certain. The Democrats had lost the 1988 election because their man, Governor Michael Dukakis, had said he was going to raise taxes. A trained political scientist, Dukakis was for "competence, not ideology." And "competent" people all agreed taxes had to be raised. George Bush had been elected because he was not going to raise taxes. His

eight years under Ronald Reagan, voters were given to understand, had left their mark on Bush. He'd learned a lot from the old
Gipper. Everything else we recall from that campaign—Bush's
visits to flag factories, revolving prison doors, Dukakis bobbling
around in a tank—was secondary to taxes. One was going to raise
them, and the other was not.

It's excruciating to recall the bravado of Bush's tax pledge, repeated over and over. But what happened later, culminating in the 1992
election, can't be fully understood unless we make the effort. Everybody remembers the "Read my lips" bit. But it was worse than that.

"My view," Bush said in October 1987, "is that when I become
president there won't be any tax increases." On June 24, 1988:
"There is a difference as plain as day between [Governor Dukakis
and myself]: tax cuts versus tax hikes. And I am not going to raise
taxes—period." Same day: "I promise I will not raise taxes as a
first or last resort." Then the famous convention address: "The
Congress will push me to raise taxes, and I'll say no, and they'll
push, and I'll say no, and they'll push again, and I'll say to them:
'Read my lips: No new taxes.'"

But surely, he was asked by reporters in October 1988, Bush
could not mean that he would not even consider raising taxes? "I
want this deficit down, but I'll say it one more time. I am not
going to raise your taxes. I am going to hold the line on taxes."
And so on, even after the election. November 21, 1988: "I don't
remember any Republicans or Democrats running on a 'Please
raise my taxes' program." November 22: "The American people,
in voting for me, have said in clear terms that the solution to the
federal budget deficit is not taxes."

Time passed. The summer of 1990 and the Budget Summit
rolled around. In my decade in Washington I don't think I've seen
a more ridiculous sight. All the participants were meeting at
Andrews Air Force Base, just outside the Washington city limits,

in order to escape the terrible pressures of the White House and Congress. They would lock themselves in a room and, in a monastic atmosphere, bring all their courage to bear to cut the deficit.

I doubted at the time that Mr. Bush should have had anything to do with the Andrews melodrama. What was the point? If the Republicans were resolved not to raise taxes, why stage a summit to discuss the matter? Why not just say, "Look, you Democrats can lock yourselves up wherever you want to escape the pressures. For me there's only one pressure—from the voters to whom I promised no new taxes—and I welcome that pressure. By such-and-such a date I am expecting a budget bill from Congress. If that bill includes any new taxes whatsoever, I will reject it and take my case to the American people. Should you still insist on a tax increase, come November 1992 you'll discover what pressure really is."

Historians of the Republican ascendance should note two things. In a sense it began at Andrews. And, in a sense, this summit was a low point in our party's history. No lofty motive could cover up one simple fact: raising taxes was a betrayal. Hearing what was up, I quickly wrote a House Republican Conference Resolution declaring our opposition to the tax deal. My colleagues joined the uprising and the Resolution passed by a two-to-one margin.

THE FIRST AND LAST RESORT

Something else for the historians to ponder is that until nearly the last moment, it was the Democrats in Congress who were most nervous. It was a setup! President Bush would send his representatives, led by Budget Director Richard Darman, to Andrews as a show of good faith. The people would like the bipartisan look of it and the administration would be seen as doing its level best to end the gridlock. The Democrats would insist on new taxes. And then the president would tell them nope, won't do it, can't break that promise to the people. In this dramatic fashion (an eco-nomic version of Reagan at Reykjavik) the talks would break down. The Democrats would have walked right into it. People would say it was all their fault. They were trying to raise our taxes again but Bush wouldn't let them!

This was a case of Democrats giving Republicans credit for thinking like Democrats. It goes back to the old verity that Democrats act so as not to upset liberals, and Republicans act so as not to upset Democrats. A compromise occurs when only Republicans are upset.

So the deal was brokered. True to Samuel Butler's saying that "oaths are but words, and words are but wind," the administration agreed to raise taxes. The Bush–Clinton Era was launched. When Democrats George Mitchell, Tom Foley, and Dick Gephardt told George Bush, "Let's put partisanship aside. We have to govern," Mr. Bush thought they really meant it. When the Grand Com-promise was offered—you raise taxes, we'll cap spending—he doubtless believed it. To refuse their noble offer would have seemed, I suppose, ungentlemanly. For weeks the newspapers had been appealing for compromise. During the campaign Bush had, as Haynes Johnson said, "told the people what they wanted to hear." But now, well, now it was time to govern.

Here's how Walter Mondale put it a few days after Bush caved, in a priceless July 3, 1990, *New York Times* op-ed entitled "The Lip-Reading Slogan Aside, Mr. Bush Deserves Some Applause." In making the famous pledge, he said, George Bush "was not quite leveling with the public." He went on:

> But now George Bush, the president, has begun to learn the difference between campaigning and governing. We should give the president credit for his statement last Tues-day about the need for "tax revenue increases." He had the

courage to change his mind, to acknowledge the truth about our nation's troubled finances, to "think anew," as he admitted.... The president should also be given credit for resisting the tremendous pressure from many of his Republican colleagues to sacrifice our nation's fiscal responsibility to a short-sighted campaign slogan.... In the 1984 campaign I tried to talk honestly about reducing the deficit. My opponent, who read the polls, declared that the deficit would disappear by reducing taxes.

A more complete medley of liberal clichés would be hard to find. Leaving aside the image of Fritz Mondale as official dispenser of credit, note the other liberal verities on display: (1) conservatives merely campaign, Democrats "govern"; (2) "acknowledging the truth" means agreeing with Democrats; (3) "fiscal responsibility" equals raising taxes; (4) "courage" means resisting Republican pressures and caving in to Democrat pressures; (5) a promise, if it's a promise not to raise taxes, is not a promise but only a "shortsighted campaign slogan" to be discarded in the name of "responsibility"; (6) agreeing with voters who want lower taxes is craven poll watching—the true leader serves them best by disregarding their little "temper tantrums"; and (7) being roundly rejected by all but two states is the natural result of "honesty."

I'm not sure anybody, not even Bill Clinton, ever dealt George Bush a worse humiliation than this little pat on the back courtesy of the *New York Times*. A close runner-up was the treatment George Bush got from Democrats immediately after he retreated. A White House press release, it was agreed by the Andrews summiteers, would be issued conceding that "tax revenue increases" were under consideration. The task of writing it fell to a Bush aide. Then the Democrats demanded to have a look at the wording. A copy was hurried over to them for approval. No, said the Democrats, not good enough. The appropriate changes were made and finally, Democrat approval secured, the thing was released. With it went the Bush administration's last scrap of dignity.

The "credit" sure didn't last very long. Within months what had once been extolled as a bold act of statesmanship became Mr. Bush's "troubling record of broken promises." From a purely psychological standpoint, I have often wondered why a man who had been elected president of the United States gave a hang what the *New York Times* or any other paper said about him. Whatever power the media have rests almost entirely on the notion that most voters care what the scribes in a few major cities think. Thus the Bush administration's habit of reading the editorial page before the sports page, like the rest of the world, proved fatal.

Most voters, if they read *Times* editorials at all, couldn't care less what editorial writers think about anything, which is why the media panicked after the 1994 elections. Suddenly these papers and networks were faced with congressional leaders who for the most part were not in the least moved by liberal scoldings and knew that the public wasn't particularly moved either. It also explains the media's resentment of Rush Limbaugh, who has tapped into the public's disgust with liberal pieties. Their big bluff has finally been called. I hope the next Republican presidential nominee remembers this.

In any event, George Bush let the scolding and flattery get to him, and the results were the second-largest tax increase in our history and the undoing of his presidency. By the terms of the Grand Compromise, taxes would be raised by $164 billion. Congress for its part would put a cap on spending. There was one minor problem. The tax increase would be immediate; the spending restraint would come a little farther down the line. Taxes now, restraints someday. The plan was to reduce the deficit by $42 billion the first year and $500 billion over five years.

It worked out a little differently. Federal spending that first year increased by 18 percent. The federal deficit reached $269 billion.

The budget deal also gave us another case study in "soaking the rich," the Democrats' luxury tax on yachts, jewels, private planes, expensive cars, and the like. This would teach those greedy types a thing or two. A friend of mine has a good term for this sort of attitude—the "gang plank mentality." Democrats have wealthy supporters who will always be rich. No change in the tax system is ever really going to alter their status. No Kennedy or Rockefeller will ever be poor. So they don't much care if anyone else gets rich. In fact the fewer new rich, the better. They enjoy the luxury of shouting, "Raise the gang plank!" Financially, they're already aboard.

A Joint Committee on Taxation had estimated the luxury taxes would bring in $1.5 billion. What they didn't take into account was that most people who buy these items are just barely able to afford them. They just might decide not to buy them if a 10 percent tax were added. This in turn would mean that fewer yachts, Cadillacs, and so on would be built. Fewer yachts means fewer workers.

The effect of it all was that 9,400 people were out of a job. The tax virtually decimated America's yacht-building industry. (The postscript: when news of this development reached Majority Leader George Mitchell from his constituents on the Maine coast, he promptly called for a repeal.) At the end of the day, if we factor in the cost to the public in unemployment insurance, this whole fraudulent gesture cost $2.40 for every $1 it brought in. As always, the middle class was left to pay the liberals' tab. It was an almost literal demonstration of Armey's Axiom: When you "soak the rich," it's the middle class that gets drenched.

GEORGE BUSH AND BUZZWORD BLACKMAIL

Many excuses have been offered for President Bush's fateful deal with the Democrats: He was absorbed by foreign affairs. He thought they were dealing in good faith. The bill for the savings and loan bailout made a tax increase unavoidable. His own staff, particularly Dick Darman, did him in. Each defense contains some truth. But none of these excuses is very flattering. We should extend President Bush the courtesy of holding him, and no one else, responsible.

Of all these explanations, the one I find least persuasive is that he was preoccupied with foreign affairs. If anything, a man looking clear-eyed at the world would have noticed that everywhere people were throwing off the burdens of government, not adding them; cutting taxes, not increasing them.

After the Gulf War gave him a 90 percent approval rating and a second mandate for leadership at home, a few people around the president argued that George Bush had been given a unique, unexpected chance to turn his attention with renewed authority to the domestic economy and put the Democrats to rout. Instead he listened once again to Darman, who said, "Let's wait for the State of the Union Address in January." There was "a rhythm" to American politics, he explained, that peaks every year with the State of the Union. A brilliant idea! So they waited for that mysterious "rhythm." Like the man in the parable burying his talents so as not to lose them, they set their mandate aside for four months until the time was right. And then the time was wrong. It was four months too late.

When Ronald Reagan left for California on January 20, 1989, George Bush was left with more assets than any president in history: A thriving economy. A world awakening to new freedoms. Socialist ideas in disgrace. All his generation's labors and sacrifices were coming to fruition. Everywhere Freedom was challenging state tyranny.

At home fresh blood in Congress was ready to carry out Freedom's mandate. Fortune had favored candidate Bush with the perfect embodiment of technocratic liberal arrogance in Dukakis. Seeing liberalism in its death throes, voters turned to George Bush and said, "Finish it off!" Instead, they got a reversal of the Reagan revolution.

Take government regulation. In the 1992 campaign President Bush lashed out at the regulatory zealots who were making life miserable for small businesses across America. But along with the tax increase, the Bush years gave us a staggering array of regulations that businesses new and old are still trying to survive. The situation became so bad and so destructive that it fell to Vice President Quayle to form within his own staff the Council on Competitiveness. The council, run by David McIntosh, was constantly harassed by the environmental fanatics in Congress. (The story has a happy ending: McIntosh went home to Indiana, got elected to Congress, and now chairs the subcommittee that formerly abused him.)

In 1992, for a Joint Economic Committee report, I had my staff look at some specific examples of the effect of regulation on business. We took a few typical small business firms, in industries employing fifty or fewer workers. Altogether, sales from these firms came to $46 billion; total payroll, $9.5 billion. Here are some of the costs these firms had to absorb from new environmental regulations alone:

- A dry cleaning operation with five workers: $62,425
- A farm supply company with fifteen workers: $64,280
- A wood preserving firm with twenty workers: $95,553
- An electroplating firm with twelve employees: $72,423

And these figures assumed that the firms did not respond to these added costs by cutting wages. That meant that all the firms had to increase their profits by that amount just to stay where they were before the regulations were imposed. Some workers must have been laid off.

The Bush administration, in other words, reversed the Reagan legacy to small business. In tens of thousands of companies across the nation, entrepreneurs decided not to invest in new equipment, not to increase their productivity, not to hire new workers. They had to divert the money to meet Washington's demands.

How did the Democrat Congress induce Reagan's successor to abandon Reagan's successes? By a tactic I call "buzzword blackmail." They'd throw bills onto the House floor with names like "the Clean Air Act Amendments" or the "Americans with Disabilities Act" and then dare us to vote against breathing clean air and helping the disabled. The Bush people knew what lay beneath these nice-sounding names. They just didn't have the stomach to explain to a hostile media how in the kinder, gentler era they'd ushered in anyone could possibly be against such measures.

We're seeing the same tactic even as I write: Republicans propose reducing the projected growth in a wide array of federal programs, which is what we were elected to do. And suddenly, the debate is about "starving kids." Never mind that a massive, inefficient, and fraud-ridden federal program costing billions, such as the school lunch program, is not the best way to feed kids. And never mind that states and localities and private institutions are perfectly capable of looking after their own. The trick is always to produce a victim—kids, the homeless, the sick—and set yourself up as their eloquent, impassioned, compassionate government advocate. On almost any given day we can see these scenes played out in wrenching thirty-second spots on the news. "The Republican party," said Democratic National Committee Co-chairman

Don Fowler the other day, "has become a right-wing, mean-spirited party. They're cutting programs for the poor, children, pregnant women, and the elderly."

After a while, the endless accusations and pleadings wear a person down. Conservatives suffer from indictment fatigue, a condition in which to even attempt a rational response seems hopeless.

THE STATE OF PLAY

But this may be a good place to make the effort and look at the precise numbers as they stand six years into the Bush–Clinton era. Scholar Stephen Moore, in his aptly titled study *Government: America's #1 Growth Industry*, notes:

- In the last forty years, every type of federal spending has grown in real dollars, excepting only foreign aid and veterans programs.

- Federal spending consumed 15 percent of our gross national product in 1950, and 24 percent by 1993. That's a sixfold increase in real dollars since 1950, a doubling since 1970, and a 50 percent increase since 1980.

- If this rate of growth is allowed to continue, federal spending alone will consume 27 percent of our gross domestic product by the year 2000. By the year 2010 it will have risen to 32 percent; by 2020, 41 percent.

- Federal entitlement spending—meaning the out-of-control income transfer programs—has doubled roughly every eight years since 1950. Health care spending, welfare programs, and Social Security are five to ten times larger than they were in 1950. The Social Security fund, although designated for Social Security and Medicare, is actually being used to fund everything from farm subsidies to pork barrel projects to the latest artistic inspiration of the National Endowment for the Arts.

- Even if state and local spending remain constant, by 2020 more than half of America's economic output will be controlled by the government.

- In 1990 dollars, the federal budget will reach $1.8 trillion by the year 2000; by 2010 it will exceed $2.5 trillion; and by 2020 the budget will reach $4 trillion.

- Entitlements will reach nearly $1 trillion by 2000; $1.4 trillion by 2010—or just less than the entire federal budget today.

- Real spending on "domestic discretionary programs"— the political spending doled out by the appropriations committees—will double in ten years and quadruple in twenty years, just as it has in the past.

- By 2020 total domestic discretionary spending programs will consume roughly twice the level of gross domestic product they do today.

- Even if federal taxes rise to 25 percent of gross domestic product, the deficit (in 1990 dollars) will rise to over

$300 billion in 2000; $600 billion in 2010; $1.4 trillion in 2020.

- Today, the federal government spends $5,030 for every man, woman, and child in America. The national debt is $13,000 for each child born in America today.

- Viewed from another angle, government spends $24,000 for every single household in America.

And all this, remember, is just federal spending. The outlook for state spending, based on past trends, is not much better. Between 1982 and 1992, state budgets rose by 50 percent, from $300 billion to $450 billion. Some state budgets rose even more. California and Massachusetts hiked their budgets by 65 percent; New Jersey by 80 percent; Arizona, Connecticut, and Florida by 90 percent.

THE ARMEY CURVE

Taken together, these figures seem to me fairly definitive proof that good intentions do not make for Great Societies. They have put us on the wrong side of what I call the Armey Curve (see the chart below). Years ago, an economist named Arthur Laffer developed the Laffer Curve to show how destructive tax policy had become. Granting that governments need tax revenue, Laffer showed that at some point taxes could become so high that they smother the economic activity that creates the tax payments in the first place. If taxes were 100 percent, for example, economic activity would cease and tax revenues would fall to zero.

At another point on the curve is the optimum level of taxes, the rate at which taxes can be levied without becoming counterproductive and reducing revenue. The Laffer Curve made an important point, but there is an even more important point to be considered: Certainly, we need government to keep the peace, prevent anarchy, run the national parks, and maybe do the odd job here and there. To this extent government bears some resemblance to its constitutional description as promoter of the general welfare and securer of the blessings of liberty. But at some point government becomes so large that it begins to smother prosperity and thus erode both our general welfare and our liberty. Here's the Armey Curve:

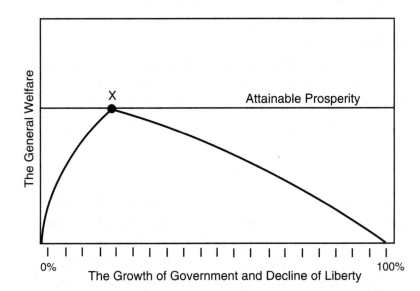

The bottom line—or the horizontal axis—is the growth of government and decline of liberty. The line on the left—the vertical axis—represents our general welfare. There is a ceiling on how well we can do at any point in time. Progress is represented by that ceiling raised through time. Our ability to raise it depends upon the optimal mix of government, savings, investment, and so on. With zero government: no prosperity, since there is chaos, no domestic or foreign security, no system of justice, no contract law. With 100 percent government: no prosperity, since there is no reason to work if the government owns everything. As you can see on the graph, up to a point, the government serves us and our prosperity increases. Past that point, however, government becomes counterproductive and our prosperity drops.

The point "X" shows the optimal mix of contained government and private activity that pushes the ceiling up, allowing maximum progress, constrained only by the limits of scientific and engineering knowledge.

We are now living somewhere far down the slope past point "X." We are looking, I think, at long-term slow growth as our economy lumbers along at a mere 2.5 percent rate by the optimistic projections of the Clinton administration—rather than the 3.2 percent rate we've traditionally enjoyed since World War II. This means that job growth is low and wages remain flat. It means that housing and education costs continue to rise. It means, in short, that the annual $1.5 trillion in "help" to the American people has hurt us almost beyond measure. This is so because American government has not gone to the appropriate place on the Armey Curve—"X"—but has traveled instead along the curve I label "the Great Society Illusion." Big Government liberals see where we are and applaud themselves for what they've done. More perceptive people see where we could have been and regret the difference—the hidden cost of irrational government.

MORAL HAMS

I suspect, though, that if we took Don Fowler from his plush Democratic National Committee office and locked him in a room until he could recite all these numbers from memory, the enormity of the situation still would not dawn on him. He would still go on and on about those mean-spirited Republicans trying to hurt kids and old folks. In the end there's just no avoiding the problem. It's always easier, more tempting, and more emotionally satisfying to play the impassioned defender of the downtrodden no matter how fraudulently. I could leave my office and with a camera crew in tow find within five minutes someone in need. I could say, pointing, "Look, in the very shadow of our nation's Capitol, this person is living in poverty! This is a disgrace! We've got to do something! We must enact a new government program!" It would make for some great footage. My colleagues might think less of me, but then again the reporters and editorial writers would say I'd "grown." You'd read long, admiring profiles tracing my conversion, my courageous break with the "darker" elements of my party. Maybe some liberal congressmen would come to my defense in the *New York Times:* "Campaign Slogans Aside, Mr. Armey Deserves some Applause."

To such temptations the Bush administration gave in, and we owe the whole charade to the tragedy of our colossal, impotent welfare state. We got here because too many politicians couldn't resist being moral hams praised for their boundless compassion. Seldom did we see much compassion extended to the people out there supporting this welfare state. Not only did the welfare state fail miserably in its vaunted "wars" on this or that affliction, it forgot who was paying the bills, who was in charge.

That's the major reason, when Mr. Bush came back a second time, middle America walked away. Few or none of the Reagan reforms were carried on. In 1992 it was harder, not easier, for Americans to start businesses, make their house payments, save for college, and give to their local church and charity. The typical family spent more, not fewer, hours filling out their tax forms. On average they were paying one of every four dollars they earned to

Washington; one and change of every ten dollars to state government. And on top of that, they had to contend with all the other taxes—property, sales, user, capital gains—that government gobbles up. In all, over 40 percent of the average citizen's earnings was claimed by government.

I said earlier that this means we're working till May 5th of each year to support government. Actually it's worse. If, according to Americans for Tax Reform, you estimate the cost of regulations to the economy, you are working for the government until July 10. Here was America, surrounded by nations embracing free-market reforms, with a Republican president, moving back toward Big Government and further away from the blessings of freedom. The voters decided it was time for a change.

FAKE RIGHT, RUN LEFT

The second part of the Bush–Clinton story is easier to tell. As Bush owed his election to the Reagan legacy of accomplishment, so Bill Clinton owes his four years in the White House to the Bush legacy of failure.

A year before Clinton's rise to power, you could have seen what was to come by reading a book called *Frankly Speaking: What's Wrong with the Democratic Party and How to Fix It* by my colleague Barney Frank. To give him his due, Congressman Frank had lots of tactical insights to offer.

Frank's point was essentially this. To "fix" the party, Democrats must discard the competence-over-ideology formula tried last time around. The voters see right through it. They know it's a way of covering the party's image of being a patchwork of subsidy hounds held together only by electoral need. In local elections, Frank continued, people tend to vote down, with a view to getting things from government, which was why Democrats would always control Congress. But in presidential elections people tend to vote up with a view to the larger interests of the country. The trick, then, was to give people a reason to vote up for a Democrat presidential candidate. "Liberals," he explained, "suffer not because of the positions we take but because of voter perceptions that our values are wrong."

The book then gave examples of how to change this perception, my favorite of which was that Democrats at the time were talking about the peace dividend. This was all wrong, only aggravating the impression voters had of Democrats as looters of the public treasury. "To many swing voters, supporters of a peace dividend are part of a movement that has frequently blamed America for many of the ills in the world, has reduced the role of our military, and may be very naive about the need for us to use force in the defense of our legitimate interests."

The solution? Call it instead America's "victory dividend," which carries "an air of triumph," and then look to the public treasury. This would make all concerned, the taxed and the subsidized alike, feel more patriotic about the whole business.

On his own terms, Frank was right. And so along came Bill Clinton with his gift for casting liberal ideas in populist language. Those swing voters, having no loyalty to George Bush, swung. Others caromed off to Perot. The choice was between a seemingly aloof president about whom we knew too much and his engaging opponent about whom we knew next to nothing. Here, it seemed, was a "New Democrat," someone who was finally going to "put people first," all those folks who "work hard and play by the rules." And just to prove it, right after settling into the White House he was going to get to work on that middle-class tax cut.

I can distill the Frank–Clinton strategy to four words: fake right, run left. Promise a middle-class tax cut, then, safely in power, raise taxes by $262 billion. Talk about new solutions to old problems, for instance, and then try nationalizing health care and putting one-seventh of the economy under government control. Fortunately, the move generally works just once.

When the first Clinton budget was about to be announced, a massive tax-and-spend package, I was again invited to the White House. Also in the group were Democratic leaders including Senator Robert Byrd of West Virginia. Byrd, when not extracting vast sums of taxpayer money for make-work projects of epochal dimensions in West Virginia, acts as a sort of unofficial arbiter of congressional manners, and I'm afraid he was very unhappy that day with my behavior. We were going around the table, each member saying his piece, and what I said when my turn came offended the senator's sense of decorum and sobriety. I told Bill Clinton, "Mr. President, if the deal goes through, you will be a one-term president."

Chapter 6

THE BIG GOVERNMENT COALITION

"**A** diverse coalition that included the nation's most influential feminist groups yesterday issued stern warnings to President Clinton and Republicans on Capitol Hill not to tamper with affirmative action, which they argued has benefited women just as much as it has blacks and other minorities..."

This was the lead sentence the other day in a *Washington Post* story—front page, top of the fold. Hardly a week goes by in Washington when you don't read a story just like it. It's one of those fill-in-the-blank news accounts we've all read a thousand times before, with different "diverse coalitions" issuing stern warnings about different programs.

There are a number of popular myths about these diverse coalitions, but perhaps the biggest is their "diversity." Whoever is taking the lead on a particular day—the (self-proclaimed) civil rights groups, the radical feminists, the labor unions, the gay activists, the environmentalists, just to mention a few—two other facts will usually be in evidence.

First, all the other groups are pitching in, even though there is no particular reason for, say, gay rights activists, to take a position on an environmental issue.

Second, whatever demand this "diverse coalition" gets together to support, the net effect would be bigger government.

This "diverse coalition" is in fact the Big Government coalition. The coalition has had a rough time of it lately. But they remain inordinately powerful and a real threat to the Freedom Revolution. In fact, second only to the possibility that Republicans themselves will blow the opportunity they have been given, these groups represent the biggest threat in the Freedom Revolution. Why? Because despite their real weaknesses, particularly a lack of generous popular support, these groups have an incredible ability to persuade not only the press, but the more timid Republicans, that they wield great political power. Once that may have been true. Today it is a myth just waiting to be exposed.

Their persistent power or appearance of power springs from another characteristic they all share. Each of these activist lobbies got its start as the voice of a genuinely popular movement—civil rights, the great labor struggles of the 1920s and 1930s, women's suffrage, and so on. Today they still rely on their origins for both their moral legitimacy and their financial and political resources. Yet each has grown distant from the original aspiration of the people and ideas they once represented, each has continued to favor Big Government solutions to problems that would clearly be better addressed by the programs of Freedom, and each is often an obstruction to the advancement of their rank-and-file supporters or former supporters.

And yet this distancing from their base of support has made the activist groups stronger in a way. Today the various members of the coalition depend not so much on their rank and file for their strength, but on each other and on a cooperative media—and of course on political action committee money. These protest groups have become in many cases the ultimate Washington insiders, every bit as representative of the old order as the hoariest Democrat chairman of a powerful House committee with the power to dole out goodies to well-behaved constituents. Real involvement by their alleged supporters would only cramp their style.

For the balance of this section I want to take a closer look at this strange array of political lobbies permanently encamped in our nation's capital, forever demanding and warning and scolding their fellow citizens.

In the next chapter we will examine chattering class of pundits without whose disproportionate attention these "movements"—with the possible exception of organized labor—would consist of little more than activists on street corners here and there railing or passing out their leaflets and manifestos.

THE NOISY ESTATE

Like house guests whose departure is always "tomorrow," the arrival of these groups to American politics seemed innocent enough. They arose to right one particular set of injustices or perceived injuries. Once these goals were accomplished, one assumed, that would be that. The activists and lawyers and public interest advocates would go home, satisfied with a job well done.

Instead, America has spent the past thirty years trying to sort through these groups' various and varying agendas, meeting those demands that seemed reasonable. On the books are thousands of statutes proving our good intentions. We could cite item upon item in the federal budget designed and funded just for them. But somehow the activists have all remained on duty. With each attempt to please them, their agendas only lengthen. Nothing we do, no amount we spend, is ever enough.

The saddest example is the civil rights movement, which is still trading on the reputation of noble leaders and causes long since triumphant. It has passed from the ideals of the 1964 Civil Rights Act—a color-blind society in which all are treated equally—to a debasing system of patronage and quotas, from segregation to integration and back to segregation. The sole difference is that this time the segregation, "affirmative action," is overseen in a more orderly fashion by bureaucrats with charts instead of sheriffs with bullhorns.

The American people in general, black and white, instinctively dislike the idea of quotas or any form of government preference by racial makeup, seeing it as an affront to their dignity as individuals. The Big Government coalition senses this, yet cannot give up quotas because to do so would mean surrendering political power. Even to raise the subject, suggest liberals such as Representative Charles Schumer, reveals the "ugly" and "racist" side of our people. This is the familiar sound of a passing order, with echoes of a governor standing on the steps of an Alabama schoolhouse. They might as well just say, quotas now, quotas tomorrow, quotas forever!

The other political lobbies trade, in turn, on the reputation of the civil rights movement, freely borrowing its words, imagery, and, for media events, the always-available Jesse Jackson. How, for example, do the radical feminists still get women classified as a voiceless, put-upon "minority"? Women today form the majority of graduate school students, law school students, and new owners of small businesses. Many who are feeling hardship do not view the federal government as their friend. Many, if they were consulted by the activists who presume to speak for them, would complain about the taxes and regulations that make it harder for them to find good jobs or the social policies that have wrecked their local schools. About the last thing on the minds of American women, I would guess, is the need for stricter quotas—quotas that assume they can't compete on their own in the job market.

Then there's abortion, where again women are represented by strident feminists without a whole lot of consultation from them. Take for example the National Organization for Women—NOW. We hear a lot from NOW. Any time abortion comes up for debate, the reporters reach for their rolodex and call NOW for comment. The TV reporters beat a well-worn path to NOW's Washington office so we can hear "a woman's perspective" on the issue. The clip is then usually paired with an interview with a white male, preferably an angry and uncomfortable-looking Southern white male. But if you wade through any large pro-life rally the first thing that strikes you are the vast number of women, young and old. The polls support this observation. The pro-life movement is composed largely of women—at the beginning it was composed mostly of Catholic Democrats, ex-Democrats, and the sons and daughters of Democrats. Further evidence can be seen in the new Congress: eleven new women were elected to the House, of whom six are pro-life. And, where NOW has 250,000 members, the conservative Concerned Women for America has 600,000.

All societies in all ages have had abortions, regarding it as a tragedy to be avoided. I cannot really claim to know how Americans or my own party will resolve the question. But one feature of the debate is truly amazing. Who could have imagined that the civil rights banner—a cause that widened our vision of humanity, defended the powerless, called upon our humane instincts—would one day be unfurled over the abortion mill? Until fifteen years ago the Reverend Jackson was eloquently pro-life (as were

Al Gore and many other Democrat leaders). But time passed, the radical feminists gained political power, Jackson decided he'd run for president, and suddenly he had a change of mind. At the 1992 convention we heard him liken Vice President Dan Quayle to Herod for holding exactly the same pro-life views Jackson once held himself. (But Herod, mind you, was the one who *killed* little babies!)

Here is how these various coalitions give the appearance of being "diverse." When NOW or the National Abortion Rights Action League (NARAL) wants to hold a press conference, or publish a public letter of protest, or schedule a demonstration, they pick up the phone and call their friends at, say, the National Education Association (NEA). To most of us abortion would not seem highly relevant to education, but having the NEA with you lends the appearance of numbers, of grass-roots strength. So the NEA steps forward and says, "We public school teachers, two million strong, join the women of NOW in warning Congress not to do such and such!" Then it comes time for the NEA to have its press conference. Say the issue is school choice. So they call NOW and NARAL, who are delighted at the chance to come before the cameras again. We then get a *Washington Post* story declaring that a coalition of women from across America issued stern warnings yesterday not to pass any legislation giving parents the right of choice in public schools, when, in fact, it was only a coalition of fellow activists from across the street. Does anyone really imagine that most women oppose having the freedom to choose the best school for their own kids? But that, in the wonderful way Washington works, is the impression left.

Often the coalitions border on the comical, as when you see big labor types avowing the devotion of their rank-and-file construction workers back home for gay rights. Or when you see NARAL, in its concern to make America more livable, coming to the defense of environmental regulation; while environmentalists, in their reverence for all things great and small, return the favor with support for abortion on demand. And every now and then, the groups will come together in resounding support for the big issues in which all have a stake—fighting against term limits and the Balanced Budget Amendment, and for government-run health care and affirmative action.

SHORING UP THE BASE

Every political party is to some extent a coalition, but I am glad these are not the components of my party. It's enough to make you pine for the days of the New Deal, when at least there was a little self-restraint, a little shame, some semblance of principle. At the last Democratic National Convention there were some four hundred members of the NEA attending as delegates—the largest single bloc. Watching the event you had the impression that all these activist groups had decided to rent an arena to meet and discuss their grievances, while a few ordinary citizens wandered around looking for each other.

Historians seem to agree that the problem began in 1972. In that election the great achievement of the "coalition" was to band together and, during the McGovern campaign, hijack the Democrat party. From that day to this, any Democrat with any hope of becoming president has had to meet the demands of these fractious interest groups.

Who can forget the sight of presidential hopeful John Glenn, the man who braved the terrors of our first orbital space flight, strutting his ideological credentials to a 1984 NOW convention: "I am a feminist, too!" And the situation has only deteriorated in the decade since. To get the radical feminists' support, a candidate must renounce any and all pro-life statements or votes he or she might ever have made. (Presumably any pro-life thoughts he or she might also have had; the Big Tent is only for those narrow-minded Republicans.) Then to avoid accusations of homophobia or violent outbursts from protesters in the audience, the candidate must discreetly flash his gay rights credentials. If he happens by New York City on St. Pat's day and joins in the parade from which that great mass of "gay and lesbian Irish Catholic Americans" are excluded—well, he'd better have a good explanation.

To lure the environmentalists, meanwhile, the candidate better not be too sympathetic to all those greedy businessmen and property owners. And to earn the imprimatur of the NEA, he'd better lie low in the debate about standardized tests for teachers or the disgraceful state of public education. He'd be wise, too, not to support laws against union violence and in general to show he is a good union man. Affirmative action? Avoid the subject as much as possible, preferably with ominous talk of "dividing our people."

Nor is this just my read of the Democrat party. By and large these are the folks Barney Frank, in his primer on presidential campaign strategy, was urging the party to hide from the Reagan Democrats until the day after the first Tuesday in November. They would all be taken care of, if only they could just sit still and keep quiet. Fixing the party consisted of wiring thousands of jaws shut until after the election, when the payoffs with federal tax dollars could be arranged.

Applying this strategy as much as possible (recall, for example, his orchestrated rift with the Reverend Jackson over the noxious views of Sister Souljah), candidate Clinton pulled it off. Apparently the strategy was skillfully applied even within his own household. And so right square in the middle of a revolution against Big Government, to no one's amazement more than its own, the coalition found itself running the White House.

This will explain a few things that might perplex future generations. They'll wonder, for example, about the sudden disappearance of the big tax cut the middle class had been promised in 1992. This has amazed even me. Looking at it from the crassest political angle, here was a New Democrat with a winning issue. Putting people first, he was going to cut their taxes. The pledge helped make him president and, if carried out, might have made him a popular president. All the more so given Mr. Bush's failure on the same score. Here was a chance to put the Democrats on the right side of the tax-cutting revolution. So why not go ahead and cut taxes?

For the simple reason that to cut taxes costs too much. To "give that money away," in the jargon of Big Government, would have infuriated the activists and party insiders who thrive on government largesse and view the power of Big Government as their personal tool for remaking society to suit their own bizarre ideological preferences. The promised tax cut was just a bromide thrown out during the campaign to soothe folks like you and me in both parties who think we pay too much in taxes. The same logic applies to the Democrats' opposition to the Balanced Budget Amendment. Popular (perhaps inevitable) as it is, it would be "irresponsible." By "irresponsible" what they mean is that it would spell the end of their party as they know it—the grand dispenser of federal favor. This isn't to say that many are not perfectly sincere in calling it irresponsible. In some cases, their visions of nation and party, of taxpayer and taxer, are so thoroughly merged that they no longer distinguish the interests of the two.

CLINTON CARE AND THE COALITION

Above all, the historians will wonder how in the months before the Freedom Revolution of 1994, the Democrat party sought to nationalize America's entire health care industry. Why choose such an unpropitious moment to try putting a seventh of the economy under government control? It was not the sort of plan anyone expected when they elected a New Democrat who preached in 1992 about learning from the mistakes of the New Deal and the Great Society. And why were all these disparate interest groups suddenly drawn together around health care reform with the fervor of revivalists at an altar call?

Well, let's think. What did each stand to gain? Let's begin with organized labor.

From bank accounts stuffed with compulsory dues, trade unions poured millions into television advertising heralding the merits of mandatory health care. They liked it for lots of reasons, not least of which was the devastating effect the bill would have on small businesses across America. I know it sounds cynical, but, well, there it is. These small enterprises don't fit in the unionized vision of America, because their workers tend to be inherently difficult to organize. The fewer of these small enterprises the better for those who run unions.

For their part, civil rights leaders liked the health care bill for its mandatory quotas on medical school admission. This was truly audacious. Most of us when we go to see a doctor don't care what color he or she is. We just want the best doctor, and assume medical schools and hospitals operate by the same principle. If race is irrelevant anywhere, it's irrelevant in the operating room. The health care bill would have introduced racial quotas even to medicine, where individual merit is a matter of life and death.

Over at NARAL and Planned Parenthood still higher hopes were riding on the health care bill and its provision to mandate abortion "services" at every hospital in the land. It would also, through federal funding, have required every taxpayer to pay for every abortion.

This was a particularly bold gambit, and its failure was quite possibly a turning point in the abortion debate. At the moment, abortion is unavailable in fully 85 percent of the counties of America; if you take rural counties only, it's closer to 95 percent. A recent Columbia University study found a sharp decline in the number of medical schools offering abortion training; a still smaller percentage of doctors are willing to teach it or serve as "mentors" to aspiring abortionists.

This is why in the medical profession they speak of a phenomenon called "the greying of the abortion provider," why the few who will do abortions have to ride circuit, traveling from town to town like frontier judges in another era. And it's why all forty-four doctors at U.S. military installations in Europe announced two years ago they would not do abortions, to the outrage of my colleague Pat Schroeder, then chairwoman of a key armed services subcommittee. Only a few doctors and hospitals want anything to do with the practice, just as few Americans want a clinic in their neighborhood. Years of debating and berating had done little to change the minds and hearts of doctors. With the health care bill, the government was going to change their minds and hearts for them.

Then there were the homosexual activists, who would have gotten rules requiring that any "household" be treated the same as a married couple with children for insurance purposes.

As for the federal employees unions—well, they seemed almost overcome by it all. For them, the health care bill looked like a New Jerusalem on the horizon, a wondrous vision of eighty new bureaucracies and forty new programs. Already, as I noted earlier, government employs more people than work in the entire manufacturing sector of our economy. And now—just think of it! Hundreds and hundreds of thousands more jobs, more patronage, more offices and cubicles and benefits! It was almost too good to be true.

Just for posterity's sake I'm going to insert here the chart mapping how this elaborate system would have operated. It's a relic that ought to be preserved somewhere.

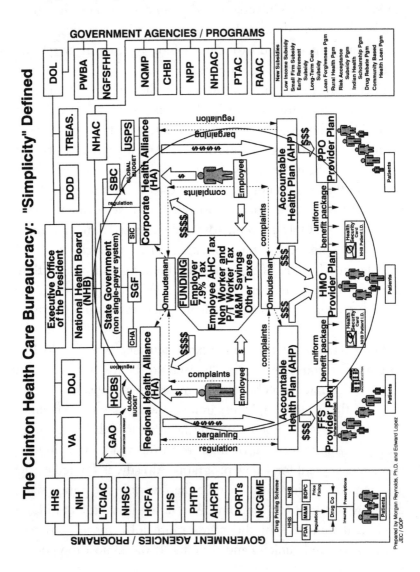

The Clinton Health Care Bureaucracy: "Simplicity" Defined

You and I and most everybody else would look at this amazing scheme with dread. That's because we picture ourselves square in the middle of it, walking (if we can walk) with papers in hand from office to office, seeing the hospital bed recede before us like a mirage. We hear voices saying, "Sorry, wrong office—you need to go see Mr. So-and-So in the office of Such-and-Such," or barking at us about incomplete forms or unavailable doctors or whatever. That's the normal human reaction. Nobody who has seen how government handles driver's license renewals would care to see how, in daily practice, it would treat us if we were waiting for a new lease on life.

NO NEW CONTRIBUTIONS

Here we come to the deep divide running through American politics today. Advocates of the bill—the Big Government coalition—looked at the same chart and saw it quite differently. Instead of complexity and futility, they saw power and money. They pictured themselves in those offices, barking those orders, stamping those papers, and in one way or another running other people's lives. One of the features of Big Government is that the bigger it gets, the more people wield its powers, and the more power those people wield, the more they feel aggrieved when they are "denied essential resources." Think back to Senator Mitchell complaining about that "phony argument that we should be treated like everybody else," and really meaning it. There's the sense of entitlement, but beyond that is something even more presumptuous. When we talk about tax cuts, they take it almost as a personal insult. It's a sign of our general failure to appreciate them and all they do for us. Under Reagan, with all his talk of scaling down government, they felt put upon, deprived, hindered in their service to the public. If all these government programs weren't working—well, it was because government workers were being denied those essential resources! Our fault, not theirs. And now, miraculously, along came the Clinton health plan. They waited tremulously. For the Big Government crowd, this "landmark reform" promised what in Texas we used to call a "boom town." This was it, the big play. Push this baby through, and there'd be resources enough for all!

But worst of all, it would have once and for all made the entire American middle class government-dependent. By enshrining health care as an entitlement, urged presidential pollster Stan Greenberg, the administration would make the middle class "like government again." In gratitude for Democrat generosity, the middle class would start behaving like a good voting bloc and stop these unpleasant temper tantrums about taxes. In fact, Greenberg advised (working overtime to earn that $4 million the White House paid him), the people could even be gulled into thinking they were paying no new taxes at all. Bob Woodward in his 1994 book, *The Agenda*, about the Clinton presidency, records the moment in 1993 when Greenberg came up with this inspiration: "Say 'contributions,' Mr. President, not 'taxes.'"

In short, an electoral revolution has deemed that the power of government be diminished. But it has not diminished the appetite for power. Slowly the pretenses are passing, and what remains of the Big Government coalition is just that, the raw impulse that I believe drove it all along, a craving for power over other people. They're quite happy with the status quo, all their little titles and privileges, and revolution or no revolution they're not about to give them up!

For the social activists, the looming trauma is even greater. Acquiring "victim" status in America, a nation founded on a belief in personal responsibility, took a lot of time and effort—years of campaigning and lobbying and shouting and threatening. They too are not about to give it all up for no better reason than that the public is losing patience with them. Some, I'd even guess, will find in the Republican Freedom Revolution only further confirmation of their resentments: the public all along has been to blame for their plight. Withheld resources are only the last of their many slights and deprivations. With electoral repudiation they feel that much more persecuted, that much more entitled to government support, that much more determined to hold on no matter what.

Over the next few years, we'll see more of this drama played out, as all the professional complainers and power seekers are driven from the temple of democracy. Indeed, I would not be surprised if the first challenge comes from within the Democrat party itself, led by the first person who comes forward to speak for the forgotten conservative Democrats who also feel they have "contributed" enough to government. People speculate about a primary challenge to President Clinton from the Left. More likely it will be a serious challenge from the Right. The reason is simple, and without it the November 8, 1994, revolution would not have happened. The Democrat establishment, dominated by the "diverse coalition," no longer speaks for most Democrats.

Chapter 7

THE CHATTERING CLASS

Much of my own outlook on the world was shaped by Adam Smith, an intellectual and man of words. "Intellectual" today carries an unflattering connotation, suggesting a lofty disdain for practical affairs, but in fact our intellectuals, writers, and journalists all belong to honored professions. Some of the greatest achievements and most profound insights have come from such people. My quarrel is not with the professions themselves, but with the manner in which they are sometimes practiced in our day.

PILOT FISH

Every age has had its scribes, sophists, town criers, and the like—people whose stock and trade consisted entirely of words. What knowledge they had was often superficial, consisting of what we would today call news—things and events the ordinary person did not have time to study. The scribe could write up public documents and so was called upon to lend his services to the king. The sophist mastered techniques of rhetoric, and the commoners would gather round to admire his cleverness. This skill too attracted the friendly attentions of the king. The town criers and heralds, for their part, knew all the latest edicts of the king. They might even relate the latest court gossip from "informed sources" to a privileged few, their listeners enthralled just to be standing near someone so close to the center of power.

To this lineage the professional political staffers of today, the publicists, public advocates, consultants, and Washington press corps may trace their origins. All are people who make their livelihoods and reputations solely with words—the chattering class. Conservatives have long accused our media and academic establishments of a liberal bias. But in a way this misses the point: the bias runs more to power itself than to any fixed, coherent set of principles. It is the bias of courtiers happy with their little corner in the modern palace. Little has changed except that now there is one big king and lots of lesser ones. So there's a lot more power and a lot more news. It's wrong to accuse them of being the lapdogs of any one party. Members of our chattering class are more the pilot fish of Big Government, drawn by instinct to follow anything big and powerful.

One trait distinguishes today's chattering class from their loquacious forebears—their sense of "independence." In older times, I imagine, the courtier was eager to make it known to one and all that his or her loyalty belonged to the state. Today, in both the media and the academy, especially our law schools, the spirit is "adversarial."

It's an odd, defiant posture that somehow always leads them to embrace the cause du jour of Big Government. Our courtiers like to carry themselves about with an air of being detached, tough-minded observers of the spectacle: They see through it all. They just want the facts. They're doing their best to keep the rest of us common folk honest. Now and then you even hear a reporter describe the media as our national "conscience."

Turn on the TV panel shows—choose any one from among the dozen—and there is our national conscience at work, mulling over the burning issue of the hour. One week we might hear them screeching loudly at some unforgivable national outrage that spells imminent ruin and starvation for the poor. A week or two later the issue is entirely forgotten. The health care bill, for example, was billed as a comprehensive answer to a national crisis of unprecedented dimensions. Its failure would mean suffering for millions. Then the issue died and, well, that was that—on to the next national outrage. The only constant to the debate that really seems to matter to the media is their own central role in it.

I can seldom walk to or from the Capitol without observing a hive of reporters and cameramen abuzz with "the latest from Washington." Wandering into the press gallery, I can observe dozens of coffee-steeped reporters frantically tapping out their dispatches, amid piles of policy papers and bills and press releases that gather like wood chips around a beaver. In moderation this would be understandable; obviously, you would expect to find a lot of reporters in our nation's capital. But it would also be fair to say that the media's presence here has swollen in direct proportion to the expansion of federal power. And like the Big Government that has created the Washington media boom, the establishment media is often detached from the everyday concerns of the average citizen. In the early eighties, ABC news came up with a slogan that captured the breathless, self-important spirit of our media types better than any description I've ever read. The ad showed Peter Jennings, head cocked a little to one side, brows furrowed, looking out beatifically from his anchor desk beneath the words, "There Is No Truth, Only News."

Turn that one over in your mind a few times. Let's see, if there is no truth, only news, then who are the most important people in all the world? Ordinary citizens and taxpayers? No, they are seldom the day's top story. The entrepreneurs, whose ideas and energy provide wealth and technological progress? No, if they make news at all outside the business pages, it's usually because they are being called to account for their "greed." So I guess the answer would have to be the people who make news and those who report and comment upon it. They, since there are no truths to give our individual lives purpose and meaning, are the big dogs in town.

Variations of the same unsettling notion can be seen in action throughout Washington on any given day, as professional talkers from every corner of the city jostle for their piece of the action. For the lawyers it would be, "There Is No Truth, Only Dispute." For the judges who have taken to refashioning our laws in their own image, "There Is No Truth, Only Judicial Review." For the academics it might be, "There Is No Truth, Only Tenure." For the activists managing all our various social crises, "There Is No Truth, Only Strife."

After ten years in Washington, my ears ring with the sound of all these people's pleadings and predictions of national ruin. From a thousand "expert witnesses" in who knows how many hearings, their voices merge into one plaintive cry: "You must pass this bill... This regulation is absolutely essential... All the data clearly demonstrate... Congress must act now against this outrage... Unless taxes are raised immediately...."

OSCAR NIGHT ON THE POTOMAC

Modern Washington, in fact, has gone the sophists and heralds of old one better. You no longer have to be knowledgeable at all to be an expert. You just have to be "concerned" or "passionate." Better still, a concerned celebrity yearning to do something "relevant." I will never forget the congressional hearing I once watched on agriculture policy. The witnesses: Jane Fonda, Jessica Lange, and Sissy Spacek—on hand to share the knowledge they'd recently acquired playing farm women in movies. Reporters, lawyers, and legislative assistants scribbled and nodded gravely as the star witnesses described the hard lot of those who reap a living from the soil. Jane's expert testimony carried particular weight because she was a second-generation Hollywood farm girl, her father having starred in *The Grapes of Wrath*. Later I sat on a subcommittee that was looking for a witness knowledgeable about aerodynamics. I suggested Christopher Reeve of Superman fame, since he must know about flying.

The Fonda–Lange–Spacek hearing was a snapshot of our chattering class at work. A few staffers on the subcommittee want a new appropriation. Substantively, that's hard to justify since farmers already get tens of billions of dollars for not producing. But with the actresses in tow, everyone flies into action. The biggest hearing room is reserved. The actresses' publicists are contacted. A media alert is sent out. The stage is set.

The testimony is heart-wrenching. Not only did they play farm wives, it turns out, but during the filming each actress actually met real farm people. So it was really a consciousness–raising experience for all three. And from the bottom of their hearts, they implore Congress to pass this all-important appropriation. This brings a flurry of excited coverage: profiles of the starlets, films of their testimony, editorials praising their concern for, well, farms. A week or two later, everybody forgets the issue, except the farmers who got their subsidy. It was all silly of course, but the flurry of attention drowned out reality just long enough to get the check written. On the phones, before the cameras, and on paper, they've produced a brief buzz of words in support of more Big Government.

I find it hard to imagine delegates to the first Congress inviting colonial stage queens to illuminate the complex matters before it. For one thing, although most of the founders were gifted in words, they were doers. Franklin was a businessman, a printer who'd met a payroll and published *Poor Richard's Almanac*, a book full of common-sense advice not sophisticated enough for the policy men of today, like "A penny saved is a penny earned." Washington, Randolph, and Jefferson were all farmers who, without ever having played farmers on stage, understood the world of sweat and toil. Jefferson could turn a phrase, but when not writing or governing he poured himself into building solid, tangible things like Monticello and the University of Virginia. All the founders thought of themselves as delegates, visitors to the capital. When the debating and orating and legislating and media interviews were over, they all had real work awaiting them back home.

This quality, I have always believed, explains more than anything else the soundness of our Constitution, the practical wisdom that runs through it. One of the sadder sights of recent times has been to see that work fall into the hands of lawyers, whose main work is not the practical wisdom of good government but the manipulation of not only the words of the Constitution, but the constant outpouring of new laws, regulations, and rulings for private or political advantage. Truly, in the flood of official words our legal–advocacy groups have found "fit tools for the designs of ambition." The framers wrote in plain language what every citizen could understand. Take, for example, the entire text of our Tenth Amendment: "The powers not delegated to the United States by the Constitution, nor prohibited by it to the States, are reserved to the States respectively, or to the people."

To cover their judicial power plays, and override the Tenth Amendment, jurists of our day have come up with "emanations" and "penumbras" hitherto well hidden in the text of the document. For reasons that leave the ordinary citizen a little bewildered, by these devices they've overridden the expressed will of the people in everything from school prayer to law enforcement to abortion—all phrased in the language of the faculty lounge, with the modern academic's gift for sounding mealymouthed, incoherent, and self-assured all at once.

A Taxonomy of Talkers

Certain liberals seem to inhabit a world of lofty phrases from which they seldom venture. In this world the great goal is "social justice." Liberals alone are its defenders and rightful adjudicators. The millions of people paying taxes to support their cherished programs must not be allowed to interfere. No conceivable data or evidence could appease them. Practical objections are dismissed with the remark that a new program will cost "only X million" or "only X billion." Never is the price quoted in the man-hours, sweat, and sacrifice it will take taxpayers to earn that money. The normal human reaction is to feel a bit humbled dealing in such large sums of money. To the talking class, it comes quite naturally; back in policy school they talked in big numbers all the time—the only difference here is that the money's real.

To all practical objections the answer is the same, repeated like a chant—social justice–social justice–social justice—as though by mere repetition they can "create" a new reality. They use such words so often and so freely that, after a while, it's as if the words were using them. One writer has captured this strange process: "At the beginning there was the Word—at the end just the cliché."

From my own brief experience in Washington, I've noticed that these vendors of words tend to share seven basic characteristics.

Splendid Isolation

Each operates in a highly insular environment, safe from the rest of the world. Take again the lawyer and the judge. They operate in the courtroom, with its own rules, its own parlance, its own legal parameters. In any other walk of life, if you began to speak of "penumbras," people would ask what in heck you were talking about. Suppose you informed your spouse you'd just discovered an "emanation of a penumbra" within the text of your marriage vow, allowing for a more "contemporary" interpretation. But lawyers who talk like that get hailed for their brilliant and incisive minds.

The educator, likewise, may today turn his podium into an ideological pulpit and then get all huffy at the mere suggestion he's strayed from his responsibilities. Before tenure he is accountable only to his like-minded peers, after tenure he's accountable to no one, least of all the public or university supporters paying his salary. Many invoke "academic freedom," having in their own educations apparently missed the simple distinction between freedom and license. They may write or teach anything they want and call it scholarship. Any criticism we might offer is "anti-intellectual." Just as today a latrine placed in a museum is "contextual art" merely because the artist declares it so, anything a tenured professor produces must be considered "scholarship."

University politics get more vicious every year—as academic life gets ever more trivial. As Woodrow Wilson observed from his Princeton years, "The reason faculty politics are so vicious is that the stakes are so small." I could never return to the battles of the academy. Dealing with congressional politics for ten years has left me too soft.

Other People's Business

The talking professions generally tend to someone else's business and are often funded by someone else's money. Here too lawyers epitomize the trait. Few things have amazed me in Congress more than the recent sight of rich personal injury lawyers lobbying against tort reform in the guise of champions of the little guy. Here are people, generous supporters of the Democrat party, who flourish in the misfortune of their fellow citizens, forever accusing, suing, claiming, counterclaiming, penalizing, and advertising for more business. America has 90 percent of the world's lawyers, and Japan, 90 percent of the world's engineers. We reward lawyers for fast-talking themselves and their clients into someone else's money; the Japanese reward people for building new products. We even have "public interest" lawyers scavenging our prisons in search of legal grievances, turning every kitchen duty dispute into a constitutional infringement. The already bankrupt Washington, D.C., for example, pays tens of millions of dollars a year to prisoners and their lawyers. America's litigation crisis is really just a massive, intricate program designed by lawyers to redistribute wealth—from us to them.

Rules for You, Not for Us

Because they dwell in a world of beautiful abstractions, people in the talking professions rarely suffer the consequences of their ideas. Does the zealous environmental regulator sitting in his comfy office ever actually meet the men and women he throws out of business? I wonder if he even thinks about them. He knows, and reminds us often, that there is "a price to be paid for protecting our environment." But it's not a price he will ever have to pay. The cause he serves is "global" in scale, which excuses him from ordinary considerations about particular people.

The ACLU attorney tells us, "There is a price to be paid for our liberties." But when a violent felon escapes justice on a procedural error, however minor or innocent, and then goes on another robbery or murder spree, whose liberties are thereby defended? Who pays the price? Usually citizens who live in neighborhoods in which no ACLU attorney would consider residing.

Phony Facts

The talking professions are almost always staffed by people who are "credentialed" by formal education in the softest academic areas—the social sciences or some of the humanities—where they have learned few facts and little true skepticism. With the occasional exception of a scientist who joins the disarmament movement or "green" advocate in the environmental movement, our chattering class has little acquaintance with hard academic disciplines. In physics, mathematics, chemistry, and even accounting abstract hypotheses can be tested against experience and objective, empirically verifiable truths and either proved or disproved.

True scientists tend to be intellectually brave but personally humble, always aware of how little they know for sure. To the contrary, the arrogance of the talkers is in direct proportion to their lack of knowledge. To hear the talkers advocate their new social programs, going on and on with their endless statistics—usually gleaned from a quick look at some think-tank briefing paper—you'd think they had spent years personally researching the subject. No chance. Most of their data comes from Washington's busy statistics industry, whose sole purpose is to tailor numbers to liberal arguments. Of course, if you torture the statistics long enough, they confess to anything. To give just one example, remember how we were told again and again that there were three million homeless people in this country? Turns out that number was literally made up by homeless advocate Mitch Snyder, and the real figure—hardly ever cited—is between 230,000 and 600,000.

Highest of the Low

The talking professions are headquartered in elaborate and ornamental places; talkers are lavishly endowed with honors (usually by peers), rituals, ceremonies, protocols, and sartorial trappings all designed to dignify their profession and elevate their importance in the public eye. Walk into any of their offices and chances are you'll find a shrine to their political (and largely second-hand) importance. Walls covered end to end with inscribed photos of themselves with all the lords of the Earth they've encountered—to make absolutely sure the visitor fully grasps how very important the talker is. Clearly here is someone with access! But what these shrines usually signify is the deep insecurity of the self-important.

The talkers like titles, too, even more than the average person. Like the scarecrow in the *Wizard of Oz*, talkers are brought to life by testimonials to their wisdom—long resumés full of dates, references, and usually trivial accomplishments. They have titles such as "Dr.," "Professor," "Your Honor," "Esquire," and "The Honorable." Some surely are appropriate and deserved, but among the talkers titles are too often a crutch to prop up unearnerd authority. I am the Honorable Dr. Richard K. Armey; B.A., M.A., Ph.D., M.C. The "M.C." stands for "Member of Congress," and I was never called "Honorable" until I came to Washington and joined the 535 people who share the distinction of being among the lowest of all professions in the public esteem.

Bad News is Good News

For the talking professions, bad news invariably magnifies their importance. Talkers need a "crisis" more than a crisis needs them.

Always when they rush up to you with warnings of our environmental crisis or the health care crisis or the day care crisis or whatever, a question comes to mind: If the "crisis" were solved, if every last reform were enacted, every demand met, every dollar allocated—what would this person do?

I don't mean to imply that, by contrast at least, conservatives are nature's noblemen, above the lure of shallow political excitements. But they do tend to view politics more as a distraction than a calling. When we use a word like "crisis," we're usually talking about something tangible and imminent, like fiscal collapse or murderers out in the street. The professional chatterers warn of crises like "our dying planet" or "our crisis of meaning," as unprovable as they are open-ended. The rule of thumb is if the "crisis" and prescribed course of action tend to elevate the speaker's importance for the indefinite future, he or she belongs to the class I'm describing, and you needn't be alarmed at the coming "crisis."

The Highest (Paying) Motives

Members of the talking profession have a gift for feigning altruism and humility even as they amass enormous personal power and adulation. Most people, myself included, freely admit to a certain egocentrism. Sometimes it's healthy, as in the desire to work and succeed; at other times, less so. Normal people are aware of this; we see our motives for what they are and try to act upon the better ones. But the professional chatterers who drive so much of our political discourse always behave as if they were pursuing only the most vital public objectives, animated only by the purest of motives, like God's little helpers.

For me, the liberals' desire for public service sometimes calls to mind an old "Twilight Zone" episode, the one where beings from another galaxy arrive on earth. They prove to be very helpful and

friendly, even offering all takers a free tour of their faraway planet, assuring everyone that "We are here to serve man." The aliens
arranging the special transport carry around little books entitled
To Serve Man, only it's in their language so no human can read it.
One copy is left behind as the transport blasts off into space with
the excited crowd aboard. Examining *To Serve Man,* a skeptic who
stayed behind on Earth suddenly deciphers it and cries out, "It's a
cookbook!"

Acquiring so much power and attention, while still being
praised for your selflessness, is quite a trick. A still greater feat is
to be known as humanitarians when, in fact, the talking professions are defined by nothing so much as snobbery: a profound distrust in the ability of other people to form their own opinions and
make their own decisions. Recall, for example, the *Washington
Post*'s description of Christian conservatives—"poor, uneducated,
and easy to command."

This last insult—easy to command—was especially remarkable
given that the conservatives' offense was their independence:
resisting liberal orthodoxy, tuning out the constant exhortations
of the talking class, and instead following their own conscience.
We saw on November 8, 1994, just how "easy to command" the
American people are. Commanded one way by the whole array of
liberal commentators and professional scolders, they went the
other way. It was a bold step, but only a step, toward regaining the
dignity of a free people.

Chapter 8

THE CONTRACT WITH AMERICA

Seeing that the American people had had it with talk, talk, talk from Washington, we decided to do something about it.

In the last few chapters, I describe how it happened that Big Government came roaring back even after the spectacular events of the 1980s. It was a temporary resurgence. Consider the whole period from 1989–1994 as the Battle of the Bulge of statism, one last lunge by a cause that was clearly lost a long time ago. Still, it's defeat was not inevitable. It took the hard work of a lot of people—and particularly the vision of Newt Gingrich—to bring us to where we are today. It required the Contract with America.

For forty years House Republicans labored in the minority, relegated to serving as a sturdy anvil on which Democrats forged their golden promises and iron mandates. No member of Congress had ever actually seen a Republican majority, though historians assured us it had once existed. Like serfs, we in the minority looked up from our plows and worktables from time to time, wondering if it had to be this way.

Among some House Republicans, the ethic had become: survive, get along, every man for himself. Each Republican, in the end, would have to cut his or her own deal. The Democrat committee chairmen had the power. The Republican role in this natural order was to take what scraps were offered and be grateful. This demeaning situation became so obvious that one ranking Republican was described in the *Wall Street Journal* as a "wholly owned subsidiary of the committee chairman." It prompted Fred Grandy, a former representative from Iowa, to remark, "The trouble with Republicans is that they don't have anything, and they won't share."

It is true that old-style Republicans often dreamed of and even aspired to becoming a majority, but that was all. I don't want to sound dismissive of these people, many of whom served their principles quite honorably. But I think the principles themselves were lacking a little fire. The Republicans' vision was of bipartisan "moderation"—a noble enough idea depending on how you understand it. Under this code the worst of all evils was "gridlock" and the most unseemly of sins "confrontation."

This was another case of letting the talking professions dictate the terms of debate, soothing Republicans with "bipartisan" pats on the back. I myself associate the word "moderation" with the virtue of prudence, meaning a sense of the good joined with a sense of the attainable. It does not mean you defer to whomever happens to have power. It does not mean you "go along to get along." In a democracy, prudence just means that at the end of the day you live with the final vote tally. But as I understand prudence and moderation, neither virtue excuses you from doing your utmost to *shape* the majority.

So the "get along" advice did not sit well with many younger members of the Republican caucus. We were the Reagan classes. When Ronald Reagan rode into town in 1981, he laid to rest once and for all the idea that only liberals are populists and idealists. He showed instead how few genuine idealists actually remained in the Big Government coalition. He embodied the optimistic, fighting spirit of modern conservatism, a side the people clearly liked.

His example gave a new mood to House Republicans. In the early 1980s the Conservative Opportunity Society (COS) was formed, led by Gingrich, Bob Walker of Pennsylvania, and Vin Weber of Minnesota, and composed of similarly "confrontational" members. These Young Turks were not "in on the deal," not part of the establishment, and not ready to fall in with the herd. These younger members gave people like me, a college professor out in the heartland, a reason to run. I knew them first as lively evening entertainment on C-SPAN and decided one day that here was a cause worth joining. Throughout the eighties the ranks of COS swelled and House politics became more confrontational, to the discomfort and even embarrassment of old Republican bulls. The Democrat majority, accustomed to quiet bipartisanship, didn't much like this development either.

Since even the Reagan administration had gotten only so far in breaking Democrat rule, it was clear to us that the Republican vision would not be fulfilled until, quite simply, the Democrat House majority had been confronted and beaten. Establishment Republicans were just not going to do the job. The Young Turks would have to take over the Republican caucus themselves and then go after the Democrats. This is how it happened.

WHIPPED INTO SHAPE

When Bush was elected in 1988 he tapped the recently retired

Senator John Tower to be secretary of defense. The Senate Democrat majority devoured Tower, and his nomination failed. Tower, it seemed, had not lived up to the rigorous standards of personal purity set by such as Joe Biden and Ted Kennedy. Bush tapped the House Republican Whip Dick Cheney for the position. (Cheney turned out to be the shining star in the Bush cabinet.)

That left House Minority Leader Bob Michel looking for a new whip, a new right-hand man. He turned to Ed Madigan, another Illinois congressman and a member of Michel's inner circle. Henry Hyde, a much stronger conservative leader, was also interested, but was urged out of the race by Michel. It looked like the pragmatist establishment would prevail once again and the House GOP would remain ineffectual.

Gingrich saw the circumstance as a perfect chance to test the depth of rebellion among the Republican minority. With Walker, he forged a coalition of conservative and moderate activist Republicans and challenged Madigan for the position of whip. Even with Michel's full and open support for Madigan, Newt won—by a single vote. Had any of this happened differently—or if a single Republican had switched and voted against Newt that morning— I am convinced we would not be a majority in the House today.

Gingrich quickly made Walker his chief deputy whip and the process of changing the Republican Conference began. Madigan was soon tapped by President Bush as his secretary of agriculture. That created an opening on the Agriculture Committee and that, in a way, created an opening for me. In the mad scramble for committee assignments after Madigan left, the position of ranking Republican on the Joint Economic Committee opened up. That was for me.

For nearly all of its existence, the Joint Economic Committee had served as little else than a propaganda arm of the Democrat party. Republicans had been bullied and passive. Since the committee moved no legislation, just issued reports, I immediately installed my communications director, Eddie Gillespie, as staff director. Eddie was tireless, smart, and bold—not one to shrink from a fight. Every time they issued a report, we issued a rebuttal. When they called hearings, we attended and questioned their assumptions. For two years we drove the chairman, Senator Paul Sarbanes, to distraction and, finally, all but stymied the Democrats on the committee. At the same time we produced report after report with which to arm our side with accurate information and sound arguments.

Meanwhile, back at the White House, the Darman-types were coping with the fallout of the 1990 budget summit and tax increase.

All through spring and summer 1990, I had argued against both the summit and a tax increase, only to be barred from the White House. Darman, I am told, was sure that Armey commanded no votes and that if the president wanted to raise taxes the Republicans would go along. The Armey Resolution against tax increases—passed by a two-to-one majority of the Republican Conference in the wake of the Darman deal—did little to shake this conviction. Frustrated, by spring 1992, I had decided to run for leadership myself.

Just as Walker and Gingrich had a special bond between them, Tom DeLay and I had ours. Until the events of 1990 both Tom and I had disdained any interest in leadership except Tom's desire to someday be whip. It was strange how we who had been so close in the big budget fight of 1990 both decided independently to run for leadership in 1992. We actually spent some time trying to talk each other into it and get ourselves off of the hook. Nevertheless, I decided to run for Republican House Conference chairman against Jerry Lewis from California and Tom decided to run for Conference secretary. We both won.

Republicans began 1993 in a blue funk. President Bush had lost, and the Democrats controlled both the House and the Senate. The Democrats were crowing about how they controlled the whole government; they were going to make Republicans irrelevant and ante up the stakes by taking over the nation's entire health care industry. Michel was now served by a leadership team made up of COS members and other activist conservatives. Gingrich was whip. I was conference chair. Hyde was policy chair. Duncan Hunter was research chair. Bill McCollum was Conference vice-chair. DeLay was Conference secretary. Bill Paxon was the newly elected chairman of the National Republican Congressional Committee (NRCC). John Kasich was the new ranking Republican on budget, having beaten another of the old leadership's inner circle.

President Clinton and his party, having "faked right" to get elected, quickly returned to the Democrat's game plan and "ran left." While they busily put the country in the mood to vote Republican, Paxon undertook the heroic task of rehabilitating the NRCC. It's impossible to give Paxon enough credit for the miraculous job he did at the NRCC. The organization was a basket case. It had been so badly neglected and so much in debt that bankruptcy was seriously considered. Paxon, Jim Nussle, and John Boehner also recruited the finest class of Republican challenger candidates anyone had ever seen. Things were looking up.

By October 1993 Michel announced his retirement. The cards started to shuffle. Newt immediately announced and quickly wrapped up the top Republican leadership spot, speaker of the House, or minority leader if we failed to take control. There was no contest against Newt (the only possible contender, the very able Jerry Solomon of New York, read the writing on the wall and withdrew after forty-eight hours). I resolved to run for majority leader or remain as Conference chairman in the unlikely case we emerged from the 1994 elections still in the minority. DeLay, McCollum, and Walker all announced for Republican whip. That meant that most of the future leadership team was already around the table in 1993.

To his great credit, Michel presided over one of the smoothest transitions of power I've ever witnessed. He could have hung on to all the levers of power until the very end, reserving for himself the right to deal with the president or Senate Minority Leader Bob Dole. Instead, he kept his hand in the big decisions but began to delegate responsibility for day-to-day decisions to the leadership at large and Newt in particular. This gave us a chance to form our own strategy—although always with Bob Michel's approval and support.

Soon after the leadership elections of 1993, Newt, DeLay, Walker, Paxon, and I began having quiet dinner meetings to plan our strategy to win a majority—and to use that strategy. These meetings were serious business. Could we forge real unity of purpose and push to victory? I was cautious at first. We were about to be in a heck of a street fight, and I wanted to know who was at my back. At my insistence, we all talked in the most personal terms about who we were, what we were about, and the reasons we wanted a majority. Talk about bonding—we practically took a blood oath. It was really all for one, and one for all, and all for the whole ball of wax.

DeLay and Walker, for instance, were in the middle of a high stakes leadership race: both wanted to be whip. They could have been petty and tried to undercut each other. They did just the opposite. I remember one night telling Bob, "I'm going to tell you just what I told Tom.... I'm on your side." We all had a good laugh. I told Newt that I knew how to fly solo and was not sure I could fly in formation. He assured me with a smile that flying in formation was easy if your wing man was resolved to shoot you down should you stray. Paxon said he doubted that two such big egos as mine and Newt's could work together. DeLay remarked that we would all have to put our egos aside. Newt joked, "Yeah, I'll put Armey's aside, and he'll put mine aside." We did have fun but, more important, we came up with a plan—one that only got better each time Newt (the brains of the mob) said, "Let me build on that, I've got four points." Those were good dinner meetings in which to plot a revolution and made all the better because Newt always paid the bill. It was at one of those dinners that the notion of what was to become our Contract with America first came up.

The dinners led to weekly planning meetings held each Thursday throughout 1993 and 1994. The Thursday team included: Newt, Walker, Tom, Bill, John Kasich, and myself. All Young Turks. They were also attended by some key staff who, in the end, always did the lion's share of the work. Ideas from the dinner were brought into the Thursday team meeting and fleshed out for execution. Our first big success was the Kasich budget for 1993. Thanks to John and the Republican members of the committee, we beat the pants off the Clinton budget. Our bigger success was developing a participation plan for the whole House Republican Conference to help raise money for the NRCC. It worked beautifully.

In February 1994 the Republican House Conference repaired to a small Maryland university, Salisbury State, to set our course for the majority. Somehow it doesn't seem right to call it a "retreat," but that's what it was. And it was no plush deal, either. We worked hard and came up with plans for action. No big hotels and banquet rooms, no lobbyists, no party donors, no press. For three days, we stayed in student dormitory rooms (vacant between semesters), ate in student cafeterias, and met in a large room in the student union building working out our plans to rebuild the Republican party.

In these humble surroundings we set the defining principles and vision for our party, writing it all up in a mission statement: "As House Republicans we will work together to offer representative governance, and to communicate our vision of America through clearly defined themes, programs, and legislative initiatives to earn us the honor of becoming the majority party in 1995." This may sound rather simplistic, but House Republicans had never before really operated as a team to accomplish a common goal.

The morning we left that little campus, I made a personal resolution. If we were going to win this thing, then we should start acting like winners right now. I announced that upon returning to D.C., I would begin preparations for a "contingency plan" to be followed immediately after we won Congress—staffing, reorganization, accounting reform, the works. Better still, I thought, let's call it the "transition plan." It would be a good phrase to have circulating around town, and I savored the image of Dick Gephardt getting wind of it.

Three things were clear when we left Salisbury. We were united around that mission statement. We meant it. And we were going to do it. The only question was how we would do it. The Contract provided the answer.

PUTTING OUR NAMES ON THE LINE

It was Newt's idea. Newt had masterminded a huge press event that had been held on the Capitol steps in 1980 where candidate Ronald Reagan had joined with Republican congressional candidates to pledge passage of the Kemp–Roth tax cuts if they were elected. Newt was a firm believer in nationalizing congressional elections, framing them as referenda on national issues like taxes and spending, rather than as a yardstick of how well the local congressman brings home the bacon. He suggested we hold a similar event and he even had a precise date in mind—September 27, five weeks before election day.

"Now that we know when it is," he said at the crucial meeting, "I want to delegate this project to my good friend Dick Armey." My first reaction was to recall Tevia's line in *Fiddler on the Roof*, "How did I come by this great honor?" But my staff and I had already learned that one of Newt's guiding priciples was to "import knowledge, export work." In fact, the arrangement served us both well.

I charged my top staffer, Kerry Knott, who had managed my first run for Congress, with drafting the overall plan for the event. We in turn delegated responsibilities since we could not legally work with candidates on political matters. Haley Barbour, chairman of the Republican party, deserves a medal for his constant support. He gave us permission to establish "a war room" in party headquarters to manage the political end of the event, which was set up in June under the expert management of Barry Jackson. There were a few minor miscalculations along the way. The first budget for the event was around $50,000, plus advertising. The final cost, as the project kept growing and growing, was around $300,000 plus $250,000 for an election week ad in *TV Guide*. Haley always believed in the goal of gaining a majority by running on issues, and he put his name on the line—the check signature line! He will live in history as one of the greatest party chairman our country has known.

We made an early and controversial decision to draw up plans for the actual bills that would make up the Contract—fine print and all. This entailed a risk we decided to run. Democrats always held back such information until the last moment. The Clinton Crime Bill, for instance, was presented to members a mere two days before the vote. It was another Democrat lesson in what a friend of mine calls "Civics for Suckers": you bring thousand-page bills to the floor and, declaring the high urgency of the issue, call for a vote before the opposition has even had time to pick out the little sweetheart deals buried in the fine print. In our case, offering the details would allow the Democrats to find cuts and budgetary hardships sure to cause untold privation, mass unrest, and bring down Western civilization as we know it. But we felt that with the value of a politician's or political party's word at its lowest point ever—thanks to Bush's "read my lips" lapse and Clinton generally—we had to be as explicit as possible. Looking back on it, I doubt there has ever been a more honest, open attempt to inject issues into a nationwide election.

In drawing up the Contract agenda, some issues were off the table from the beginning. Obviously, nothing that increased by one paperclip the operations of the federal government was to be considered. Neither would any tax increases be considered. But neither, on the other hand, would issues to which most of us were committed be included in the Contract—abortion, for instance. Not that this is unwinnable; on the contrary, I believe abortion weighs upon the party only as we shade and equivocate on our principles. It didn't seem to hurt Reagan any to have clear convictions on the subject. But for this, the point was to unite the party in a referendum on the scope and cost of government.

Likewise, it occurred to some to put in my flat tax bill, ridding America of our entire tax code and replacing it with a fair, across-the-board 17 percent rate—with the personal and family deductions I'll explain in chapter 9. Some colleagues and many outside supporters and editorialists argued for putting it in the Contract. I was actually the one who decided to leave it out. Its hour, I believed, had not yet come.

My staff and I brainstormed and came up with a lengthy menu of policy options. This was then distilled into questionnaire form

and sent to all incumbent Republicans and all Republican candidates. Two-thirds of sitting members and half the candidates
responded.

We then appointed members to working groups to draft the actual legislation. Generally, they were chosen based on their previous
interest in the issue, their level of enthusiasm, and their ability to
work hard. We shied away from more senior members (in most
cases) because they had more committee responsibilities and frankly
took the project less seriously than did the younger members.

What we ended up with was the following:

- A Day One "Checklist." We wanted to show dramatic
  change from Day One. A working group was charged
  with listing procedural reforms to be enacted at the first
  crack of the gavel.

- Term Limits. Congress should be a place where citi-
  zen-legislators came but then went back home to real
  jobs.

- Regulatory Reform. Start putting some common sense
  in our regulatory policies.

- Balanced Budget Amendment/Line Item Veto. These
  were longtime Republican goals and a centerpiece of
  our economic agenda.

- Stronger Defense. Halt the Clinton administration's
  march to a hollow military and set in motion a Republican defense agenda for 1996.

- Economic Growth. After fighting the Democrat tax

and spend agenda, we wanted tax cuts and other reforms to get the economy moving again.

- Pro-Family Reforms. With the assault on the family by Big Government reaching its peak, we knew families needed relief.

- Tough Crime Legislation. This was easily the biggest concern for most Americans and another issue on which the Clinton administration had fallen short.

- Common Sense Legal Reforms. We needed fewer lawyers and frivolous lawsuits and more justice.

- Senior Citizens' Reforms. Our seniors need some relief from high taxes and age discrimination policies.

- Welfare Reform. Work and personal responsibility should be encouraged, not dependency.

The actual day of the event turned out to be fairly dramatic for us. Early that morning, just after my staff awakened Representative Jim Talent from a sound sleep to discuss the final welfare reform language, the rain was coming down and the wind was howling. We had been forced to gamble since the two indoor backup sites had fallen through. If the rain continued, we would have to cancel the event or hold a scaled-down version without the backdrop, band, or banners. Fortunately, Newt's weather forecaster proved correct after all, as the sun peaked through the clouds early in the morning and provided us with a beautiful fall day as temperatures reached the 70s.

Candidates were bused to the Capitol steps from the hotel and proceeded to file through the stage, signing the Contract in groups of four. At the top of the Capitol stairs, members saw for the first time the elaborate staging, the huge Contract with America backdrop, the band, and the crowd. I saw on their faces the realization that this was not a typical press event but was instead one of those defining moments that come seldom in this business.

The Contract was like a reversal in a college wrestling match. Before it, the Democrats had us down. They were the ones with a "positive" agenda, we were just the malcontents, the "nay-sayers." As soon as we unveiled the Contract on September 27, 1994, everything turned around. Now their backs were to the mat. Now we had a hopeful agenda. Now they were the nay-sayers, the pessimists. And they played right into our hands. They attacked the Contract.

CLINTON VS. REAGAN

Everything in the Contract, after all, had the approval of the American people. The whole idea implied prior agreement. You don't "contract" something with people that they don't want. Most of the Contract spoke to the long-standing frustrations of the voters, things the Democrats had snarled up in red tape for years. Again it goes back to Barney Frank's thesis I mentioned earlier, which I mentioned earlier. You could see it in the continuing pattern: in presidential elections people thought in terms of the national interests, of which party most reflected their own vision of life. Hence the two Reagan landslides and ascension of his presumed heir, George Bush. But moving down the ballot, the people tended to honor Tip O'Neill's maxim about all politics being local. They vote down, in my colleagues' candid phrase, meaning for Democrats, who promise one or another subsidy or program. The Contract changed this state of affairs. Suddenly all politics was national—and therefore, strangely enough, personal. The Contract persuaded voters finally to bring their national vision to local elections.

Bringing still greater clarity to the election was President Clinton, who obliged us by setting his reputation on the line. Not only did he lash out at the "Contract on America," but in a move doubtless inspired by Stan Greenberg—again earning that hefty fee—Clinton invited America to compare him with President Ronald Reagan. Not a good idea. Six years of Democrat propaganda about Reagan hadn't quite done the trick, it turned out. He was, and remains, beloved by many in America today, all the more by contrast to those who followed in his great wake. Hearing the attacks, I didn't worry for Reagan's reputation. I just thought, "Beautiful!"

Ever since the world was young, Democrats could be counted on at election time to recite the usual campaign accusations, as unchanging as the calendar. So it was in 1994. Those greedy Republicans were going to destroy Social Security and lower taxes for their rich friends! Alas for them, no go this time. It did not take the average voter long to see that a child tax credit, a family Individual Retirement Account, and a tax credit for home care of the elderly and the afflicted were not "tax breaks for the rich." It did not take long to figure out that repealing the Clinton tax increase on Social Security benefits of 1993 and raising the level of earnings a senior could enjoy without losing Social Security benefits did not "abolish Social Security." When the old reliable Democrat campaign rhetoric bounced off actual Republican proposals, it gave a hollow ring. Watching their empty expressions as the old tricks failed, as the people walked away in disgust, was for me a delight equaling the coming Republican majority victory.

Democrats, over the years, have been better with words than us, if only because to them the meaning of words was so much more flexible and they had better echo chambers than we did. Every so often a Republican might dare to question one of their programs or tax increases or ideas, only to disappear in a cloud of moralistic liberal clichés, like a clumsy bear enshrouded in bees— "Stop him! He's declaring war on our poor! He's looking out for his rich friends! He's going to destroy our safety net!"

Reagan alone was immune to this treatment, which the Left explained away as some mysterious personal quality possessed by the Great Communicator. But there was no great mystery about Reagan's appeal. What the liberals never quite understood was that Reagan had only said to America, in essence, "I agree with you." And being a principled man, he meant it.

The Contract proved the point. Republicans are always haunted by the fear that the public will not understand and are, therefore, reluctant to state their views bluntly. Democrats, on the other hand, are always afraid the public will understand, and so they distort information early and often. With the Contract, we turned the tables on the Democrats. We asserted a legislative agenda in full faith that the public would understand. And you did. The result was the greatest Republican electoral victory perhaps ever.

On September 27, 1994, we laid an offer on the table, and on November 8 the nation accepted it. Five people at dinner took a bond and extended it first to an entire minority conference of 178 members of Congress, then to a nationwide slate of candidates, then to an entire nation. The glue that held it all together was honesty. Like any contract, it was a promise to keep our promises. The novelty of it was the acceptance of a specific obligation: no more grand promises, no more visionary bravado, no more lip-reading, no more vague visions of what government will do for us. Just a binding pledge to do our level best to accomplish specific things in a specific time—on our sacred honor—and to free

Americans to pursue their own visions. Like any contract, it is not only a path before us but a bridge burned behind us.

We have made our choices, and now we have no place to go but forward. The rest, as they say, is history. When the 104th Congress was sworn in on January 4, 1995, we set about fulfilling the Contract. With a hundred-day legislative blitz unparalleled since at least 1933, we brought every item in the Contract up for a vote, exactly as we said we would. More than that, we passed nine out of ten items, failing only to get the two-thirds vote for the term limits constitutional amendment (although that issue is far from finished). The big question is, what's next?

Part Three

BEYOND THE CONTRACT

Soon, all public policies will be judged as either backward or progressive according to a simple criterion: do they narrow or enlarge individual freedom and responsibility? Those policies that rely on government coercion will be seen by our grandchildren as primitive and retrograde. Those that trust the individual will be welcomed as rational and humane. The following chapters cover among the most crucial reforms needed to restore limited government and unlimited opportunity for all Americans.

Chapter 9

THE FLAT TAX

"Congress shall have the Power To lay and collect Taxes...."
How, from these ten words in our Constitution, did we get an income tax code with hundreds of sections, 6,439 pages of regulations, and 480 tax forms?

All those pages and volumes and rules are a monument to the breathtaking claims of Big Government and the narrowness of its vision. If, in that simple clause, the framers intended that government should shape broad social policies with its tax power or manipulate economic behavior or redistribute wealth or replace private decisions with political ones, they never got around to saying it. All they said was that Congress shall have the power to tax. To a reasonable person of that day, or any other, this meant tax enough to support the essential operations of government. Like any other delegated power in the Constitution, it is intended to be used moderately and for a specific purpose.

If we know anything about the founding fathers, it is that they were not social tinkerers who believed the people needed constant watching. They were men of principle and independence who believed the government needed watching. Other countries have suffered worse under their social engineers, but perhaps none has ever undergone such minute fine-tuning. Seldom have the citizens of any nation been subjected to so many rules and treated with so little regard.

THE SEVENTEEN PERCENT SOLUTION

"We are not the bosses of taxpayers, they are ours." These are the words of T. Colman Andrews, director of the Internal Revenue Service in the 1950s. At the time he offered this reminder: the typical household paid about $7,000 annually in taxes, as opposed to today's $16,000. Just when we strayed from the idea of the IRS as a servant is hard to fix. What is clear, though, is that we have strayed very, very far. The most enduring revolutions usually bring about the simplest reforms. I believe this lesson should guide us in Congress. We should scrap our entire income tax code and replace it with one flat rate that applies to all Americans. We should have just one deduction—to ensure that every family keeps enough of its own income to support itself. Beyond that, everybody pays a flat 17 percent rate on all income. No other deductions, no loopholes, no tax breaks. You calculate the percentage, fill out a postcard-size form, make out the check, and you're done with the IRS until the next year. And best of all, no tax attorneys, no lobbyists to plead your special case, no IRS agents to harass you. All these barnacles on the ship of state are dislodged with a single bold sweep and forced to take up more productive occupations.

I suppose if someone were presenting this idea to me for the first time, I would immediately ask, given the simplicity of the idea, and given people's general disgust for our current tax system, why has it never happened before?

Shortly after Andrews and his humble vision of the IRS departed Washington something went seriously wrong. In 1930 American workers surrendered about 12 percent of their paychecks to the government; in 1950 they surrendered 25 percent; in 1995, with the new Clinton taxes, they will contribute a full 36 percent. For this we get to hear the president's eloquent tributes to those who "work hard, pay their taxes, and play by the rules."

President Carter, as I noted earlier, took up the cause of tax reform fifteen years ago, calling our code "a disgrace to the human race." Every now and then Washington tries to appease our frustration with "tax reform," as politicians understand that term. As recently as 1986 we rewrote much of it only to invite a host of new problems and then reverse what few genuine reforms there were.

The next practical question might be, why 17 percent? Early in our history Chief Justice John Marshall wrote, "The power to tax is the power to destroy." His warning was prompted by a case involving a tax proposal of just 2 percent. If my reform should be enacted, let the historians note the following words very carefully: I believe even a 17 percent income tax is far too high. Offhand I'd say it's about 7 percent too high. I hope others after me will carry the flat tax principle further. The goal should be a universal income tax of 10 percent. It's never been clear to me why the biblical tithe, representing an amount good enough for God, should not be good enough for government.

Next practical question: But didn't we cut taxes under Reagan?

I have paid Ronald Reagan many tributes here, but he had only limited success in actually cutting taxes. While he cut taxes in

1981, his original policy was short-lived. Congress raised taxes in 1982, 1983, 1984, 1987, 1990, and 1993. Thus every dollar of tax cuts enacted by Reagan in 1981 has been replaced with $1.25 in new taxes passed by Congress. Consequently, from 1980 to 1991, total federal tax receipts and tax burdens have actually risen. What the right hand of government giveth in tax cuts, the left hand taketh away with continuous tax hikes.

We can thank "soak the rich" reversals of the original Reagan policy for our current highest marginal rate of 42 percent. When state taxes are factored in, many people confront a marginal tax rate of 50 percent. Who pays these "soak the rich" taxes? Senators Mitchell, Kennedy, Rockefeller, and company gave us a case study in this with their luxury tax. Punitive tax rates designed to soak the rich have tended to destroy economic opportunities for lower-and middle-income workers. Studies also show that high income tax rates apply in large part to small business owners who are a major source of new jobs. In the 1980s, after President Reagan cut income tax rates, the share of income taxes paid by the wealthiest 1 percent of Americans rose from 18 to 26 percent. But since the 1990 tax rate increases, the share of taxes paid by the rich has fallen.

How do taxes affect the forgotten middle class? Millions of middle-income earners are in a 28 percent federal tax bracket, a 15 percent payroll tax bracket, and a 5 percent state/local tax bracket. This means that the tax collector snatches 48 cents of every additional dollar a worker earns.

Even the working elderly fall prey to our punitive income tax rate structure. Senior citizens in the work force have high marginal income tax rates, special earnings penalties, and—courtesy of the Clinton tax policies—higher taxes on Social Security benefits. The National Center for Policy Analysis calculates that some working elderly face marginal tax rates of up to 82 percent. In other words, of each additional dollar the senior citizen earns, the government tax is as much as eighty-two cents and the worker keeps eighteen.

Children are hurt even more. The IRS, too, looks upon our children as a most "precious resource." Their arrival into the world is met with two responses. The parents must earn more money, so they work harder. Then the government taxes more of those earnings, caring little why it was earned—the new child the parents have to foster. The Heritage Foundation notes that a typical middle-income family of four paid just 2 percent of its income in taxes to the federal government in 1948. Today, the same family pays 24 percent (again, just to the federal government, leaving state and local taxes aside). The reason is that the tax exemption for raising children has been eroded by inflation over the past thirty years, dropping from 42 percent of family income to only 12 percent. If the value of the dependent deduction had increased simply to keep pace with inflation, it would be worth over $8,000 today. As matters stand, it's worth only $2,400. This means that there has been a massive shift in the tax burden away from single and older people and toward young families struggling to raise their children.

Do these high marginal tax rates affect economic output? As we have seen, they do. Innumerable economic studies show that high marginal tax rates are inversely related to productivity and economic growth. Productivity and thus wages tend to rise when marginal income tax rates are low, but productivity falls or grows very slowly when marginal income tax rates are high—as they are today. Since productivity is a primary engine of economic growth, high marginal tax rates serve only one purpose: they make Americans poorer.

And finally, the most insane feature of the tax code today: it punishes savings and investment. When you buy a consumer good, your income is taxed once, at the time it is earned. If you buy stock in a company and earn a return, that investment income is taxed twice. First, it is taxed at the company, when the business pays its corporate income tax, and then it is taxed again when the individual receives the dividend and reports it on his personal income tax forms.

This is sheer lunacy, discouraging investment in new and existing companies. When the cost of investing became dramatically lower in the early 1980s—at least compared with what it had been under President Carter—economic activity sprang to life. But under the current system, the government is as good as saying, don't invest in America's future. Until we rid ourselves of the current tax code, we will never know what new products, new technologies, and new jobs have lain fallow, waiting to be created. It's safe to say the loss has been great.

The $618 Billion Headache

The original 1913 income tax was a two-page form, with a two-page instruction sheet. Back then the top tax rate was 7 percent, prompting fears that it might one day reach 10 percent. And less than 1 percent of Americans had to fill out an income tax return.

Today, just looking at our tax forms makes us weary. There are hundreds of tax forms, hundreds of pages of instruction booklets, and countless tax attorneys and accountants trained to make sense of it all for us.

One economist, James L. Payne, recently calculated the total cost in work time across America because of these complexities. Relying on research carried out by the research team of Arthur D. Little, Payne put the total number of working hours Americans devoted to federal tax compliance activities in 1985 at 3.6 billion hours for businesses and 1.8 billion hours for individuals. That's a grand total of 5.4 billion man-hours spent by workers and businesses just to figure out their taxes—more man-hours than it takes to build every car, truck, and van manufactured in America. Since a typical employee works 1,844 hours per year, this monumental waste of time comes to nearly three million Americans working full-time on nothing but tax compliance. That's thirty-two times the number of employees in the IRS and roughly one-and-a-half times the number of people in our armed forces.

Next, Payne converted those man-hours into dollar terms. The typical worker at a major accounting firm in 1985 (when Payne's data were first collected, in a government study incidentally) earned $35.47 an hour, while a civil servant at the IRS earned about $21.14 an hour. An average of those two—or $28.31—is a good estimate of the hourly cost of a typical tax preparer. Converting that figure into 1990 dollars and adding a few other incidentals, Payne concluded that America today spends roughly $232 billion just to support our army of three million people working on filling out tax forms.

It gets worse. Payne points out that "every tax amounts to a penalty for engaging in the activity of being taxed." That's why when we want to discourage something like smoking we slap heavy taxes on tobacco. Using the most credible studies conducted in the past fifteen years, Payne estimates that taxation creates an extra burden on economic activity of about 33 percent. This means that for each dollar collected by the government in taxes, society loses thirty-three cents because of lost economic output. Across the entire economy in 1990—our sample year—this "excess burden" totaled $315 billion.

Finally, Payne added sundry items including the cost of tax audits, the cost of running the IRS itself, the huge cost of litigating tax disputes in court, and, most significantly, the real economic costs of the efforts taxpayers make to avoid paying some or all of their taxes.

His conclusion: *Our heavy and complicated tax collection system imposed a $618 billion cost on the economy in 1990. That's nearly half of the tax revenue we collect today, twice the cost of running the Defense Department, and over three times the cost of Medicare.* Economists call this cost the excess burden of the tax system because it represents what taxes cost the economy, above and beyond what the government actually nets. In other words, sheer waste—taxpayers lose it, but the government does not get it.

IT'S A GIFT TO BE SIMPLE

My flat tax plan to fix all this is based on the pioneering work of Hoover Institution fellows Alvin Rabushka and Robert Hall. It would work as follows:

Unlike the hundreds of different forms and schedules of today, the flat tax would have exactly two—one for individual income and the other for business income.

When an individual fills out his form, he would list all income from wages, salaries, and pensions, take a generous allowance for himself and his family, and pay the flat 17 percent rate on whatever is left over—end of process.

I included the family allowance because I firmly believe that a person should be allowed to support himself and his family before he begins to support the government. When the plan is fully phased in, three years after enactment, this allowance would be $13,100 for an individual filing separately, $26,200 for a married couple, and an additional $5,300 for each dependent child. This means that a family of four would have to earn $36,800 before it owed a penny in federal income tax.

While the average family today spends eleven hours filling out its individual 1040 form, under this system you could do it in eleven minutes. In fact, if you like, you can do it right now:

Form 1 ARMEY-SHELBY FLAT TAX FORM 1997

Your first name and initial	Last name	Your social security number
Present home address		Spouse's social security number
City, Town or Post Office Box, State and ZIP code	Your occupation	
	Spouse's occupation	

1. Wages, Salary, and Pensions..	1	
2. Personal Allowance..		
a. $26,200 for married filing jointly..	2(a)	
b. $13,100 for single...	2(b)	
c. $17,200 for single head of household...................................	2(c)	
3. Number of dependents, not including spouse............................	3	
4. Personal allowances for dependents(line 3 multiplied by $5300).	4	
5. Total personal allowances (line 2 plus line 4).............................	5	
6. Taxable wages (line 1 less line 5, if positive, otherwise zero).......	6	
7. Tax (17% of line 6)..	7	
8. Tax already paid...	8	
9. Tax due (line 7 less line 8, if positive)..	9	
10. Refund due (line 8 less line 7, if positive)...................................	10	

Business income would be handled with equal simplicity. Typically, a business would simply subtract expenses from revenues and pay the 17 percent rate on the remainder. Revenues would be defined as corporate, partnership, professional, farm, and rental income—virtually all money generated by business activity other than employee compensation. Expenses would include purchases of goods and services, capital equipment, structures, land, and wage and pension contributions to employees.

A couple of points are important here. First, this is not a business tax; it is a tax on business income. The distinction is important. Businesses, in the end, do not pay taxes. People pay taxes, businesses collect them.

The point of this tax on business income is to "catch" the income that people receive from business activity. For example, if a wealthy stockbroker invests in a company, that company doesn't pay him in wages or salaries—it pays him in stock dividends. That's exactly the sort of income this tax applies to—but it will be collected at its source, the business, instead of later on. This way, little of it will escape taxation through the many loopholes, accounting tricks, and outright tax evasion that are so prevalent among some investors today.

Second, this is much simpler than the current business income tax. Right now, if a business purchases a new piece of equipment, it is allowed to write off most of the cost—but only gradually, over a period of years, according to a complicated depreciation schedule. Unfortunately, there's a different depreciation schedule for dozens of categories of equipment, which means a small business owner (or a large one, for that matter) needs to read reams of federal regulations to decide which schedule applies. Quite often, he guesses wrong and ends up in court.

But under this system, he writes off the entire cost of a new equipment purchase in the year it is made. If he buys a new computer for $2,500 to handle his bookkeeping, for example, he simply deducts $2,500 from that year's taxable income. Does the government "lose" money on the deal? Not at all. As that equipment makes him more productive and he earns higher profits, the government makes up the difference—and all without subjecting the small business owner to the incredible complexity he puts up with today.

For both the individual income tax and the business income tax, the principle is the same: except for the generous family allowance, all income is taxed at the same low rate of 17 percent.

WITHOUT WITHHOLDING

My proposal contains one other feature I find particularly alluring. It puts an end to income-tax withholding.

Ask anyone how much his car payment is or the size of his rent check or utility bill, and chances are he can tell you the figure to the dollar. But ask him how much he paid the government last month, and he typically has no idea. I first realized how insidious this was when I noticed that my then-teenage son David became excited as April 15th rolled around. Thinking I'd raised him better than that, I couldn't understand why he wasn't upset that the government was taking so much money. Then he explained to me that at tax time, the government sends him money. We had a little talk in which I explained that not only was the money the government was giving him his money to begin with, the government took even more than it was entitled to.

Withholding was the boldest and shrewdest power play ever conceived by the federal government. Without it, Big Government could never have expanded so relentlessly. It began as a "temporary" wartime measure in 1943. And without any great national debate that I recall, it just stayed in place. If there were protests at the time, I have little doubt they were answered by appeals to the "efficiency" of this arrangement. "Efficiency," in Big Government terms, means that only the people who get money from government know the exact amount, so the benefits seem very tangible. The people who give money to government usually do not know the amount, so the costs seem vague and abstract.

The flat tax would also have the virtue of visibility—another way of saying honesty. Right there in front of us, we would each see how much we're paying. In Europe, where value added taxes are the norm, citizens have no clear idea how much they pay for government. In fact, Europeans are notorious for greatly underestimating their actual tax payments, because they never see the bill. It's reasonable to wonder how far they would have strayed into socialism without this hidden device.

TAX AND SPIN

When I first came up with the flat tax plan, I wasn't sure how it would be received. I was a little concerned it might be brushed off as an old idea, since as a free-market economist I knew the idea had been kicking around for years. But President Clinton came to my rescue by raising income tax rates yet again. He did not choose a propitious time to do so. The majority of Americans understood that more taxes were the last thing we needed. So I decided to introduce the flat tax in order to yank the whole tax debate in the other direction.

Almost immediately my office was flooded with thousands of letters praising the idea. I've seen a lot of mail come into my office in my time in Congress but never anything like this. It wasn't only the sheer volume of mail but the intensity and enthusiasm of each letter. They contained phrases like, "at last," "it's about time," "a breath of fresh air," and "wow." To me, it was an encouraging reminder that the American people are as fed up with our complex tax code as I am.

Then came the public criticism from my detractors, filling me with more hope than even the highest accolades could have done. Only days before the November elections, with candidates around the country campaigning on the flat tax, the Clinton Treasury Department released a report charging that the flat tax would expand the deficit. A quick check of their figures revealed that Treasury's best and brightest had made a $500 billion error in their calculations. Maybe it was deliberate, maybe not—but it boomeranged. In fact, with the flat tax, the government should "lose" only about $40 billion a year—an amount that can easily be made up with spending cuts.

Right here, let's take up the criticism that a flat tax is somehow "unfair." In other words, "unprogressive." I reject this whole way of thinking. What is unfair about everybody paying exactly the same tax rate? The reasoning completely eludes me.

Part of the confusion, I think, is the application of private criteria to public questions. In ordinary life we tend to measure generosity by what's left after a contribution has been made. If you were walking down the street with a hundred dollars in your pocket or purse and gave one dollar to a needy person, no one would call you miserly. You didn't have to give anything at all. But no one would call you a living saint either: you kept $99 for yourself. If I had $50 and gave $1 to the needy, that too would be praiseworthy. But if a third person came along with only $1 and dropped it in the tin can, he would receive high praise for his generosity. Even though we all gave the same amount, everyone would understand that his was the greatest sacrifice because the guy with only a dollar was left with nothing.

The problem is that taxes are not charity. The federal government is not the Salvation Army. And paying taxes is not a voluntary act of generosity. It is a civic duty. To say that we want a society in which generosity is encouraged is not the same as saying we want a tax code in which generosity is enforced. Indeed, the moment such acts are compelled, they cease to be acts of generosity. They become minimal acts of compliance. By its very nature generosity is voluntary. By their very nature taxes are coercive. Government does not encourage generosity, it kills it. You can't be praised for what you had to give under threat of punishment.

This is why it's fraudulent to go around saying that some folks are not paying "their fair share" in taxes. It is my understanding of civic duty that everyone, by definition, carries an equal share. Where duties are concerned, fair means equal. For example, observing laws is a duty and exactly the same laws apply to all. We wouldn't put up extra stop signs in an affluent neighborhood just to slow the people there down on the grounds that they should observe "their fair share" of laws. Likewise, voting is a right and also a duty. But we don't give some people two votes and other people only one. Everybody's vote constitutes the exact same share of total votes. Serving on juries is also a duty to which all, theoretically, must be prepared to contribute the exact same time and effort. For some people it poses an inconvenience, while some have extra time on their hands and are less inconvenienced. But we don't devise a "progressive" jury requirement to right this situation, singling out those with extra time on their hands to carry "their fair share" of the time burden.

This leads to the other fallacy of progressive taxation, the idea that the untaxed balance of one's income is merely left over for private indulgence. Obviously, the very wealthy have lots of money to spend. That should not bother us a bit. So far as I'm concerned, they can do with it as they please. I neither admire them excessively nor salivate at the sight of them.

But that said, the flat tax plan would in fact be "progressive." The crucial point is that under this plan, the first $36,800 of the income of a family of four will be exempt from the income tax. For example, a family making $36,000 would pay zero percent of its income in income tax, a family making $50,000 would pay 5 percent of its income, and a family making $200,000 would pay 14 percent of its income. This will remove as many as ten million people from the tax rolls.

The personal exemptions, in other words, cover a far larger portion of a middle-class taxpayer's income than a wealthy person's. Therefore, that 17 percent flat rate will apply to a much smaller part of his income. In fact, by any reasonable estimate, my plan would give us a tax system as progressive as the tax system in place when John F. Kennedy was president. Moreover, it is a fact of history that whenever the upper rate has been lowered, the revenue collected from the rich has increased. We saw that with the Kennedy tax cut of 1963 and the Reagan tax cut of 1981. And we learned the lesson in reverse with the Bush tax increase of 1990.

As for investment income, some union activists are laboring under the misconception that my plan does not tax capital gains and investment income at all. False. True, my plan eliminates taxes on individual's income from his savings account, money market, mutual funds, or other investments. But that income has already been taxed at the business, not the individual level. The reason is that it's vastly more efficient to do it that way. Today, huge amounts of taxable income fall through the cracks of the tax system. For instance, more interest payments are claimed as deductions than are claimed as taxable income. My system will catch that revenue (which will mostly come from wealthier tax-payers, by the way). If we tried to tax stock dividends at the individual level, for example, we would need to retain today's army of IRS auditors to compare business receipts with personal returns. The elegant simplicity of the flat-tax plan would be lost.

Others wonder if removing the home mortgage interest deduction would hurt the real estate industry. The answer is, not as much as removing the double-taxation of savings will help it. While the targeted tax deductions for homes will be removed, we will no longer double-tax capital gains and interest, which will cause the savings pool to expand dramatically. This will lower interest rates, make capital available for housing purchases, and keep housing prices stable.

Finally, what about deductions for charitable contributions? Here again it's the government man who reveals the lowest opinion of his fellow citizens, always assuming that without government throwing incentives in our path we would never do something nice for others. Almost half of all charitable contributions today are not even claimed as deductions. To me this suggests the tax code has less to do with private charity than we generally assume. Other evidence confirms this. During the 1980s, as Ronald Reagan steadily lowered the top rate from 70 percent to 28 percent, the charitable deduction became proportionately less valuable. When the Tax Reform Act of 1986 expanded the personal exemption, the number of taxpayers itemizing the deduction dramatically declined. Yet charitable contributions did not decline during the Decade of Greed, they doubled!

A growing economy gives people more money to give away and the dignity of giving freely. Churches, medical research foundations, homeless shelters, and other places of genuine charity will thrive as we move away from the compulsory compassion of Big Government.

And the country—the people—will also thrive.

Chapter 10

FREEING THE ECONOMY

The flat tax must be accompanied by a radical rollback of government regulations. It isn't enough to give the American people's
money back to them; with that they must have the freedom to use
it as they think best, without harassment and endless "directives."

When a government bureaucrat or his local deputy comes
strutting up to dictate what we may keep or not keep, use or not
use, do or not do, we don't take it very well. Without a clear constitutional mandate, we wonder, what's he doing here? When he
lays his mitts on our property or earnings or business, he's edging
close to our person, our sense of who we are and what we're called
to do. And in most cases the regulator hasn't even done us the
courtesy of learning about our work—the practical matters of
profit margin, operating expenses, and the like. He seems to
regard it as beneath him to fret over such things. A chilling com-

ment by Hillary Clinton herself captures this condescension well. When critics objected that her health plan would destroy small business, she haughtily sniffed, "I can't be responsible for every undercapitalized small business in America." The result of the bureaucrat's regulatory labors, across the most productive and intricate economy on Earth, are lots of "little" losses that add up to one enormous burden that must be removed to create jobs and higher wages.

DEATH BY A THOUSAND PAPER CUTS

When I was campaigning in Washington State in fall 1994, I heard some stories about these "little" losses. One, for example, came from a man named Dobbe Spasojevich, the proprietor of Sno-King Electric in Arlington, Washington, a small firm with twenty-two employees. One day Spasojevich sat down with his wife and their accountant. They couldn't quite figure out why their business costs were rising beyond what people were willing to pay for his work. Since they were hardly getting by, it was not a case of gouging customers. So they put the pencil to it, adding up all the money they were losing to government. The state Labor and Industries Department had raised workman's compensation assessments by administrative fiat. State employment security assessments were increasing, again by an administrative mandate. The state legislature had once again raised the business and occupation tax. Permit fees had to be paid to the government of each city and town Spasojevich worked in. And finally, there was the ever-rising paperwork cost of complying with federal, state, and local mandates of all kinds.

His solution to the problem? He decided he had no choice but to lay off his employees and accept only jobs that he could do himself. He let all twenty-two employees go.

It was much the same story from David Holmes, owner of Eagle Securities. While he once employed eight to twelve people installing security systems, the rising cost of employing people, thanks to government regulations and taxes, forced him to let his employees go as well. He now works alone, hiring only an occasional "subcontractor."

Then there was Gene Boere of Gig Harbor, Washington, who repairs diesel engines and heavy equipment. For the same reasons, he refuses to hire any employees at all.

These are not the sort of numbers that land on the countless little desks at the Labor Department or Environmental Protection Agency (EPA) or the Occupational Safety and Health Administration (OSHA) or even the White House. Yet it happens every day, hardly noticed at all by the national economic writers, the politicians, the planners, and the environmentalists. Add them up, though, and what you have is a national tragedy. Here are the reliable estimates of Thomas Hopkins, an economist at the Rochester Institute of Technology:

- The direct costs of regulation to the private sector come to about $580 billion annually. And this figure doesn't take into account the secondary and tertiary effects of the cost of regulating the economy.

- Of this general burden, $189 billion (in 1991) came from "process regulation," meaning government-mandated paperwork.

- Second most burdensome was the cost of regulations on transportation, international trade, communications, and other sectors—about $130 billion in 1991.

• Next, and growing fastest, was the cost of environmental regulations, which reached $115 billion in 1991.

RISKY BUSINESS

As for health and safety regulations, who is not for those? In the upcoming chapter on health care reform, I offer the suggestion that we charge the Food and Drug Administration (FDA) chiefly with testing new products for safety, basically to make sure they are not harmful or worse. I do not think it the business of government to examine products for efficacy—how well they work. This should be done by professional licensing boards and, ultimately, by market forces. Products that work will always beat out products that don't.

In any case, what health and safety regulators do now is for the most part more destructive than useful. They operate with little regard for practical consequences. If, for example, any pesticide poses a hypothetical lifetime cancer risk of more than one in a million, our present EPA will attempt to ban it. This is bureaucratic logic in action. You and I go out every day and do things—drive, cross the street, ride airplanes—that involve a more tangible risk. The regulator getting up in the morning and walking ten blocks to work has undertaken greater risks than one in a million. The regulation of these minimal risks raises the cost of countless things we buy. If all the pesticides carrying those hypothetical risks were taken off the market, the price of fruits and vegetables would increase an estimated 50 percent and the incidence of both cancer and heart disease would increase as people switched to less healthy diets.

Similarly, some agencies, including OSHA, classify crystalline silica as a carcinogen. Do you know what crystalline silica is? It's the stuff you find in beach sand. One-quarter of the earth is covered with it. So why not pull everybody off the beaches and restrict travel to those other danger spots, like the Painted Desert? Of course, there's no evidence that sand and cancer are related, but crystalline silica is still on the government's growing list of cancer-causing substances.

Sometimes these regulations to reduce risk in one area end up increasing risk in another or precluding a better solution to the same problem:

- In one instance, the Americans with Disabilities Act required many cities to install wheel chair elevators on public buses. Although a well-meant idea, in practical terms it would be cheaper and more convenient to provide disabled people with door-to-door subsidized limousine service.

- Another instance came in a federal mandate to remove asbestos from the walls of buildings. We now know that removing the asbestos has caused greater risk for cancer than leaving it where it was.

- In Southern California, the federal government put the kangaroo rat on its list of endangered species. That sounds like a kind gesture—give our furry friends a break. However, worried about the habitat of this vanishing rodent, the Fish and Wildlife Service then banned the use of "disking" to till property and remove brush in order to contain wildfire. As a partial result of this policy, raging fires damaged or destroyed hundreds of homes; one man and untold kangaroo rats were killed.

The Office of Management and Budget's (OMB) Office of Information and Regulatory Affairs estimates that one premature death occurs for every $7.5 million in regulatory costs imposed on the U.S. economy. Regulations kill jobs, slow economic growth, and lower most everyone's standard of living. These conditions in turn produce correspondingly higher mortality rates.

What do I mean by a radical rollback of regulations? I mean we should dismantle the whole irrational regulatory structure, firing most of the 124,000 federal employees whose full-time jobs are to think up and write regulations. We should leave only the few reasonable safeguards a free economy needs. When I last looked the *Federal Register* was at about 70,000 pages. We could easily aim to halve that, a preliminary goal of 35,000 pages of regulation. The guiding principle should be to keep those regulations that are demonstrably protecting the health and safety of Americans and scrap the rest.

As of this writing, Republicans in Congress, joined by many Democrats, have already taken the first step. The House passed a one-year moratorium on federal regulations, amounting basically to a restraining order on the Clinton administration. This, incidentally, was not even part of the Contract with America.

We also passed the Regulatory Reform Act. First, the act requires government to estimate the cost of each particular regulation before it goes into effect. Until now regulators dwelt largely in the realm of abstraction. If their experts and policy people determined that some new regulation was essential, then that settled it: regulate. "Cost" was a word that seldom entered these calculations. Second, the new law requires that regulators determine whether there's some more practical alternative to the proposed edict. Basically the law instructs bureaucrats to think before they act. And third, if some federal regulation has diminished the value of private property by 30 percent or more, the government now must compensate the owner for the difference. This too should make the regulator think again. Even better, the compensation will come out of the regulatory agency's own budget.

UP FROM REGULATION

Conservatives in both parties object to regulation for the practical reason that constant state supervision is deadly to the economy. Regulations are the underside of each new program offered to us. They add to the cost of just about everything. They throw people out of work. And they crisscross the economy like a thousand little tripwires, breeding a litigious, fearful, defensive spirit throughout our society.

Far deeper than these inconveniences is the gross insult of it all. Americans do not dream, strive, sacrifice, build, and produce in order to one day find themselves answering to an army of little potentates on the Potomac. People who do not see the great insult at the heart of Big Government do not, I think, fully understand their own country.

The American people deserve a government that has the ability to see their goodness and the decency to respect it. Big Government implies either that the American people are not capable and therefore need the protection of their government or that they are not to be trusted and therefore need the regulation of their government. Both are wrong.

To a certain cast of mind, regulations ultimately make us more free. This is why the debate about government regulation, like so many other modern disputes, presents the spectacle of two opposite factions vying for their claim to the word "freedom." The regulators, in their own view, attempt to free us from corporate excess, free us from dirty water, free us from smog, free us to roam in pristine parks and forests, free us from danger, free us from risks, free us from faulty products, and so on. This is a case of the old saying that nothing is so false as a half-truth.

To rational minds in both parties at all times it has been taken as a given that some activities usually occurring in public places require regulation. Stop signs, street lights, zoning codes, and laws against littering are, for example, all regulations. No one would feel more free without them. The absence of such regulations would form a sort of tyranny, as is the case when a court strikes down a zoning ordinance against setting up adult book shops near the local school.

The critical distinction has once again to do with power and who has it. Healthy, common-sense regulation is generally self-regulation. No one seriously disputes stop signs because they are the product of democratic consensus. Being rational people, we understand that Freedom is synonymous with a certain amount of self-regulation—meaning nothing more complex than orderly self-government. Usually this sort of natural self-regulation occurs at the local level, where the people have direct knowledge of whatever problem might be at issue and where they can best weigh the costs of regulation versus the public good. "Regulation" has taken on a bitter connotation today only because everybody understands that we, the people, are not doing the regulating. There's been a radical disconnection between ruled and the rule-maker, the people engaged in productive activities and the people engaged in regulating productive activities.

How it all came to pass, reaching today's 70,000 pages in the *Federal Register,* is one of the sadder stories of modern American history. In most cases the citizen has been the innocent party, absorbing costs and decrees that just seemed to come out of nowhere. But in some cases the citizen has not been so innocent. Some have been complicit in circumscribing their freedom, as for example in the case of our government-supervised agricultural industry, an issue I'll address below. One of the horrible effects of regulation is that while at first it engenders healthy resistance, as we still see in most businesses today, after a certain point it instills abject dependence. The regulated, unable to compete meaning-fully against one another in the marketplace, compete instead for federal favor. At the extreme, as with agribusiness, the regulated can scarcely imagine a world in which government does not give them their orders; they're afraid to even contemplate the possibil-ity. Alternatively, the regulation ethic has given rise to a peculiar modern figure Ted Forstmann calls "the apologetic capitalist," the one who escapes the Big-Government net, turns a profit, and yet feels almost guilty for having been spared. But often, the story of government regulation is the story of unwelcome acts of caprice and arrogance at the expense of our people. Congress took to passing big, sweeping laws. And then they simply left it to an obscure, eager class of government careerists throughout various departments and agencies to interpret the details. Those details, not surprisingly, licensed the constant involvement of the regula-tory interpreters in our daily affairs.

The failed Clinton health care plan, I become more convinced, will mark the turning point in our subservience to government. The administration's cherished hope to leave its very own land-mark gave us, to the contrary, a landmark for Freedom. One figure from that debate will always stay with me. If we were making a movie about the arrogance of a federal power and called central casting for a guy to play the supporting role of self-assured bureau-crat, they would have sent us Ira Magaziner. In case you've already forgotten, he was the fellow who ran the big 500-person health care task force and conceived the grand design—and who alone understood precisely how the 1,370-page scheme would work.

His credentials for that assignment are worth pausing over. At the time his big moment arrived, Magaziner was a "management consultant" to various corporations, none of which notably prospered through his labors. A career highlight came when he was engaged to design an economic development plan for Rhode Island. The plan he came up with, known as "The Greenhouse Compact," called for massive government involvement and power over the economy. The governor liked his plan. State experts thought it a work of brilliance. Editorial writers praised its visionary scope. And so the plan was put to the people of Rhode Island, who overwhelmingly rejected it. Before going into the "planning" business, Magaziner attended an Ivy League school in the sixties. A *New Republic* profile published during the health care debate recounted some early political high jinks. Caught up in the idealism of the day, Magaziner and a horde of friends moved into the quiet working class New England town of Brockton for the express purpose of forming a majority voting bloc, taking over the town, and making it a model of "social democracy."

What in this resumé suggested an ability to redesign the world's greatest economy? Even on the most charitable reading his is not the profile of a man competent to order the affairs of the nation. By the logic of modern government, however, the fellow whose big regulatory plans had just got him run out of the smallest state in the Union was promptly anointed to craft a still bigger plan for the entire nation. How did it happen? Having made a few million dollars in the "consulting" business, Magaziner got involved in Democrat politics, organizing campaign events and raising money. He apparently found an intellectual soul mate in the future first lady. After the election he put in for a big important federal job. Vaguely knowledgeable about health care, he was deputized to remake the health care system.

Right here is what really, really gnaws at ordinary Americans—the sheer nerve of modern Washington, a hubris directly inverse to ability. At random you could pull any ten Americans from the streets of any small town, explain the basic facts of the health care problem, and nine of them could come up with a better idea than Magaziner. And yet all across America the people with initiative and common sense are shunted aside like so many bit players. The people who do the working and paying and creating and producing find themselves answering to the commands of people who "plan," "consult," "analyze," and campaign for a living, but who produce and create exactly nothing.

THE TV POLICE

Our computer industry, thank goodness, is hardly regulated at all. I suspect the reason is it simply grew too fast. It was grossing billions before the bureaucrats realized it existed. But the government controls our other cutting edge technology industry, telecommunications, with volumes of rules that in some cases date back to the days when Americans listened to Elliot Ness on the family radio.

The government polices the airwaves as if the ether itself were a government resource. It decides who may broadcast, for what purpose, and on what terms. It finds real and imagined monopolies throughout the industry, destroying some, protecting others, regulating them all. By decree—sometimes sanctioned by Congress, sometimes not—government bureaucrats have banned local phone companies from competing with local cable companies, long-distance phone companies from competing with local phone companies, local TV stations from buying an arbitrary number of other local TV stations, and on and on.

The end result is to needlessly hobble a truly revolutionary industry that promises to make our lives far richer while creating millions of new American jobs and adding literally trillions of dollars to our nation's wealth.

Whether they realize it or not, millions of Americans can see the results of this every time they open their monthly cable TV bill. Throughout the country, Americans are served by local cable companies that charge exorbitant rates, a pointlessly limited selection of channels, and often surly service. Why? Because, thanks to regulation, they are by and large government-protected monopolies, free from any real competition. As used to be said of the phone company when it too was a monopoly, to a large extent the cable companies don't care about customer satisfaction—they don't have to.

The full story is actually quite complicated, and there's more than one side to it. In fact, the recent history of cable TV provides a tantalizing hint of the great promise of deregulation at the same time it shows the high cost and frustration of having the government on the industry's back.

There's nothing particularly high tech about stringing wire to people's homes and sending a television signal through them. Various firms have been doing that since the 1960s, when cable first began as a way of bringing television service to remote areas with poor broadcast reception. The only reason cable exploded relatively recently rather than two decades ago is in fact a result of an early deregulation—a deregulation sadly incomplete.

From the moment in the late sixties when it became clear that cable could compete with local television broadcasters even in urban areas, those local broadcasters sought government protection from competition. Being powerful and well-established, they got it as the government began writing rule after rule designed to prevent cable from offering the same service as broadcast TV stations. Throughout the seventies, most people were stuck with about five stations, three networks, and maybe one or two low-budget independents. This era was captured in the movie Network, with NBC, CBS, and ABC offering little choice of programming, most of which was aimed at the lowest common denominator of the Nielsen audience. "Charlie's Angels"—not Discovery Channel documentaries—was the typical fare.

Then, in 1984, the government passed legislation billed as the Telecommunications Deregulation Act. For the first time, cable companies were able to enter local areas with more or less freedom, and suddenly the nation was being wired for cable from coast to coast. In the beginning of the 1980s 15 percent of American homes were outfitted for cable service; today it's more than half. But though the government allowed cable companies to compete with local broadcasters, it virtually forbade other cable sources from competing with the cable companies. Specifically, it banned any cable competition from the most obvious source, the phone companies. The phone companies, of course, already were in the business of stringing wires to people's homes, and it would have been fairly simple for them to expand their services to carry cable. This would have given consumers a choice between two or more cable services and instantly costs would have dropped and service improved. Instead, the opposite happened as cable wallowed in its government-granted preserve.

By 1992 the situation had reached a boiling point as Americans became fed up with their indifferent cable providers. I remember some colleagues of mine preparing for town hall meetings in their district that year, expecting questions on the economy, foreign affairs, and other great issues of state. Instead, all anyone wanted to talk about was cable service. Congress had to do something—and naturally it chose to do the wrong thing. Instead of simply ending the monopoly, it tried to regulate the industry even more tightly. The Federal Communications Commission (FCC) immediately opened a new Cable Services Bureau, and asked for and received $11 million to hire 240 new accountants and economists. The result: cable rates went down by an average of $2 in most areas, while many cities saw rates increase, by 15 percent in Baltimore and 17 percent in Detroit, for example. As one consumer advocate put it, "Few people could buy a McDonald's Happy Meal with the money they saved from the cable legislation." The option of simply deregulating and letting market competition do the rest hardly came up for discussion.

Traditionally, the government has distinguished three kinds of communications and drawn up a different regulatory policy for each: the print media, mainly newspapers, magazines, and books; the so-called common carriers who transmit information over wires, telephone companies and the cable TV industry, for example; and those who use the broadcast spectrum, notably radio stations and broadcast television.

Since the print media had the good fortune to be invented before the rise of the modern regulatory state, it is hardly regulated at all, being governed by little more than the First Amendment of the Constitution, which guarantees freedom of the press. Anyone today can start a newspaper or publish a book, and he can say almost whatever he wants, provided only he stay on the right side of the libel laws.

It's a different story altogether for broadcast television and radio stations. Here, the government argues that since the electromagnetic spectrum is limited, it should be treated like a public road with the FCC as the ethereal traffic cop, ready to issue citations. When you're driving to work and you tune to your favorite country music station, only to find yourself listening to the news instead—that's your government at work. As a condition for being granted the "privilege" of broadcasting on the airwaves, the country music station has had to agree to devote a certain amount of its time to broadcasting "public interest" news bulletins. The idea that people who might want to hear the news could turn to a news station apparently did not occur to the bureaucrats.

Then there are the common carriers, the people who carry information over wires, such as the telephone and the cable TV companies. In this case, the government has decided that these by nature quickly become monopolies, since it is presumably impractical for two or more companies to string wires to every home. That's a dubious theory to begin with. Actually, as we saw in the case of cable, if common carriers are monopolies, it's because the government makes them monopolies by law. Still the "natural monopoly" theory serves the government's purposes well; it's used to justify all sorts of regulation.

As a result of these and other rationales, the government today controls telecommunications more tightly than almost any other industry in America. Among the rules it issues are the following:

- Huge parts of the broadcast spectrum are reserved for established TV and radio stations, with little left over for newer ventures, such as cellular telephones and personal beeper devices (and this despite the fact your broadcast TV dial is full of UHF and VHF stations that are not being used).

- The long-distance phone companies are forced to pay huge fees to local phone companies for the privilege of connecting with the local networks. This not only raises long-distance rates, it allows the subsidized local phone companies to undercut any potential competitors, thereby solidifying their current monopoly status.

- The local companies themselves are prohibited from trying to offer long-distance phone service, as well as cable television and a host of other information services. This prevents further competition in long-distance calling and, as I've mentioned, practically guaranties monopoly status to the cable companies. They are also prohibited from manufacturing telecommunications equipment.

- No firm may own more than twelve TV stations, eighteen AM radio stations, and eighteen FM stations. Although we generally appreciate economies of scale in other areas, we inhibit them in telecommunications out of a wholly unjustified fear of monopoly. At a time when there could be 500-channel cable systems, this makes no sense.

- And let's not forget the chill created by the ever-present threat of future regulations. For years the government imposed the unfair Fairness Doctrine, which required broadcasters to give equal time to all opposing viewpoints. If something like that had been around in colonial times, *Poor Richard's Almanac* would have had to carry King George's propaganda. Although it was thankfully rescinded by Ronald Reagan, House Democrats—irritated by the continued popularity of Rush Limbaugh—have threatened to impose it again. Broadcasters seeking license renewal—watch out.

One of the many problems with all this is that the three-part division of communications is a relic of the vacuum tube era that has little relevance to the world of digital information. Newspapers are now eager to supplement paper and ink with electronic messages straight to home computers. Broadcasters are sending their signals over cable as well as the airwaves. Phone calls are now carried through the broadcast spectrum as well as by wire.

Technology has changed our world, and the sluggish regulatory beast, while dimly aware of this, can hardly move fast enough to adjust. Its solution, of course, is to stifle the changes long enough to write a whole new set of rules.

But why regulate at all? If we completely opened up places on the broadcast spectrum to a public auction, the market itself would determine the best use of this supposedly limited highway far better than the bureaucrats can. More important, we would provide a huge financial incentive for entrepreneurs to find a way to compress signals. In time, the broadcast spectrum would for all practical purposes become infinitely large. If we eased the burdens on the phone companies, particularly the scrappy "Baby Bells" that lead the field in innovation, the resulting competition would produce products that Dick Tracy and even Bill Gates himself never dreamed of. We need only glance at the computer industry, which has remade our world in ten years' time, to sense the limitless possibilities now opening.

The stakes are high. According to the respected economic forecasting firm, WEFA Group, if all telecommunications markets were opened to competition immediately, 3.4 million American jobs would be created in ten years. At that time our gross national product would be $298 billion higher and consumers would save $550 billion. Without deregulation, according to technology writer George Gilder, the United States will lose up to $2 trillion in economic activity through the 1990s.

IDLE YOUR LAND, KILL YOUR COWS

Since coming to Congress, nothing has held quite the same morbid fascination for me as our farm programs. Resisting all attempts at reform, growing angry even at the suggestion of change, the smallest hint that maybe the system is irrational,

182 ★ THE FREEDOM REVOLUTION

defenders of our federal agriculture policy simply trudge on to the next subsidy—counting on the rest of us to grow bored with the whole arcane subject.

Farm program lobbyists use a bureaucratic lexicon indecipherable even to fellow bureaucrats. They talk of "base acreage," "target prices," "nonrecourse loans," and "deficiency payments." Usually their calculation is correct—it does get very boring. It's a technique I call "esoterrorism." They deliberately make the discussion of farm programs so esoteric that few members of Congress, much less the general public, dare enter into the debate. But there's no reason to be intimidated. Farm programs, at least in concept, are as simple as they are ludicrous. Here's how they work:

First, the U.S. Department of Agricultuer (USDA) benevolently sets out to help farmers by guaranteeing them a high return on their products. Sometimes the bureaucrats simply write farmers checks directly. Other times they set a price support to keep farm prices artificially high, in which case American consumers subsidize the farmers. And quite often, they do both. The farmers, naturally, then produce as much as they possibly can to get as much of that federal money. The more they grow, the more money they receive.

This, of course, leads to big trouble. In no time, following the USDA's signals, farmers produce far more than can possibly be sold at the government-set high price. Before the bureaucrats figure out what's happening, they find themselves buried in surplus farm products, which under the terms of the farm programs the government is obligated to buy. Frantically, they try to dispose of it. Some, they hand out in nutrition programs for the poor. Some they dump overseas in the guise of foreign aid. Much they simply allow to rot in government silos. But in the end, the vast government-induced surpluses become completely unmanageable.

At this point Armey's Axiom kicks in: one bad government program creates the need for a worse one. The bureaucrats begin paying farmers not to farm. The USDA actually pays them to take huge amounts of their land out of production—and I do mean huge. In a typical year, the U.S. government pays our farmers to idle sixty million acres of farm land, an amount equal to the entire land area of Indiana, Ohio, and half of Illinois combined.

After years of careening from one policy to the other, the government has now settled on its final solution to the mess, which is today considered modern "market-driven" farm policy: It pays farmers to produce nearly as much as they can and at the same time it pays them not to produce as much as they can.

For example, if you are a midwestern corn farmer, the government will send you a check for the corn you produce. But as a condition for receiving that check, you must agree to take one-quarter to one-third or more of your land out of production, depending on how much corn the bureaucrats in the USDA think the country needs in a given year. In theory, this incentive to produce is supposed to somehow cancel out the incentive not to produce and some equilibrium will be reached. But in practice, it works about as well as trying to drive a car with one foot on the accelerator and the other on the brake. We end up paying enormous amounts in subsidies, millions of acres of good farm land lies idle, and our government warehouses are full of surplus grain anyway.

We all used to snicker at the insanities of central planning in other countries, like the time Soviet bureaucrats ordered a factory to produce left shoes but forgot to issue an order to make any right ones. But I am not at all sure the Soviets ever came up with a program quite like our farm policy. The irony of it all is that while these programs were designed to help the small family farmers, evidence shows that they are actually hurting them. By their nature, they tend to reward large farm operations, since they are based on acreage. The more land you have to farm on—or not to farm on—the larger your subsidy. The great advantage of family farms is their ability to cut costs by having in many cases the entire family help out (they're fortunately exempted from most federal labor standards). What happens, sadly, is that the corporate farms get the money and buy out the family farms.

Some farm programs, of course, are worse than others. The award for the most primitive farm programs goes to the peanut subsidy. This is nothing less than a government-operated cartel, doing to peanuts what the old OPEC cartel used to do to oil. It works like this. The government simply decrees that an American farmer must have a government-issued license before he is allowed to grow and sell peanuts in the U.S. domestic market. By issuing these licenses only to a select group of privileged growers, the government keeps the supply of peanuts scarce, thus artificially jacking up their price. As a result, U.S. consumers pay $553 million a year in higher food costs to support a relative handful of generally well-off peanut producers. It's estimated that this government-sanctioned consumer rip-off adds 40 cents to the price of a typical jar of peanut butter. If any group of businessmen tried to organize an arrangement like this on their own, they would be charged with collusion and sent straight to the federal penitentiary.

The real crime is in how these government-issued peanut-growing licenses are distributed. There are many ways to get one, but one of the most common is to simply inherit it from a father or grandfather who was growing peanuts when the program first began fifty years ago. You could be a stockbroker in Atlanta, but as long as your grandfather was growing peanuts in 1941, you are one of the privileged few allowed to grow peanuts today. If you don't want to get your hands dirty, you can rent this license out to a real farmer, who in turn will pay you a tribute for allowing him to grow peanuts on your behalf. This isn't a farm program—it's an

American form of feudalism.

In the category of the most extravagant legal looting scam, we have the sugar program. In this case, the government simply blocks foreign sugar from entering the country, which gives U.S. sugar producers a protected market and allows them to sell their sugar to their fellow Americans at close to double the world price. Again, were the government not sponsoring this scam, federal agents would have long ago closed in on the operation. According to Congress' General Accounting Office, American families pay $1.4 billion in higher food prices each year as a result of the program. The truly amazing thing about the sugar program, though, is the outrageous profits that individual sugar producers are allowed to enjoy at the consumers' expense. A single sugar growing family, the aristocratic Fanjuls of south Florida, receive $64 million annually in artificially high profits thanks to the program. (Needless to say, the Fanjuls and their employees dole out hundreds of thousands of dollars in campaign contributions to politicians to keep the program in place.)

For shamelessness, the place of honor must belong to the dairy program. The dairy program works like many of our other farm programs in that the government supports the price of dairy products at an artificially high rate—thus forcing consumers to pay more for milk. But the dairy bureaucrats added a new twist to the usual desperate effort to avoid government-induced surpluses: they have actually paid dairy farmers to kill their cows. In the mid-1980s, USDA financed a thing called the "whole herd buy out" in which dairy farmers were paid $900 million to either export or execute some 1.1 million animals—which incidentally had the unintended effect of instantly knocking the bottom out of the U.S. meat market as the nation was suddenly inundated with tons and tons of red meat. (The bureaucrats answer to that fiasco: they proposed a new farm program for meat producers, too.)

This captures the essence of our farm programs. Leaving aside that the programs cost taxpayers roughly $20 billion a year in taxpayer subsidies and $10 billion a year in higher food prices, the truly staggering aspect of the programs is that, taken together, they amount to a government-sponsored war on American productivity.

SUPERMARKET TO THE WORLD?

The farm program lobby is quite frank about that. When our biochemists recently discovered a hormone that would allow cows to produce more milk, the Agriculture Committee wanted to outlaw it. As one member saw it, "The dairy industry needs more productivity... about as much as a drunk driver needs another drink." Only the government could compare higher productivity with pathological behavior.

Take a moment and grasp the economic absurdity of idling our own farm land, creating a peanut shortage, killing our cows, and banning technological innovations. Can anyone imagine the government paying Detroit to shut down its factories and destroy its machinery? Yet this is exactly what our farm programs do to rural America. And our farmers, and all those who would work to support them, pay the price.

The United States has a clear competitive advantage in agriculture. Unlike poor countries throughout the world, we already have a highly advanced farm infrastructure in place, with excellent modern equipment, grain elevators and other storage facilities, extensive road and rail networks, well-equipped ports, and the most educated farmers on the planet. Left to their own devices, without anachronistic government regulations and subsidies, our farmers could blow away the competition and capture markets that would be ours for generations. Instead, thanks to the government, we are deliberately shutting down our agriculture industry.

There's a whole world out there that should be desperate to buy the farm products that the U.S. government is telling our farmers not to produce. As we pay our farmers not to farm and pull millions of perfectly good acres out of production, foreign nations are bringing millions of new acres into production to meet the demand that we are ignoring. They are incurring huge costs to do so. Not only do they have to build the infrastructure that we already have, often they have to cut down fragile rain forests or construct elaborate irrigation networks. If our farmers were allowed by our government to meet foreign food needs, these nations would never make the investment. But once they do, they will do everything they can to keep our farmers out of their markets. Thus, the markets that we are losing as a result of our federal war on productivity are being lost for good. Even barren Saudi Arabia has now invested billions in developing its own agriculture industry when the Saudis could have filled their needs from the bounty of the American Midwest.

The solution is obvious. Phase out farm programs as quickly as we reasonably can, and eliminate the government regulations that go with them. Our farmers can then produce to meet the needs of the world's soaring population. Rural America, far from being the depressed and declining area it is in places today, will become the home of an economic boom. Not only will farms greatly expand, but the farm supply industry will expand, creating hundreds of thousands of jobs as American workers rush to produce the equipment, the fertilizer, and the machinery a growing farm economy needs. Much as some farmers today cling to the programs, misled by the great agribusiness lobby that supports them, scrapping these programs altogether will seem the best idea since harnessing plow to ox.

TAKING LIBERTIES

Whatever the enormous cost of regulations to the economy as a whole, to individuals the cost sometimes overtakes the sum of everything they have. In extreme cases citizens have had their property completely devalued when the regulators denied them its reasonable use. These "regulatory takings" are often carried out with no compensation and without due process of law, in cavalier disregard of the spirit, if not the letter, of the Constitution. The most notorious cases of this scenario have been carried out in the name of preserving wetlands.

You probably know of some examples of this abuse in your own towns and neighborhoods. The term "wetland," for most of us, connotes frogs, lilies, flamingos, and maybe a few gators prowling about. Yet a piece of land could be considered a wetland if it is dry for 355 days a year. In other words, your backyard could be a wetland. We find this definition nowhere in the 1977 Clean Water Act; that's just how the regulators "interpreted" the law, with no one in Congress or the White House bothering to correct them. So across America people have been going about their business when suddenly the EPA shows up talking about "hydrolic soils" and the like, takes little tests and samples on their property, and declares the place in need of federal protection—from the owners. Some examples of this definition in action follow:

- In Maryland, the Phillips sold their house, withdrew their life savings, and bought a forty-four acre farm to use as their retirement home. They planned to raise part of the money for their purchase by selling off a portion of the land for development. Then the Army Corps of Engineers stepped in and declared the farm a wetland, barring all further construction, rendering the property useless. The government did not recompense the Phillips for their loss.

- An elderly woman in Wyoming wanted to plant a bed of roses on her own land. Federal bureaucrats prevented her from doing it.

- In Pennsylvania, a couple built a tennis court on their own land and were threatened with a lawsuit by the federal government. The charge: polluting a waterway.

- James and Mary Mills of Broad Channel, New York, built a deck on their house and were fined $30,000. One of the charges against them: their deck had cast a shadow on a precious wetland.

- The federal government once held up a license for a residential project because the bureaucrats in charge wanted to protect a wetland. The wetland they were guarding was .0006 acres—about the size of a ping pong table.

Almost as disgraceful as these abuses of power is the silence of our chattering class as they happen. The chatterers are supposed to be the big champions of the powerless. Talk about the Fourth Amendment, and they can rhapsodize for hours about the right of criminal suspects to be free of unlawful searches and seizures; any evidence taken from a suspect's home must be taken according to strictest procedure. But for years the Fifth Amendment rights of property owners have been trampled over by regulatory zealots, with hardly a word from our civil libertarians.

This "regulatory takings" issue crystallizes what excessive government regulation is really all about. Whether we're talking about the government seizing alleged wetlands, destroying small businesses with regulatory fees, telling farmers not to farm, or hamstringing communication entrepreneurs, what we're really talking about is the government infringing on property rights.

Here, I guess, we come to another of those deep fissures in our politics, where both sides invoke the same words while meaning opposite things. Think about it for a moment. Why would someone who passionately argues that violent criminals should go free on account of evidence illicitly obtained, not bring the same fervor to defending a family whose land has just been ruined by government intrusion or whose business has been ruined by government red tape? I do not have time here to explore every mystery of the liberal psyche, but I think it all has something to do with their notion of property.

By any common-sense definition of property and freedom, you would think a defender of one would be a defender of the other. We could invoke all sorts of big-name thinkers on this point. John Adams observed that "the moment the idea is admitted into society that property is not as sacred as the laws of God... anarchy and tyranny commence." George Mason, said that "all men are created equally free and independent, and have certain inherent rights... among which are the enjoyment of life and liberty, with the means of acquiring and possessing property." Lincoln observed that "property is the fruit of labor; property is desirable; it is a positive good." And it might interest our regulators of today that Franklin Roosevelt laid down this principle: "The function of government must be to favor no small group at the expense of its duty to protect the rights of personal freedom and of private property of all its citizens."

But really these words just reinforce something we all know by simple intuition. You are not free unless you are free to own things. If you work for something and another party comes along regularly to regulate or confiscate a portion, to that extent you are working for the other party, not for yourself or your family. It goes back to my point in the introduction: there's no snob quite like the one who looks down on "things." The liberal thinks of property (other people's, at any rate) as a reflection of something aggressive in the owner, something anti-social, grubby, materialistic, unseemly, undeserved. But earners regard his and other people's property very differently. When they look at a house or piece of land, they see years of planning and sacrificing and waiting. When they look at their car, they see years of car payments and the work it took to pay them. When they look at a shop or business, however great or however humble, they see the product of a lot of thought and hard work.

So profound is the feeling, in fact, that it has withstood two generations of windy class-war rhetoric. Perhaps the biggest failure of all liberalism's great hopes for America has been to set the owners of small property against owners of large property. The reason for this failure is simple. To earn any property at all is to understand what property is. The average American doesn't resent the wealthy because he or she is striving for the same things. Striving not just for "things," but for the freedom and accomplishment those things typically represent. Most of us understood that money is not the end-all of human existence long before liberals told us: We'd heard it from far more trustworthy sources, as in the warning that wealth alone will get you into Heaven as surely as a camel will pass through the eye of a needle. But Americans in general aren't preoccupied with money so much as with earning it. Wealth is admired less for its material advantages—although they're okay too—than for the effort and vision it usually takes to get them. Who except a few social levelers in the

Clinton Justice Department begrudges Bill Gates, the founder of Microsoft, his billions? It's the liberal who looks only at his bank account; the rest of us look to his achievement. As a matter of fact it's unlikely a guy like Bill Gates could have accomplished what he did if, like the liberal, he were consumed all the time by thoughts of "things" and money. People who merely covet money seldom get it—unless they go into government. In the free market, the people who value money are the ones who succeed. People like Bill Gates succeed because they are thinking of something beyond themselves, a personal goal beyond self-enrichment. What the political left has never quite grasped is that liberty, not luxury, is the theme of it all. The free market is about freedom not just to have things, but to become something.

Easing the regulation of small business, phasing out farm programs, deregulating telecommunications, protecting property owners from regulatory takings—all this is only the beginning. We must as part of any Freedom agenda examine the whole catalog of regulations at all levels of government and reduce them to their bare minimum. Cutting the entire burden in half is to my mind a modest proposal.

Chapter 11

FREEING OUR CHILDREN

The problem with our public education system is very simple: too often it is run by people more concerned with protecting the system than serving the public. The solution is even simpler: break this monopoly of power, give parents the power to choose where and how their children will be taught, and let our teachers and students flourish once again. I believe this reform is all but inevitable as the Freedom Revolution runs its course. As we free our incomes and businesses and health care from the grasp of government, why should we not also free our own children?

There is no reason why America's schools, public and private alike, should not be the finest in the world. We have many able and devoted teachers doing the best they can, often under hard circumstances, as in our inner cities. We have more wealth than any other society, and a willingness to invest it in public education, so that even in our poorest neighborhoods we spend some $7,000 to $10,000 per student. In many public schools, perhaps even most, we still have an ethic of hard work and achievement; some of our brightest university students today come from public high schools. We have, moreover, something like 6,000 colleges and universities, public and private, offering further incentive to good performance in high school. In material terms, nothing is wanting. Whatever needs fixing in America's public schools today is not primarily a matter of money.

FREE TO CHOOSE

The very idea of public education is in many ways uniquely American. Our public schools began as an idealistic attempt to extend the benefits of education to all. Everyone would get their swing at life's plate. No one would be consigned to a life of drudgery and lost opportunity merely because the family could not afford a private education. Generations of Americans got their big break in life from a first-rate public education. Eight of our last eleven presidents went to public schools. If you had graduated from a public school, in the past that meant you knew the fundamentals of math, science, history, geography, and literature. Not only did you have the precise penmanship and habit of good spelling that marked the era, you could write pretty well, too. You had, in short, the skills to see you through life, to apply for a job and hold it, plus a lot more. Magazines appeared tailored to literate high-school graduates—*Reader's Digest, Life, The Saturday Evening Post*. An entire book publishing industry arose just to accommodate this market of people who had missed college but were ambitious enough to want to educate themselves. There were eagerly awaited series like Will and Ariel Durant's popular histories of the world or Mortimer Adler and Charles Van Doren with their *Great Treasury of Western Thought*. No image captures the spirit of those times better than the sight of encyclopedias sitting proudly on the shelves of the laboring family.

I believe we can restore our public schools to their former greatness. Using Freedom as our guide, we can rebuild our poor schools and make the good public schools better. The key is choice. Our schools suffer from a lack of competition. Instead of forcing parents to send their children to one particular school, we should give them vouchers with which to purchase an education at the school of their choice, public or private.

America's colleges and universities are the best in the world, period. People from all over the world flock to our campuses. The reason is that these colleges must compete for students. Indeed, among the best are public universities forced by the market to compete against private ones—Texas A&M and the entire Utah system being a case in point. Always the customer is free to turn elsewhere, forcing each college to offer better academic goods.

Why should our public schools remain under a power monopoly, protected from the private individual choices of the marketplace? How could more Freedom not help all parties involved? Who is served when the choices are narrowed, when people are less free? The answer, in one very narrow sense, is that the teachers unions are served. The decline of our public schools has coincided remarkably with the rise of teachers unions, who have come to view our schools as their own private domain. I reject the very suggestion that parents, children, and teachers could ever have conflicting interests. This conflict is purely political, arising from the unions' increasing reliance on partisan favor and government coercion. Individually, we have, surely, just as many wise and devoted teachers as in former times. Although some teachers do seem more preoccupied preserving turf and various political causes, I cannot believe they form any kind of majority. I have met too many good teachers to believe that.

The problem is the union as an institutional force. Once it would have been inconceivable to find teachers unions organized against parents and taxpayers. Teachers, it was taken as a given, worked for parents and for the public generally. Yet politically, this is the situation we have today: parents seeking more choices for their children's education, and the unions, trading on their political connections, thwarting those parents.

It doesn't have to be this way. Education can and should be above politics. School choice is, I believe, not only in the interest of parents and students, but in the interest of teachers also. If there are any two groups who should, absent the false conflicts of politics, be working together, it is parents and teachers. Choice is the way to restore that natural alliance.

WHAT HAPPENED TO EDUCATION?

The influence of power and politics has not been good for our schools. The public schools have so deteriorated that four in ten public school teachers send their own children to private schools. And who can blame them? What our founders would make of these schools is suggested by the fact that fewer and fewer public school students today could even name more than one or two of the founders. If the distinctive mark the public schools used to leave on graduates was good citizenship and a belief in hard work, today the distinctive mark seems to be "self-esteem" and an inability to get on in the world. Just like the old public schools, today's have given rise to a publishing industry, but now it comes in the form of dozens of remedial books on how to write letters or term papers or address envelopes or apply for jobs. It's one thing to talk in diffuse terms about "saving our children" or to proclaim the great reforms to come—"Goals 2000" and the like—but when the issue turns specific, to their particular children—well, that's a different matter. They're just being responsible parents.

You have probably heard of Bill Bennett's *Index of Leading Cultural Indicators*. It is pretty depressing reading, surveying as it does the intellectual and social damage our young people have sustained. Here are a few key findings:

- "While expenditures on elementary and secondary education have increased more than 200 percent since 1960, SAT scores have declined 73 points."

- "In a 1989 National Geographic survey of geographical knowledge, Americans between the ages of 18 to 24 finished last among nine countries, including Mexico."

- "In the 1988 International Assessment of Educational Progress exams in science, U.S. students scored last among tested nations." (Korea, the United Kingdom, and Ireland all finished well ahead of the United States.)

- "But when students were asked about their attitude toward math and science, more than two-thirds of American students responded that they were 'good at math,' compared with less than one-quarter of Korean students."

- In 1992, only 6 percent of high school seniors could understand the reasoning and problem-solving techniques involved geometric relationships, algebra, and fractions—all necessary prerequisites for college math.

- During this same period of precipitous decline, grades have gone up... and up... and up. In 1966 teachers handed out twice as many Cs as As. By 1978 they were handing out more As than Cs. By 1990, more than one-fifth of all entering college freshmen had a high-school average of A minus or higher.

- "Twenty-one to 23 percent (40–44 million) of adults demonstrate skills in the lowest level of proficiency (25 percent of these people were immigrants, and two-thirds had ended their education before finishing high school), and 25 to 28 percent (50 million) of adults demonstrated skills in the second lowest level of proficiency."

- As with our math students, most of those who were functionally illiterate thought they were doing just fine. Only 14 million out of 40 million said they didn't read or write well.

- Perhaps the most astonishing revelation of all: "Only 10 to 13 percent of high school graduates reached the two highest levels" of reading and writing proficiency.

It does not have to be this way. There's a temptation to say, "Ah, well, so much for the public schools. They've been in decline for a long time, but then so has the whole culture, and, well, there's not much anyone can do about it...." This attitude is known to many a public school parent. It is exactly that weary, overwhelmed, out-organized feeling the teachers unions are counting on. But the situation is not hopeless. There is one organizing principle stronger than the unions' own organization, and that is the principle of free choice. We can, if our political leaders have the backbone, restore that choice to parents. Indeed, the grateful public reception to Bennett's other well-known book, *The Book of Virtues*, proves how desperately parents long for the day when public school children will again learn the great truths and parables and poems that define our culture. Just as in 1994 we dismissed the arrogant people who ran Congress, we can now dismiss those who have nearly ruined our public schools.

BREAKING UP THE EDUCRATS' MONOPOLY

Considering this state of affairs, union complaints about inadequate resources seem a little hollow. The United States spends more on education than any nation on earth. Resource upon resource has been poured into public education. In most every state it's the first or second highest item in the budget, and every state has its own department of education. In the eighties our total education investment grew by a third in real terms. In 1992 America spent almost as much on elementary and secondary education ($257 billion, $32 billion of it federal) as we did on national defense ($300 billion). Public school spending in real terms has quadrupled since 1950, rising to $6,500 per student, compared to just $4,100 per student in private schools. In Washington, D.C., it's $8,200 per student—more than the tuition of many elite universities. However, in 1993 nine of the top ten states in student performance were in the bottom half in school spending.

And what about our federal Department of Education? One vaguely remembers that it was supposed to turn things around, reverse the decline in public education. As with the National Education Association building in Washington, you drive by the huge block-shaped structure and wonder exactly what's going on inside. It is a Carter legacy, a 1976 campaign promise fulfilled to great fanfare in 1980. Finally, we were making education a national priority! The education establishment, which had pitched in during the Carter campaign, would now have a cabinet secretary, sitting right there next to the president to advise on the issue. Eighteen years, countless billions of dollars, and who knows how many conferences and reports and education bills later, everything is worse. In every category public education is in decline, with the sole difference that we now have federal experts to trace it, committees to study it, and a cabinet department to declare it official.

The situation led at least one union leader recently to something of a public confession. To his great credit, Albert Shanker, longtime president of the American Federation of Teachers, put it this way: "It's time to admit that public education operates like a planned economy, a bureaucratic system in which everybody's role is spelled out in advance and there are few incentives for innovation and productivity. It's no surprise that our school system doesn't improve: It more resembles the communist economy than our own market economy." He estimated that "ninety-five percent of the kids who go to college in the United States would not be admitted to college anywhere else in the world."

Why is school choice not simply *a* reform, but *the* reform? Because monopoly control is the problem. Only school choice restores consumer sovereignty over what goes on in the classroom. Only Freedom can radically change a school's incentive structure, bringing the parents' values and expectations and standards into the classroom. It is worth noting that none of the bitter conflicts troubling our public schools—multiculturalism, liberal sex education, school prayer, creationism—are found in schools not monopolized by the unions. They are problems peculiar to government-run schools, because only there is such coercion possible.

A LITANY OF FOILED SOLUTIONS

The current school reform movement was sparked by the 1983 "Nation at Risk" report of the National Commission on Excellence in Education. But that widely publicized report was not the first by a panel of national educational "experts" to lament a rising tide of mediocrity in our schools nor the first to warn of the superior German and Japanese educational systems. Nor was it the first to call for longer school days, a return to the basics, or renewed emphasis on science and mathematics. An almost identical report issued by the so-called Committee of Ten, led by Harvard University president Charles Elliott, included the very same assessments and recommendations—in 1893.

These tired ideas for reforming the current system, rather than replacing it with a system of free schools, have failed before and are doomed to fail again. Here's a list of the most familiar suggestions and why they won't work.

More money

The United States spends more on education than any nation on Earth. Yet objective researchers can find no correlation between spending and student performance.

One reason school spending has no effect on performance is that much of it never reaches the classroom. The New York City school system, which enrolls about a million students, spends $9,000 per student, of which no more than a third ever reaches the classroom. The system employs a central district staff of 4,000, housed in eight buildings, and employs an army of school custodians who are paid an average of $58,000 a year to clean classrooms twice a week and mop the floors three times a year. By contrast, the city's Catholic school system, educating 110,000 students, employs a central office staff of just thirty-three—and gets far better results. How can private schools manage to do so much better with so much less money? Perhaps it is for the reason given by the principal of a dirt-poor, academically outstanding black school, who, when asked to explain the school's excellence, reportedly answered, "We're so poor, all we can afford to do is teach the basics."

Higher teacher salaries

Paying teachers more on average is also not the panacea many think it is. From 1960 to 1990 average teacher salaries grew by 45 percent in real terms to $35,334 a year, which is faster than average wages for the rest of the work force. In 1993 Utah ranked forty-ninth in teacher salaries, but scored first in the nation on the National Assessment of Educational Progress. Clearly, we should reward the better teachers through the merit system, but simply raising pay without other reforms is not going to be the solution.

Charter schools and private management

Two reform ideas currently gaining popularity are charter schools (public funding with reduced bureaucratic oversight) and private management (public funding with private administration), but neither proposal promises real change because neither breaks the government's financial monopoly. Nor does either idea do anything to restore consumer sovereignty. They are at best partial reforms.

Public school choice alone

Public school choice (letting parents choose among competing government-run schools) is a promising idea that is showing encouraging results, although it, too, fails to break the government monopoly. First tried in East Harlem, New York, in 1974, this idea has spread, in various forms, to fourteen states and 100 cities. After implementing its program, East Harlem's graduation rates rose dramatically from less than 50 percent to more than 90 percent, and its students have shown improvement in basic reading and math skills. But in most other respects, East Harlem schools remain mediocre. Ultimately, public school choice promises only limited improvement because it does not provide the true competition between government and private schools that only genuine school choice can offer.

Now many people who oppose or are at least apprehensive about school choice do raise objections that deserve to be answered in good faith. But all these arguments dissolve under closer examination.

School choice will bankrupt the public schools. We are told that choice would be too "costly," that it would "drain precious resources" from the government schools. This is an odd objection given how the public schools use their present resources. In any case, one virtue of competition is that it always lowers prices. Costs rise where power is monopolized, because the consumer has no choice but to pay what is asked. Just as in private business nonessentials and incompetents are cast off, so in education would schools competing for students have to reform themselves in order to attract students. The threat of "bankruptcy," as critics of school choice use it, actually translates into the imperative to provide better service at lower operating costs. Moreover, with each student who moves to a private school, the cost of running his former school goes down by that amount (less such fixed costs as electricity and bricks and mortar). So this reform could actually leave the public schools financially better off.

School choice will enable private schools to "cream" the rich and bright students off the top, leaving the poor and hard-to-teach behind. Taken to its logical conclusion, this argument is a case against the existence of private schools, period. Yes, the bright kids of rich parents have the option of private education. But the whole idea of school choice, after all, is to extend the advantage of private schooling to as many non-rich kids and parents as want it. Our public schools are not charged with leveling natural or material advantages; they're charged with helping all our kids do the best they can and fulfill whatever gifts they have. It helps no one to force the brighter students down. Moreover, public schools currently spend considerable extra funds on slow-learning students. There is no reason that money could not be used to "sweeten" vouchers for such children, giving private schools an incentive to take them on and meet their special needs more effectively than the public schools do today.

School choice will undermine the "common school" tradition of American democracy. The term "common school" invokes the old tradition of bringing together a diverse, stratified citizenry to be steeped in the attitudes of democracy. This objection seems absurd considering how "democracy" is practiced by the teachers unions themselves. Essentially what the unions are saying to parents is, "We must teach democracy, therefore please be quiet and let us run your children's lives as we see fit." Another falsehood in this argument is apparent in any urban public school. No schools are more segregated by race or class than are urban public schools, which is why liberals have had to rely on forced busing to change things. The moment any family in these districts has worked and saved enough to get out, they get out.

Parents won't choose wisely. The argument asks us to envision the worst possible parent, sitting around swilling beer and haggling with the wife while the browbeaten kids go neglected. Such people cannot be trusted to make important decisions on behalf of their children. Most of us, I think, have a somewhat higher opinion of the average public school parent. Of course there are unconscientious parents—or worse. But we cannot plan an education system taking them as the norm. To do so is to insult the vast numbers of good parents who do take an interest in their children's education—more interest, in fact, than the unions encourage. If the great majority of parents were not conscientious, there wouldn't be a school-choice movement and we wouldn't even be debating the issue.

School choice will give rise to extremist schools. This was the accusation that did in Proposition 174, the 1993 California initiative to restore school choice. As Democrat Assembly Speaker Willie Brown put it, "Can you imagine a KKK group, skinheads, witches, or other cult groups setting up schools to teach their philosophy and using taxpayers' dollars to do so? This country has a history of blocking religious and dangerous cult groups from using public funds, which must be continued." It was the only argument left to Speaker Brown, because the initiative had accommodated all other conceivable practical objections to school choice. It proposed using only some of the state's $30 billion in education funds for vouchers, to see how the idea worked before going further. It was carefully drafted to ensure that public schools would be reimbursed for all fixed costs. And it required that any private school accepting a voucher conform to all anti-fraud, civil rights, and safety rules. So, lacking reasons, the speaker came up with his vision of witches and the Klu Klux Klan setting up schools of their own.

There were a few problems with this argument. First, private schools are reviewed and certified by professional accreditation agencies. Without that imprimatur, no student attending the school may be accepted into college. Second, neither skinheads nor the Klu Klux Klan are known for their hunger for knowledge, making it unlikely they would take the trouble to found schools. Third, an awful lot of skinheads and other troubled youth are the products of the moral chaos of urban public schools. On balance, school choice would certainly reduce the numbers of sad, troubled children. In any case, exit polls revealed that voters would have voted for the measure provided it were amended to guard against such groups, so Speaker Brown will soon have to come up with something else.

School choice will produce unaccountable "diploma mills" and "fly by night" schools. Translation: "We'll run the diploma mills, if you don't mind!" Free-market schools could not possibly be any less accountable than are our public schools today. As with private colleges, schools under a voucher plan will have to compete for good reputations. College admissions departments and employers can weigh the value of a diploma for themselves. That's why they interview applicants, to compare academic history with direct impressions.

School choice will destroy the private schools. The notion here is that if government, through vouchers, is effectively funding private schools, it will soon come to control and perhaps destroy them—a valid enough concern. The first reply is that, of course, many laws already apply directly or indirectly to private schools. Under the 1988 Civil Rights Restoration Act, for example, acceptance of government education funding, even the mere admission of students who receive federal student loans, makes an entire private college liable to all federal civil rights laws. A future liberal Congress (may it never happen!) might try to apply this same principle to elementary and secondary schools. However, Milton

Friedman, who first proposed the idea of school choice vouchers back in the 1950s, argues, and I agree, that it is possible to build a legislative "firewall" against the attachment of federal or state strings to vouchers. California's Proposition 174 contained a provision building just such a firewall right into the state's constitution. But, of course eternal vigilance will always be the price of liberty.

School choice violates the separation of church and state. "Congress shall make no law respecting an establishment of religion, or prohibiting the free exercise thereof...." This means, Supreme Court rulings have held, that government cannot give money to private schools—good news for most private schools, which want nothing to do with government money. But under school choice reforms government would not be giving money to private schools; it would be giving parents the money and allowing them to choose any school they like, public or private. It offers something modern government rarely offers, an entirely noncoercive arrangement.

Chapter 12

FREEING HEALTH CARE

Most Americans today think that our health care system is private, free from government interference. Unlike our European friends, our doctors are not government employees, our hospitals are not part of the government bureaucracy, and we still have a vast medical supply industry that, driven by free enterprise, gives us the best medical devices and cures in the world.

But if our health care system is really free, why doesn't it feel that way? A typical American cannot choose his health plan; he can only accept whatever plan his employer offers. Most likely, his employer is trying to herd him into some sort of health maintenance organization (HMO) whether he wants to be in one or not. He cannot change jobs, moreover, because there's no guarantee that he won't lose his health coverage altogether. (At any given moment, forty million of us have no health insurance coverage.)

All the while, he is paying exorbitant amounts for health care and is powerless to take his business elsewhere.

If that feels more like a government health care system than a functioning free market, there's a good reason. To a large degree, it *is* a government health care system.

The truth is that the government, even without the Clinton health care takeover, is deeply involved in our health care. The best way to bring costs down, increase choice, eliminate job lock, and put the American citizen in control of his own health care needs is to get the government out.

Government's Assault on Health Care

Americans face an odd situation. On the one hand, the average American has access to the finest medical system in the world, with the most advanced technology, the latest drugs, and the most efficient and humane hospitals anywhere on earth. On the other hand, for many it is difficult to buy their way into that system. Typically, Americans purchase nearly all medical services, even the smallest items, through third-party payment, a highly inefficient system fraught with moral hazard (third-party payment schemes are especially liable to abuse, since they involve spending other people's money).

Still more problematic, the average American, assertive and self-reliant as he may otherwise be, becomes, at the mere mention of health care, as limp and passive as if he were already on the operating table. He lets his employer buy an insurance policy for him, settles for whatever policy the employer chooses, and lets the employer decide which specific procedures and providers that policy will cover. In no other area of insurance do we find such remarkable passivity. Whatever the product—life insurance, fire insurance, car insurance, homeowners' insurance, renter's insurance, or the like—virtually all of us buy it out of the yellow pages, as with any other useful or desirable commodity. But not health insurance. Why?

One reason is that, while nominally held in private hands, America's health care system is swiftly becoming another province of Big Government. Even without the Clinton plan, government at all levels spends forty-two cents of every health care dollar in America (fifty-three cents, if the $70 billion-a-year tax subsidy for employer-purchased insurance is counted as government spending). Thus, nearly $400 billion of the $950 billion health care economy is bought and paid for by federal, state, and local governments. And the government's share is growing.

That involvement comes in the form of a three-pronged assault on the medical sector. The three prongs are Medicare, the government's health insurance program for the elderly; Medicaid, for the poor; and the archaic employer-based, third-party payment system, which the feds keep in place through a generous income-tax subsidy.

After thirty years of steady growth, the combined effects of these three prongs have produced a medical inflation disconnected from the rest of the economy. General price levels rise and fall, but medical prices only rise. Spurred by "compassion," the government channels ever higher amounts into the system. The resulting inflation, in turn, causes people to go without coverage, which provides a further pretext for "reform," which in Washington translates as full-scale government takeover. What President Clinton tried to do in one bold stroke is happening gradually anyway. While ailing Canadians, who have a government-run system, look with yearning to our system, we proceed inexorably toward replicating theirs.

To avoid Canada's fate, America must privatize its public health care system and free its private one. We must once again put consumers in control of their health care choices and move away from today's employer-based system. Almost overnight we'll see job lock evaporate, competition blossom, and price increases slow down or even stop. We must also reform, radically, government health spending. If we replace today's exploding Medicare and Medicaid with more sensibly structured programs that put consumers in charge, our medical inflation will abate still further.

ROOTS OF THE PROBLEM

Historically, our health care inflation problem has its roots in a minor administrative decision made during the Second World War. Wartime bureaucrats chose to exclude employer-provided health insurance from the definition of income for tax purposes. One of history's best examples of the law of unintended consequences, this seemingly innocuous choice is the principal cause of what is today called the "health care crisis."

Without this decision, there would never have been an employer-based health insurance system. There would never have been our present heavy reliance on third-party payment with its inherent invitation to overconsume; no job-lock problem (since job lock can only occur when employment and insurance are linked); less need for government health care subsidies (since the pure market system, had it not been supplanted by the employer-based system, would have kept insurance affordable for the poor and elderly); no soaring medical inflation (caused by Medicare, Medicaid, and the tax subsidy); and far fewer uninsured Americans—in short, no health crisis.

Here perhaps we have the best possible illustration of another Armey Axiom: compassion without understanding can be cruel. The wartime bureaucrats thought they were doing an obviously good thing. To decide otherwise—to declare that employer-provided health benefits were a form of income (which by any rational measure they are)—would have suggested the government did not regard health care as a right.

Not surprisingly, this nobly intentioned policy was a response to an earlier, noble intention—wartime wage and price controls. With the demand for war materials shooting up after December 7, 1941, the price of labor (wages) rose as well. The government, rather than let the market clear, resorted to the age-old temptation to outlaw higher prices. Throughout forty centuries of human history, from Hammurabi to President Nixon, price controls have produced the same results: scarcity, lower quality, evasion of the law, black markets, and bigger government. President Roosevelt's wartime price controls, dictating the official price of everything from labor to meat to gasoline, fared no better; they turned all these commodities into scarce, rationed goods. Naturally, in the labor market, employers, experiencing shortages of workers, sought incentives to attract manpower. Health care seemed the perfect incentive.

In 1942, the War Labor Board, charged with fighting wage inflation, ruled that fringe benefits up to 5 percent of wages would not be deemed inflationary. The following year, the IRS ruled that employer-provided health insurance, already tax-deductible to employers as a legitimate cost of doing business, did not have to be declared as income by workers. Thus, cash wages would be taxed, but health benefits received from employers would not. The combination of these two decisions was economic dynamite. Employers seized on health benefits as a way to attract workers. Workers eagerly opted for tax-free fringe benefits. By the war's end, total enrollment in employer-provided group health insurance plans had more than tripled from seven million to 26 million members. The first rumblings of today's "crisis" could be heard—but no one was listening.

After the war, despite powerful new incentives to buy health insurance during the 1950s and early 1960s, the third-party payment system didn't swell to its modern proportions. Insurance remained, for most Americans, merely a backup method of financing medical purchases. Close to 50 percent of all health spending was still paid out of pocket. But with the creation in 1965 of today's twin medical mammoths, Medicare and Medicaid, that self-reliance began to fade. Americans relied on third parties to pay all their bills. And health spending took off.

Between 1940 and 1960 health care spending rose modestly, from 4.2 percent of the annual gross national product to 5.2 percent. From 1960 to 1992, however, the percentage of gross national produce spent on health care almost tripled, reaching an estimated 13.4 percent in 1992. Spending on Medicare and Medicaid rose from 5.9 percent of total health care spending in 1967, the first full year these two programs were open for business, to 28 percent of total health care spending in 1990.

Third-party payment has grown so rapidly that today every time an American spends a dollar on health services, he pays only twenty-one cents out of pocket. The rest is paid by third parties. In this sense Americans are overinsured, not underinsured. We have acquired an addiction to spending other people's money, with the usual destructive results addictions bring.

I witnessed an example of this the other day. A member of my staff was stung by a wasp. She went to the doctor and was given a simple ice pack. When the nurse brought it out, my staffer asked how much it would cost. "Oh, don't worry," said the nurse. "Your insurance will cover it." Her innocence lost, my assistant then got to thinking what other ailments she might have that required attention. Later, when she told me her story, I reminded her of a favorite Armey Axiom: no one spends other people's money as wisely as he spends his own.

PREDICTABLE UNPREDICTED COSTS

There is probably no better example of this principle than the two federal health programs: Medicare and Medicaid. In January 1967 the Johnson administration projected that Medicaid would cost $2.3 billion in fiscal year 1968. Its actual cost was $3.5 billion—off by a third. And the program has been galloping ever since, to roughly $140 billion in fiscal year 1995. Likewise, Medicare's hospital insurance in 1965 was projected to cost $9 billion in 1990. It wound up costing $67 billion—a disparity of a mere $58 billion. The demand for Part A, the hospital-insurance portion of Medicare, was so underestimated, it became evident as early as 1967 that the program would soon go broke. Congress chose to raise taxes rather than control costs. As a result, by 1975 the payroll taxes needed to pay for Part A were double what Congress had anticipated.

As Medicaid hid from poor Americans and as Medicare hid from elderly Americans the true costs of their medical purchases, the use of these services began to rise, and so did prices. Rising prices, in turn, spurred the development of expensive new technologies and drugs, fundamentally changing the nature of health care and further raising its price. Because the tax code was encouraging people to overinsure and prefer first-dollar coverage with little or no out-of-pocket expense to the consumer (biases carried over into Medicare and Medicaid), people demanded more health care relative to other goods, driving prices still higher.

Soon the government could not keep up with the explosion of public medical costs, and by the early 1980s Congress imposed a complicated system of price controls to rein in these monsters. In an absurdly complex scheme, Washington fixed hospital charges on the basis of hundreds of "diagnostic-related groups" and later fixed doctors' fees according to something mysteriously known as "relative value units." Each procedure was given a code number and assigned a price based on formulae whose details fill page after page after page of the federal code of regulations.

Predictably, these fixed prices were set below doctors' and hospitals' actual costs, typically paying only 60 to 70 percent of hospital costs. Soon a desperate Congress began ratcheting them down still further. Doctors and hospitals also responded predictably. They began shifting their unreimbursed costs from government-insured patients to privately insured patients. This cost-shifting pushed up the price of private insurance still higher, putting it beyond the reach of millions of Americans who were either ineligible for Medicaid but did not have access to the income tax subsidy or so young and healthy that insurance was no longer a good buy for them. Indeed, many of today's uninsured are really self-insured, preferring to rely on personal and family savings than overpriced insurance.

Thanks to the employer-based system, the unemployed and self-employed got no tax subsidy at all, so insurance is about twice as expensive for them as it is for those with employer-provided insurance. And when people lose their jobs, the discriminatory tax policy makes sure they lose their insurance too, temporarily expanding the number of the uninsured and making the employed afraid to leave their jobs. Thus when the economy weakened during the Nixon–Carter years, the number of uninsured began to rise noticeably.

FROM CRISIS TO NEAR-CATASTROPHE

For a time in the mid-1970s some states settled on the theory that health costs were rising because there were "too many hospitals." The result was a rationing scheme called "certificates of need." Anyone who proposed building a hospital would have to get from the bureaucracy a certificate attesting to the "need" for a hospital in that neighborhood. The result: fewer hospitals, less competition, higher prices, and higher mortality rates in the states that had these regulations compared with states that did not.

Also in the 1970s lobbyists for medical providers began nagging state legislatures to require insurers in those states to cover specific services, such as acupuncture, hairpieces, and even marriage counseling, regardless of consumer need or desire. From 1970 to the present these mandates multiplied from thirty to more than one thousand, each adding incrementally to health care premiums. (Understandably, as soon as some new procedure or therapy was added to the list of covered services, a great and hitherto unsuspected need for it immediately arose.) The National Center for Policy Analysis estimates that as many as one in four of the uninsured has simply been priced out of the market by these laws.

As the 1980s arrived crisis loomed. By the time of his 1988 presidential campaign the governor of Massachusetts, Michael Dukakis, was speaking regularly of the "tragedy of 37 million uninsured" Americans. It was an exaggeration. For one thing, half the uninsured were merely temporarily without insurance, being between jobs for four months or less. One-third were voluntarily uninsured, in other words, self-insured, usually because being young and healthy they found insurance too expensive compared with their likelihood of needing it. Only about six million could be called chronically uninsured—people who went without insurance involuntarily for more than a year. The figure also implied that people were not getting medical care. In truth, doctors were still honoring their ancient ethic of not turning away the seriously ill, even when they arrived at the doctor's door poor and uninsured. Although doctors make fewer house calls, there are still many "Dr. Welbys" in this country who simply tear up the bill and send the patient off with a handshake. Indeed, this ethic was codified in the 1985 federal budget law requiring all medical providers that do business with Medicare (i.e., virtually all of them) to treat emergency cases without regard to ability to pay. Today, hospitals annually give away billions in charity care. People were not, as Dukakis suggested, dying on the hospital steps. And so, unmoved by his cries of a "crisis" demanding more government supervision, voters, still enjoying the glow of the Reagan years, spurned Dukakis.

Four years later, however, the Bush recession gave more resonance to warnings of a "crisis," and Governor Clinton was able to win votes with promises to "squeeze waste" out of the health system and devote the savings to covering every American—a seemingly costless solution.

Once in the White House, the new president moved quickly to make health reform the centerpiece of his presidency, convening a huge, but secretive, thousand-member task force chaired by the first lady to come up with a plan. As the task force's myriad "working groups" pushed pieces of the proposal through dozens of "tollgates," presided over by the president's old friend and management guru Ira Magaziner, the plan grew in size and complexity. Indeed, by the time of its unveiling on October 27, 1993, Magaziner was said to be the only human being able to make sense of it.

And what was this brand new Health Security Act? My own reading of its 1,342 pages persuaded me that it was the desperate final attempt by Big Government to bring about the "Statist Millennium." It is amazing to think back on the bravado with which this sweeping legislation was billed. Each of us would to be given a "health security card." This card would entitle us to lifelong government-provided health care. It would be *our* card, the president declared in his 1994 State of the Union address, "something no one can ever take away from you." It struck me, sitting in the

House chamber that night, that this was not the best sales pitch for reminding people of what they really wanted to keep in their wallets.

This was to be the final fulfillment of the New Deal vision of lifelong "security" under the management of the state. Three of the five postwar Democrat presidents—Truman, Johnson, and Carter—tried and failed to add this capstone to the welfare state, the final piece that would consolidate middle-class dependence on Big Government forever. Now it would finally happen; that goal and all the powers it would bring were within reach. It would have set up the most bewildering bureaucracy in history and required 100,000 bureaucrats to operate it. The repudiation of this monstrous proposal was one of the best moments in our history. And to their party's credit, it was centrist Democrats who made the decisive difference in killing it.

FROM "FREE" HEALTH CARE TO HEALTH CARE FREEDOM

Having dodged this bullet, how do we fix the health care system?

We can start by clearly identifying the true cause of our current medical inflation and insurance problems, overwhelmingly caused by government.

The test of market-oriented health reform is simple: to what extent does it give Freedom to people?

Let us begin by discussing that 60 percent of the health care system that is still at least nominally private. The most direct and effective solution to our medical inflation problems is simply to reverse the World War II policy that began it all. Repeal the tax exclusion for employer-provided health insurance. While employers would still be allowed to deduct it as a legitimate business expense, employees would now have their health benefits taxed as income.

With the tax exclusion removed, three things would happen. First, employees would demand that their now-taxed health benefits be converted into cash wages, since the advantage of health benefits over cash wages would be eliminated. All things being equal most people prefer cash they can spend as they choose over payment in kind. The glue binding insurance and employment would be dissolved. Job lock would vanish. Employees, not their bosses, would control their own health care dollars and purchase health plans that more truly suit their needs. Rather than pool through their workplace for group rates, they could join voluntarily with members of their church, union, college alumni association, professional association, or others to obtain group coverage.

Second, many people would cut back on the amount of insurance they buy. They would drop their costly and wasteful first-dollar coverage with low deductibles (typically as low as $250 today) and switch to more basic coverage with high deductibles (say, $1,000 to $5,000). So they would use their insurance only in a true emergency. Overnight, patients would be asking their doctor how much suggested procedures cost and whether the generic version of a drug might be just as effective as the brand name and weighing the cost of a proposed test against the cost of some other good—say, a child's college tuition or a down payment on a house.

Some proponents of government medicine fear this change would mean the end of preventive medicine. They say that people faced with paying a fee out of pocket for each doctor's visit would choose to stop seeing the doctor except in emergencies and that costs would rise since illnesses would not be treated early on. This argument fails to distinguish between two kinds of preventive medicine. The first kind consists in frequent, seemingly free visits to the doctor—the hit-or-miss approach, which can be wasteful. The second kind of preventive medicine consists simply of living a healthy life which is more efficient, producing immediate as well as long-term benefits. When people are allowed to choose between medical services and other goods, they will reduce the first, less efficient kind of "prevention" and encourage the second, more efficient kind. All of which would produce the third and most important effect of this simple tax-code reform: healthier citizens.

According to a famous Rand Corporation study done in the 1970s, people asked to shoulder more of their health-care costs through higher deductibles and co-payments use up to 40 percent fewer medical services with no significant worsening of their health. States and private firms that use incentives to encourage their employees to live healthier lives have seen dramatic results. *Forbes* magazine, for example, pays each employee $2 for every $1 of medical claims they do not incur, up to a maximum of $1,000. The result: *Forbes'* health costs fell 17 percent in 1992 and 12 percent in 1993, while enrollment in the company's wellness program shot up. People literally ran to the treadmills to make sure they got that $1,000 at the end of the year.

Another criticism leveled against ending the tax subsidy is that it would amount to a tax increase on the middle class. This need not be the case. Enacting the flat tax (which would end the preferential treatment of all fringe benefits, not just health insurance) would ensure virtually all Americans a significant tax cut, leaving them with more money to spend on health care, not less.

Still other critics are concerned that the poor would be hurt by the end of the employer-based system. Actually, the poor would greatly benefit from the lower prices, higher take-home pay, and greater mobility and choice that a liberated system would offer.

A number of other secondary reforms could dramatically cut health care costs. Republicans have long advocated medical malpractice reform as a way to bring down medical costs. We believe doctors working in good faith should not have to order additional, wasteful tests and procedures solely from fear of a future lawsuit. Such "defensive medicine" adds billions each year to the nation's medical tab. In our first hundred days in the majority, the Republican Congress voted for the first meaningful medical malpractice bill ever, imposing a stiff $250,000 cap on pain and suffering awards, the massive sympathy prizes that bear no relation to the actual costs required to make a malpractice victim whole. And this is just the first step.

So much for the 60 percent of the health care economy that is in private hands. What about the other 40 percent, dominated by Medicare and Medicaid? My suggestion, put in Washington policy jargon: block-grant Medicaid and create Medicare choices. Or in plain English: fire the bureaucrats and free the consumers.

PALEO-CARE

As I write these words, Part A of Medicare, which pays for retired people's hospital services, is on the brink of receivership, and the Clinton administration is doing absolutely nothing to save it. The president's written policy prescription for Medicare is for it to go belly up. The Health Insurance Trust Fund, upon which Part A depends, will spend more than it takes in next year and is projected to become insolvent in 2002. To save it, the current Medicare payroll tax would have to be more than doubled from 2.9 cents to 6.5 cents out of every dollar of wages earned in the country. If the tax is not raised, pressure will grow to raid the main Social Security retirement trust fund, endangering even further the security of soon-to-retire baby boomers.

Medicare Part B faces similar problems. Premiums for this voluntary program, which pays for retirees' physician services, barely cover 25 percent of its actual costs. General revenues cover most of the rest. The premiums would have to be increased from the $36.60 a month they were in 1994 to $144 a month just to keep those proportions where they are today. I would not bet on members of Congress voting for that one. Most still remember the last time Congress tried to raise Medicare premiums—without my vote—as part of the 1988 Medicare Catastrophic Coverage Act. That bill made seniors so angry, it had to be repealed within a year. One crowd of particularly virile senior citizens even tried to overturn the car of the then-chairman of the Ways and Means Committee, Dan Rostenkowski—with Rostenkowski still in it.

As I write this, House Republicans are preparing legislation to create what we call a "Better Medicare," to place alongside the current 1965 paleolithic version of Medicare. Better Medicare would give every beneficiary the option to keep his current coverage or choose from a host of private insurance plans. A beneficiary could choose a managed care plan that offers more benefits or a high–deductible plan, and then pocket the premium savings and self-insure for the deductible. He could choose the benefits package that best suits his needs, trading a less useful benefit for pharmaceutical coverage instead, for example.

The range of options will reflect real prices and reward consumers for shopping frugally. Government shouldn't dictate a limited number of options from which retirees must choose. The point is to turn consumers into wise shoppers and let the market rise up to meet their demands. By harnessing the awesome power of consumer self-interest, we will not only make Medicare less wasteful but improve quality and patient satisfaction and keep the system sound and able to serve the future generations of retirees.

Medicaid, too, is in terrible shape. The joint federal-state program for the poor is driving state budgets across the country into the red, and state spending on Medicaid could easily quadruple by 2000. Believe it or not, the $90 billion-a-year federal share of the program is growing nearly as quickly, by more than 10 percent a year, which means it will double in size by 2000 if nothing is done to fix it.

Since Medicaid serves a quite different population from Medicare's (one that, unlike the elderly, cycles on and off the program based on income), saving this program will require a different approach. The best option for saving Medicaid is turning it over to the states, with the federal government providing its fair share of the funding in the form of block grants. Under the House Republican plan being prepared for consideration later this year, we would repeal the current detailed Medicaid rates and regulations (about which the states are forever complaining) and instead give the money to each state in the form of one big annual check. That state could then use the grant as it sees fit, provided the money goes to provide medical care to the poor. By cutting out one full layer of bureaucratic waste and freeing states to innovate, block grants would enable us to direct more money, in real terms, to the medical needs of the indigent, while getting costs under control. My guess is we would be able to set a realistic cap on the program's growth rate (at, say, 5 percent a year instead of the current unsustainable 10 percent).

Finally, one of the best things we could do for American medicine in the next couple of years would be to reform the federal Food and Drug Administration (FDA), the agency charged with approving every new drug and medical device sold in the United States. The FDA's approval process is notoriously slow and bureaucratic, sometimes taking as many as nine years to approve a new drug—or reapprove an old drug for a new use. A charitable estimate is that the FDA's sluggish approval process doubles the cost of bringing a new drug to market. It now costs more than $231 million and takes an average of twelve years to bring a single new drug to the local pharmacy. This process results in hundreds or even thousands of premature deaths each year because vital cures are withheld from the sick.

Instead of a massive, old-style bureaucracy testing drugs and devices for years to verify both their safety and efficacy (meaning whether they work as advertised), why not let the market decide whether that drug or device is effective while restricting the FDA to the simple task of issuing a seal of safety? As with UL–approved electrical devices, a drug or medical device bearing the seal of safety would be considered safe for public use. Doctors could begin prescribing it as soon as it received this seal—even before the agency's routine paperwork had been completed, which currently adds needless months and years to the approval ordeal. This new FDA would actually fulfill its purpose of saving lives, instead of just employing bureaucrats.

We must stop judging government programs by the professed motives of those who offer them and instead judge them by their results. Any objective analysis of government-funded health care is bound to reveal the truth—that such an approach is ultimately more costly, less efficient, and less beneficial to the sick than health care in a free market.

We are now living in a half-way house—somewhere between medicine as practiced by family physicians of fifty years ago and the government-controlled medical systems of socialized nations, where patients wait for months to have crucial surgery and doctors engage in collective bargaining.

We can, I believe, bring back the day when doctors were the most respected members of the community, when employers did not begrudge their workers' illnesses, when most people could pay their hospital bills out of their salaries, and when the term "health care crisis" did not even exist. We can make the world's finest health care system still finer, still more life-saving, still more miraculous in its healing powers—if only we can muster the discipline to set it free.

Chapter 13

FREEDOM FOR THE POOR

Thus far, we have been discussing proposals that dare to assume that human beings can be trusted with Freedom and responsibility. But can Freedom cope with the crime, poverty, dependency, and other pathologies that are destroying the lives and the futures of children in our inner cities?

The answer is an unequivocal yes. There is no "natural" rate of poverty, crime, or illegitimacy that simply must be endured. Nothing in logic or the peculiar circumstances of cities should require that Americans tolerate, in Newt Gingrich's memorable litany, "twelve-year-olds killing each other, fourteen-year-olds getting pregnant, seventeen-year-olds dying of AIDS, and eighteen-year-olds graduating with diplomas they can't read." The poor, we are reminded on the Highest Authority, will always be with us. But nothing ordains that their poverty be the Nightmare on Elm Street. With the right policies, America can again be a nation with no permanent underclass—no group of people condemned as if by fate to remain at the bottom of the economic and social ladder forever.

Good public policy begins with recognizing what approaches have already failed. We can without hesitation dismiss proposals for additional wars on poverty, model cities, urban Marshall plans, public housing projects, job corps, job search centers, government child care, summer jobs programs, early childhood intervention strategies, Head Starts, Even Starts, self-esteem classes, national service corps, or anything with a name like Operation Hope. After spending three decades and more than $5 trillion at the federal, state, and local levels ($350 billion in 1994 alone), a sum in real terms greater than the entire cost of World War II, we have seen the outcome of such government "solutions"—they do not work. Total welfare spending is now more than twice the level needed to raise the incomes of all poor Americans above the official poverty line.

The language of modern government—war, corps, campaign, operation, strategy—suggests a military understanding of a problem that, at its root, is economic, moral, and spiritual. Bureaucracy is the natural tool of Big Government, but the effects of bureaucracy on our cities evoke images of round-the-clock aerial bombardment.

To end poverty, reduce out-of-wedlock births, and give poor children hope for the future, we must scrap today's failed welfare system and replace dependency with work, marriage, and personal responsibility. To end crime, we must put police back on the street, reform our justice system, abolish parole, and double the number of prisons. If this sounds like a radical agenda, it is. But it is not an unrealistic agenda. It is no different from the norms that prevailed in America from the founding right up through the fourth decade of this century.

This "Tough Love" option is truly compassionate because it trusts in the inborn abilities of people. It assumes they are capable of handling Freedom's responsibilities and that, to the extent they are not capable, the natural safety-net—family, friends, churches, and charities—will supply, with few exceptions, what is lacking. Indeed, society's safety net will grow stronger when no longer displaced by government largesse.

WHERE HAVE ALL THE FATHERS GONE?

The Tough Love option addresses the welfare engine's prime fuel, out-of-wedlock births. Half of all unwed teen mothers go on cash welfare within a year of their first child's birth—77 percent in the first five years. This is disastrous. As sociologist Charles Murray argues, "Illegitimacy is the single most important social problem of our time—more important than crime, drugs, poverty, illiteracy, welfare, or hopelessness because it drives everything else."

The statistics bear him out. A child who grows up fatherless enters the world more likely to live with trouble—to be sickly, join a gang, quit school, become addicted to drugs, break the law, conceive children out of wedlock, and go on welfare—than a child with a loving father (or even the cherished memory of a deceased father) in the home. Illegitimacy fosters moral weakness, ruins young lives, and leaves families and neighborhoods devastated. And our government promotes illegitimacy through the welfare system.

Today, three out of every ten American births take place outside of marriage. That is four percentage points higher than the rate that, in 1965, prompted a sociologist named Daniel Patrick Moynihan to warn of a coming black underclass. Tragically, when only blacks suffered high illegitimacy rates, liberals tended to disregard it, blaming black poverty on racism and other causes. But they can no longer look the other way. White out-of-wedlock births have now reached 22 percent. The black rate is an unimaginable 67 percent. As single motherhood loses its stigma and we build a culture of illegitimacy, the prospect of underclass problems spreading into comfortable suburban neighborhoods cannot easily be dismissed.

The current welfare system can make fatherless homes an attractive option. The typical welfare basket of benefits, including Aid to Families with Dependent Children (AFDC) cash benefits, food stamps, public housing, and Medicaid, is worth a good deal more than a minimum wage job. Under this system, if an unwed mother with one child has an additional child out of wedlock while on welfare, the government rewards this behavior with additional benefits, which can reach $13,000 a year on average. But if this same young woman should marry, she loses some or all of her benefits, depending on her husband's income. And of course his income is taxed, while her welfare benefits are not. As the Heritage Foundation's Robert Rector has quipped, the two rules of welfare are "you must not work, and you must not marry someone who works." The welfare recipient quite rationally concludes that work and marriage are irrational.

Every president since John F. Kennedy has tried to escape this logic, promising to reform welfare, "break the cycle of dependency," "make welfare a second chance, not a way of life," and so forth. And after every reform, the only thing that changes is the size of the welfare rolls—they grow. Seven years after the 1988 reform, hailed by now-Senator Moynihan as the first step to replacing welfare with "workfare," the AFDC rolls have swelled by forty percent to five million mothers with ten million children, while only about 1 percent of recipients actually work for their benefits. And welfare remains a way of life. Today 93 percent of AFDC cash-welfare recipients are on the program for more than two years; 65 percent stay on for more than eight years. The more welfare is reformed, the more welfare grows.

Tough Love was the approach to poverty favored throughout the nineteenth century—with far more success in solving difficult urban social problems. The Philadelphia and New York of 1840 faced problems of crime, gangs, and substance abuse not unlike that found in those cities today. Yet society, with almost no government involvement, created a remarkable network of flexible institutions that reduced these problems.

DESTROYER OF THE HUMAN SPIRIT

Because the statistical record of nineteenth-century social welfare efforts is so spotty, Professor Marvin Olasky has painstakingly documented it one charity at a time, poring over annual reports and contemporary newspapers to find out what really went on. In the course of the research that produced his classic study, *The Tragedy of American Compassion*, Olasky discovered that nineteenth-century humanitarians achieved real reductions in, among other things, drunkenness, illegitimacy, and abortion rates. Both the selfless optimism and the hard-nosed realism of nineteenth-century America leaps from the very names of its organizations: Erring Woman's Refuges, Baltimore Female Association for the Relief of Distressed Objects, Asylum for the Relief of Half-Orphan and Destitute Children, Memorial Union for the Rescue of Homeless and Friendless Girls, House of Industry and Home for Discharged Convicts, New York Christian Home for Intemperate Men, Ladies' Society for the Female Poor and Especially the Relief of Poor Widows with Small Children (which latter group, Olasky tells us, "tried to have a reach as long as its name").

As the wonderful particularity of these names suggests, nineteenth-century Americans were determined to know their beneficiaries by name and to approach them in the spirit of relatives rather than strangers. For example, the rule book of the St. Louis Provident Association instructed its volunteers:

- To give relief only after personal investigation of each case

- To give necessary articles and only what is immediately necessary

- To give what is least susceptible of abuse

- To give only in small quantities in proportion to immediate need, and less than might be procured by labor, except in cases of sickness

- To give assistance at the right moment; not to prolong it beyond duration of the necessity which calls for it

- To require of each beneficiary abstinence from intoxicating liquors

- To discontinue relieving all who manifest a purpose to depend on alms rather than their own exertions for support

These earlier Americans understood what we have forgotten: the moral nature of poverty. They took it for granted that "outdoor relief" (indiscriminate handouts to the able-bodied) would encourage destructive "pauperism" (dependence). They were careful to scrutinize alms-seekers, to distinguish the "deserving" from the "undeserving" poor, and to make personal moral reform a condition of any aid, which they gave in kind, never in cash. Often prompted by religious precepts, they understood that compassion in its true, original sense means "suffering with" the poor, as opposed to merely providing impersonal "income maintenance" to the poor. That our century has utterly forgotten this rich body of wisdom is indeed the "tragedy of American compassion."

In 1935 the other President Roosevelt, Franklin, laid the foundations of today's welfare culture by signing into law two major new poverty programs. The first, public housing, was hailed as a humane and decent alternative to the slums. The other, Aid for Dependent Children (ADC), would give cash assistance only to households in which the breadwinner was "dead, disabled, or absent."

Roosevelt expressed misgivings about even these limited measures. "The lessons of history," he warned the nation, "show conclusively that continued dependence upon relief induces a spiritual and moral disintegration fundamentally destructive to the national fiber. To dole out relief in this way is to administer a narcotic, a subtle destroyer of the human spirit." But with relatively small amounts being doled out—and to such deserving recipients—the risks seemed negligible.

At first most states restricted ADC. These restrictions soon broke down, however. By 1939, absent-father families (as opposed to the deceased-father variety) made up one-third of the ADC caseload. That year, Congress shifted most deceased-father families into the new and quickly growing Social Security system, making ADC a program almost exclusively for absent-father homes. Still, fewer than 4 percent of ADC children were illegitimate. Today, 92 percent are.

By 1964 absent-father homes made up two-thirds of recipients of the program, which had since been renamed Aid to Families with Dependent Children, and the welfare's subtle narcotic effects were becoming increasingly apparent. The popular press had discovered a new stereotype—the welfare mother with children conceived by various fathers. Social scientists began to talk of a "poverty crisis" unknown just a few years before.

Disregarding these warning signs, President Johnson, declaring a "War on Poverty," forged ahead and expanded the welfare state in a flurry of bill-signings in 1965 and 1966. More important, the welfare state took on an entirely different rationale with what the *New York Times* called the "new philosophy of social welfare": government hand-outs were not a privilege, they were a right. The new Office of Economic Opportunity (OEO) actively sought to strip the element of shame from welfare. OEO bureaucrats branched out across the country, establishing one thousand neighborhood service centers to identify people eligible for benefits and disseminate the belief that everyone is entitled to a share of the common wealth, without regard to any moral causes of poverty. Meanwhile, two ambitious new programs—food stamps and Medicaid—joined FDR's AFDC and public housing to create the generous basket of benefits that today goes by the shorthand term of "welfare." To avoid confusion with the seventy-four other nutrition, education, housing, community development, and other welfare programs for low-income people, or the 154 federal job-training programs that currently exist, let us call this foursome by columnist Ben Wattenberg's term, Greater Welfare.

GREATER AND GREATER WELFARE

From 1965 to 1992, while the country's population grew by 33 percent, spending on Greater Welfare grew by 1,000 percent, surging from less than $15 billion to more than $156 billion a year (in constant 1992 dollars) and more than tripling from 1.5 percent to 5 percent of gross national product. With greater spending, dependence surged. Today, Greater Welfare recipients number in the tens of millions. While the exact figure cannot be determined because of overlaps, the following gives an idea of the vast extent of the now permanent government-sponsored underclass:

- Public housing   5 million recipients $ 22 billion
- AFDC   15 million recipients $ 25 billion*
- Food stamps   27 million recipients $ 27 billion
- Medicaid   33 million recipients $140 billion*

(The asterisked dollar figures include the state share of these joint federal–state programs.)

And just what has Americans' generosity wrought? *The Index of Leading Cultural Indicators,* compiled by former federal education secretary and drug czar Bill Bennett, provides a sobering answer. From 1960 to 1990 the teen pregnancy and suicide rates doubled. The crime rate and the percentage of children living with only one parent (flat from 1880 to 1960) suddenly tripled. The divorce rate, juvenile arrests, and out-of-wedlock births quadrupled. Violent crime quintupled. And just as all these destructive trend lines are concentrated in a narrow thirty-year window, 1960 to 1990, they are also concentrated in a narrow geographic location, the cities—the exact time and place in which the War on Poverty was waged. Another Armey Axiom: anytime you find an identifiable population under the care of the federal government, you find a population that suffers every socio–economic malady known to man.

And yet at the same time the economy grew strongly and, in real terms, material poverty virtually disappeared. This point bears explaining.

Most Americans do not realize the extent to which we have won the "war" on poverty, because our knowledge of the relative comfort of the American poor (compared with other nations and America's poor of past decades) is filtered through the media and, more important, because the statistics are rigged to make material poverty seem like a large and growing problem. It is not.

Washington rigs the welfare statistics in two ways. First, it does not count non-cash welfare transfers as income or any household assets as potential income. If it did, official poverty would shrink dramatically. Second, the federal poverty line overstates poverty because it is based on a formula that no longer reflects reality. Set in the early 1960s, the formula is based on a "typical basket of household goods" arbitrarily selected by federal bureaucrats, who assumed, for example, that a poor family spends one-third of its income on food. That may have been true in 1960, but food prices have fallen steeply since then. Today poor people have additional funds that were not available in 1960 with which to buy non-food items, including luxuries like color televisions and VCRs.

Poor Americans, the one-fifth of Americans with the lowest incomes, spend more per person today than the median American household did in 1960. Nearly 40 percent of the "poor" own their own homes; 60 percent have air conditioning; 91 percent have color televisions (29 percent, two or more color televisions); and 64 percent own a car (14 percent, two or more cars). A poor American today eats more meat and enjoys more living space than the general population does in Western Europe. The poor's greatest nutrition problem is not hunger, but obesity.

Today's poverty is thus paradoxical. In an age of material plenty and economic growth, fourteen-year-olds murder eleven-year-olds, gang members go "wilding" in Central Park, and a Chicago mother leaves her children alone in a locked apartment for five days without food. Researchers have coined a term for this paradox: "behavioral poverty," that is, poverty produced by one's own choice. All evidence points to Greater Welfare as the prime engine of behavioral poverty. Allow me to suggest a plan for changing this.

TOUGH LOVE FOR UNWED MOTHERS

The House Republican welfare bill contained in the Contract with America, the Personal Responsibility Act, takes a giant leap by ending out-of-control welfare entitlement spending and sending these programs—lock, stock, and barrel—back to the states, which are much better suited than Washington to help needy people. At this same time, the legislation promotes work and marriage. As a condition of receiving the money, the states would impose work requirements for benefits. They must impose a five-year lifetime maximum eligibility for welfare. And they cannot use the money to give cash payments to unmarried mothers under eighteen or to give unwed mothers additional cash payments (which amount to $4,000 per year) for additional children born while the mother is on welfare. (New Jersey obtained federal permission to experiment with this so-called "family cap" in 1993. Initial results show a 13 percent drop in the number of out-of-wedlock births.)

Thus we encourage the states to send a clear message to young people: "In this state, unwed motherhood will no longer be a ticket to a free apartment and a welfare check for life. We will not subsidize irresponsible behavior. If you find yourself in a difficult position, we will help you, of course, with food, housing, and health care, so you can keep yourself and your baby healthy, but do not expect cash payments. This, we hope, will encourage you to marry, find a job, move in with your parents or friends, or turn to a church or charity for assistance. But once your five years are up—which is more than enough time to make necessary arrangements—you will no longer have any choice. You are going to have to exercise personal responsibility. We respect you too much to expect anything less."

Phasing out welfare for unmarried teens may produce some social disruptions and even a few cases that will inevitably be magnified into horror stories. But experience indicates most people will do just fine. In 1991 Michigan's governor John Engler succeeded in cutting off general assistance to 100,000 able-bodied single men, 82,000 of whom had never held a job in their lives. The press struggled in vain to find even one clear case of someone dying or going hungry as a result of the cutoff. In Charles Murray's terse phrase, "People survive."

Critics will also say there are not enough jobs for the unskilled, or alternatively that such jobs are "dead ends." Nonsense. As Governor Tommy Thompson's Wisconsin and Riverside County, California, have demonstrated, when welfare recipients are required to look for work and "take the first job offered," they tend to find work. (To be sure, these "work first" programs are aggressive in helping with job searches, but this could as easily be done by private job placement services.) Far from being "dead ends," entry-level positions in, for example, fast-food restaurants are a port of entry into the world of work, a first step on the ladder of opportunity. For those who work but still cannot support a family, direct subsidies that foster responsibility would be better than government programs that promote dependency.

As George McGovern has argued, "We forget that too often a job—any job—is the best training for a 'better' or more specialized job." And anything on which George McGovern and Dick Armey agree may be regarded as the practical definition of a self-evident truth!

Unlike bureaucracies, private charities must be efficient because they are subject to the discipline of the market. Charity's charlatans, fakers, and incompetents, like those in any other line of business, are generally held accountable by their "investors," the donors. Government charity, by contrast, is rarely held accountable, and so is inefficient and impersonal. The greatest testimony to the superiority of private charity, of course, is the tax code. For example, even though under current law a charitable donation of $1,000 is only worth around $300 in tax relief to the donor, Americans still gladly choose to part with the other $700. Why? Because they know the money is likely to be well spent, with little administrative overhead taken out. Who would say the same about $1,000 given to the welfare bureaucracy?

BOOKS OF VIRTUE

Ending the current crime wave will require two kinds of toughness, one external and one internal. By external toughness I mean abolishing parole, doubling prison space, and making criminal justice vastly more harsh and efficient. By internal toughness I mean encouraging moral habits and self-control—or what used to be called character. Here again, our nineteenth-century ancestors did better than we, practicing a combination of external and internal toughness—prisons and Bibles, if you will—and produced remarkable results.

In the early years of American history, crime rates were low. But in the early 1830s, an unprecedented crime epidemic swept across the growing cities. Waves of immigrants from Europe and young men from the country searching for work created a growing pool of rowdy and sometimes drunken day laborers. Saloons and boarding houses proliferated. Violence soared.

But then a striking thing happened. Beginning around 1850, crime rates began to fall off again and remained generally low for roughly the next fifty years. In his book *Thinking About Crime*, James Q. Wilson notes that "late nineteenth-century Boston was a less violent and disorderly place than the Boston of 1840, and homicide rates in Philadelphia declined throughout much of the late nineteenth century." Why? Undoubtedly the invention of urban police forces helped. And certainly the opening up of the West in the 1850s provided an important release valve for criminal elements. But far more effective than any of these, in my view, was a sustained national movement to civilize the young through character formation.

Nineteenth-century Americans placed the blame for crime on no one else but the actual criminal. They paid the wrongdoer the high compliment of holding him personally responsible for his misdeeds. As their diagnosis was moral, so was their prescription. For example, the Sunday school, in those times a day-long affair, spread literacy and biblical truths, while giving youngsters lessons in "decorum and restraint." The Sunday school movement became so popular that, by 1829, 40 percent of New York City's school-age children were said to attend. Harder-to-reach children benefited from the Young Men's Christian Associations, which boasted two hundred chapters with 25,000 members by 1861, providing urban youths with wholesome diversions and mixing athletic activities with religious instruction. And of course generations of American children grew up with William H. McGuffey's *Readers*, among the best-selling books of the century. Not only did McGuffey's *Readers* teach the educational basics at what would today be regarded as astonishingly challenging levels, but they also stressed the moral dimension, suffusing nearly every story with valuable lessons in such virtues as honesty, integrity, dependability, constancy, courage, order, cleanliness, punctuality, and hard work.

By far the most influential of the nineteenth-century moral reform efforts was the temperance movement. Through campaigns to persuade drinkers to sign the "pledge" and get on the temperance "wagon," as well as through legislative restrictions, temperance advocates succeeded in dramatically reducing Americans' alcohol consumption with all its destructive effects. Between 1830 and 1850, Americans' per capita consumption of spirits dropped from more than seven gallons a year to less than two, a 75 percent reduction in a generation. What united all of these movements—the Cadets of Temperance, the Cold Water Army, the Gospel Missions, the revivalist tent meetings, the Sunday school, YMCAs, Children's Aid Societies, and all the rest—was the characteristic nineteenth-century emphasis on personal responsibility. These movements cultivated an interior power of self-restraint. And they were all completely private.

In the absence of a revival of the traditional moral virtues, all our government-centered crime prevention programs are bound to fail. But government does have two very limited, but very important, roles. The first is to provide moral instruction by way of the statute book. As the saying has it, the law is a teacher. Government's second role is to deter crime by threat of punishment. To deter, punishment must be virtually certain, swift, and severe. Today's criminal justice fails on all counts.

Crime Pays

The 1960s witnessed a revolution in criminal justice. Young punks just starting on their careers of violence were treated gently, their punishments light, their criminal records torn up on reaching adulthood. In place of chain gangs, work release programs were created to "reform" prisoners through trust. In place of rock-breaking, parole and early release programs were instituted to "rehabilitate" the socially maladjusted by encouraging good behavior. The brains at the American Civil Liberties Union took this thinking to its logical conclusion and proposed that prisoners be allowed to unionize and take over the operation of their jails.

All this was done on the "root cause" theory of crime. This theory was once perfectly expressed by actress Jane Fonda, in a 1971 antiwar speech: "If any of you have been in jail, you probably have realized that everyone in jail is a political prisoner, because we have a system which makes people commit crimes. Most people don't have any choice. They have to steal to eat. They have to get spaced out on drugs because they can't face the kind of decay of our society, because their needs aren't being met."

These words were spoken smack in the middle of a historically fierce crime wave taking place during one of the most prosperous eras in American history. Then, in the 1970s, the federal government decided to test the "root cause" thesis for itself. In an experiment called the National Supported Work Demonstration, the government took large numbers of high school dropouts and low-income men with prior criminal records and divided them into two groups. Half the men were given a guaranteed job and a wide array of expensive social services worth about $21,000 (in 1992 dollars). The other half received no job and no aid. What happened? The men with the guaranteed jobs and benefits committed just as many crimes, used just as many drugs, and showed just as little interest in steady employment as they had before the experiment began. The researchers found this surprising.

Criminal behavior today can be explained in two words: crime pays. It pays, in part, because crime is cheap. A murderer can expect a mere 1.8 years in jail. A rapist, just sixty days in the hoosegow. A robber, twenty-three days. For all serious crimes taken together, the expected average punishment is just eight days—about the length of a Club Med vacation, with free room and board.

As punishment goes up, crime goes down—and vice versa. As

recently as 1950 expected punishment for all serious crimes was as high as twenty-four days, triple the current level. By 1974, however, it had plummeted to a scant five and a half days. During the same quarter-century the crime rate tripled. When expected punishment began rising again after 1974, crime leveled off, falling slightly in the 1980s. What all these numbers tell us is simple: criminals are rational. They respond predictably to rewards and punishments. For half a century, we have been reducing the punishments, and criminals have been taking us up on the invitation. We cut the marginal tax rate on wrongdoing and launched a supply-side boom in criminality.

Only by restoring the proper balance of rewards and punishments can we take the profit out of crime. Here's how:

- Make apprehension certain. The fear of getting caught has been shown to be a more powerful deterrent to criminals than the fear of being punished. Urban police departments need more police on the beat. The mere presence of a law officer can change an urban street's entire feel, even raise its property values, by scaring off ne'er-do-wells who fear apprehension.

- Make conviction certain. Appointing tough law-and-order judges is essential. The president should make a judicial appointee's inclination to mete out stiff punishments a top consideration, and the Senate, in confirming judicial nominees, should give the recommendations of the Fraternal Order of Police at least equal weight with those of the Left-leaning American Bar Association. At the same time, Congress should curb the ability of criminal defendants to escape conviction on technicalities. For example, police should be granted a "good faith" exception to the so-called exclusionary rule, which currently keeps even the most incriminating evidence out of court when there is so much as a typographical error on a search warrant—never mind that the Fourth Amendment itself says nothing about excluding evidence.

- Shift the balance of fire power. Criminals should be disarmed without remorse. Ten years in prison should be tacked onto the sentence of anyone who uses a firearm in the commission of a felony, no exceptions. At the same time the rights of law-abiding citizens to own guns should be unquestioned. As Senator Phil Gramm puts it, "I want that would-be mugger or burglar to wonder if my Mama has a gun."

- Make incarceration certain. Eighty percent of all violent crimes are committed by 7 percent of urban males. Translation: most crime comes from a few criminals who break the law again and again. The median number of reported felonies by a given felon in a given year is fifteen. But the probability that the felon will actually go to prison and serve most of his time behind bars has fallen to only one-fifth of what it was in 1960. Thanks to easy parole and judicial overcrowding decrees, hardened repeat offenders are released to the streets, mugging and killing, stealing and raping. Clearly, keeping this tiny cast of professional lawbreakers off the street as long as possible would dramatically reduce the crime rate.

It is time to abolish parole and double the amount of prison space. Our choice, in the words of former Attorney General William Barr, is between "more prison space or more crime." While we are at it, we should abolish pretrial release for anyone accused of a major felony, and abolish early release and work release programs for prisoners. And to throw some sand in today's swiftly revolving door of justice, states should pass "truth in sentencing" laws requiring that convicts serve no less than 85 percent of their sentences. That is to say, lock 'em up and get a good night's sleep. I am happy to report that most of these ideas are either contained or encouraged in the House Republican crime bill that was passed and was part of the Contract with America.

Granted, doubling prison space will cost money. (The current U.S. prison population is 900,000 inmates, of which 80,000 are federal.) But total spending on prisons consumes just a half-penny of every public dollar spent. The entire criminal justice system consumes only three cents of every dollar, and though it is true that incarceration costs taxpayers approximately $19,000 per offender and $70,000 per cell, jail is a very good buy compared with the costs of leaving criminals on the street. Given that the average inmate has committed an estimated 187 crimes in the year before going to prison, at an average cost of $2,300 per crime, society gets a pretty good return on a $70,000 investment.

MAKE WAR NO MORE

Making this the last welfare generation, abolishing parole, building more prisons, recovering the notion of character, encouraging private charity, and reviving group homes for children and unwed mothers—it must seem by today's standards a radical agenda. Some will call it heartless, though what is the current system but heartless toward victims? But the Tough Love option is the opposite of heartless, for it dares to respect the potential of every human being, regardless of his or her station in life.

As the Frenchman Alexis de Tocqueville observed more than 160 years ago, we Americans have a unique penchant for forming useful private associations. The recent mania of our ruling class for government-run "wars on poverty" and Washington bureaucracies mapping out "campaigns" and "operations" from "headquarters" on the Potomac is totally out of character with our traditions. A century hence, this tragic detour will seem a bit scary and a bit bizarre.

Let us hasten the day when the word underclass will be so unfamiliar, it will send people running to the dictionary. Let us give the citizens of today's welfare communities hope and dignity by bringing them into the same free society most Americans expect for our children, the society of the flat tax and consumer-based health care and education and all the other logical applications of Freedom. Let us end the welfare culture and save our children, not through the false compassion of government action, but through the authentic compassion of Tough Love.

Chapter 14

FREE TO TRADE

Among the more divisive issues conservatives face is whether our borders should be open to trade and immigration. For myself, I am not in the least divided on the question. As the guiding principle in our affairs with other nations, I trust Freedom as much as I do in guiding our domestic affairs.

As I've tried to explain to my fellow conservatives, governments don't trade with governments, people trade with people. When someone calls for trade restrictions, he or she is saying the federal government should interfere in the personal affairs of fellow Americans. Such government intervention, moreover, will affect our prosperity as much as the prosperity and fate of other nations.

The world is a new and vital marketplace. Many of the enemies who once menaced us are gone. And half the world is made up of developing economic frontiers—Latin America, the Pacific Rim,

China, India—all eager to have what the United States has always offered: Freedom, prosperity, self-betterment. As they develop, these nations can be increasingly prosperous trading partners for generations. Those people with a defensive and uneasy attitude toward foreign trade picked the wrong century in which to be born.

It's not a proud nationalist boast, but a pretty humbling thought, that despite all our troubles other nations still look to the United States as their model. We can spend the next few decades shipping them the products and services that made our living standard the highest in the history of the world. We can be a chief exporter of ideas and technological skills, helping them build better, freer nations. We can accept them as full trading partners, competing product for product. Or we can just back away from the whole challenge—which is not my understanding of the American character.

As I see it, the question of free trade versus protectionism is the ultimate contest between backward-looking support for special interests and forward-looking support for the general interest.

TRADING UP

I'm for free trade. What I am most definitely not for is anything along the lines of a government-managed "New World Order." George Bush could have done us all a great service by striking that pretentious phrase the first time it came marching in from the White House speech-writing shop. It was one of those attempts by government to name something and thereby assume command of it. The greatest thing about our post-Cold War economy is that it arose from the decline of government-planned economies.

As a general rule, international trade has always created wealth for all involved, made new goods available to domestic markets, and given local merchants the opportunity to seek new markets abroad for their products. But trade has also spread civilization throughout the world.

Among the first international traders were the Phoenicians, who rose to power and prominence around 1100 B.C. and were known as great sailors and traders for a thousand years. They brought several skills and products to the Western world, among them a dye called Tyrian purple and the secrets of glasswork, textile manufacturing, and metalwork. They also brought to Europe the useful thing I'm using right now—the alphabet.

Americans should keep the Phoenicians in mind. The United States is already the world's largest trader, and there's every reason to believe this will continue—unless we go out of our way to alter current trends. Now, faced with the potential for the greatest economic growth in our history, we should keep in mind three points:

- First, it would take a bold and conscious effort by the American government to stop American manufacturers and entrepreneurs from entering into international business markets. Americans are now all over the world, buying and selling, bringing back new orders for American goods, creating new jobs for American workers. Attempting to stop that activity in this age of instant global communication and rapid transportation would be futile. Why would anybody want to try?

- Second, deliberately pulling back from current international markets will only diminish American influence in the world. If we don't take the lead in world trade, someone else will and profit accordingly. The likely candidate would be Japan.

- Third, America, of all nations, has the least to fear from the inevitable cultural exchanges that come with trade. We are today's Phoenicians, exporting our ideas and culture to the rest of the world. For years, blue jeans have been sold for many times their value in Eastern European black markets just because they have the prized "American look." American television is watched all over the world. American songs are sung by the young people of every continent. When the students of Red China revolted in Tiananmen Square, they briefly and heroically raised up a self-made papier-mâché Statue of Liberty, because even behind the Bamboo Curtain they knew what America stood for. Let all who would "protect" our national identity bear that in mind.

In the nineteenth century it was far easier for America to close its shutters on the rest of the world. We had an exploding economy the size of a continent. Shipping was difficult and costly. Great empires, like France and Great Britain, offered powerful and ruthless competition abroad. Better to develop our domestic markets to the greatest level of efficiency and sophistication.

But since World War II, we've been the greatest producer of goods in the world. Our economy is by far the largest in history. The United States is the only superpower left, and our industrial strength is overwhelming. In 1960 trade in goods and services equaled 9.3 percent of the U.S. gross domestic product. In 1993 the value of trade was 21.7 percent. During this same period world trade rose from $200 billion in 1960 to over $3 trillion today.

Production itself has spread across national borders. The personal computer, a product in which American firms lead the world, is composed of many parts—half of which come from foreign countries. That prompts truculent union leaders to warn of a "job drain" that will inevitably put American workers in unemployment lines, but exactly the reverse is true. Because some computer parts are imported from nations with more primitive economies, American companies can manufacture PCs at a much lower cost and price them competitively in the world market. The result: larger sales, increased orders, greater productivity, more jobs. If they didn't import foreign parts, U.S. manufacturers would have to sell at a price above the world market, sales would cease, orders would stop, and companies would fold. This is the sequence that threatens the jobs of American workers.

And by the way, in case you're worried about Japanese ownership of American business, remember that it runs both ways. American companies are also buying shares of Japanese companies, just to diversify their holdings.

Nevertheless, many Americans' apprehensions about international trade, though perhaps mistaken, are based more on sound political instincts that make them suspicious of the high-flown rhetoric often used to promote world trade. Too many American politicians and corporate executives take their cue from the clichésmiths in the media, who go on and on about "global villages" and "our interdependency" and the New World Order. The ordinary guy is rightly distrustful of this communitarian cant. Americans don't want their sovereignty auctioned off in the global marketplace, and they don't want the big thinkers in Brussels, The Hague, or any other foreign capital telling us how America should run its own affairs. The United Nations is an instrument of the United States and other member nations, not the other way around. But fears for U.S. sovereignty, like most other apprehensions about free trade, can be addressed by a few sound, simple principles.

Countries don't trade, individuals do. Restricting free trade restricts individual freedom. We can talk loosely about trade between the United States and Japan or the United States and Germany, but that's not really what's happening. In the civilian economy governments don't produce goods. Individuals and companies from various countries are the traders, with governments often hovering nervously over the transactions, ostensibly to protect their citizens, but more often to make sure they get their cut in the form of taxes.

Thus, when we speak of a nation opening up "its" market, we really mean that government has removed restrictions on its own citizens to buy and sell goods. Free trade transfers sovereignty not to the United Nations or the New World Order, but to American citizens.

When the United States Congress approved NAFTA, news accounts suggested we had made "concessions" to Mexico. Put in more precise economic terms, our government conceded to individual Americans the right to dispose of their own property by buying from foreigners. But American entrepreneurs also gained the right to sell to Mexicans. Ross Perot said that the Mexicans would have no money to pay for American goods. An American discount chain opened a branch in Mexico City and sold all its wares in a matter of days, so hungry were Mexicans for goods their own economy was failing to produce.

Free trade, not protectionism, made America a great and prosperous nation.

Some contend that America grew strong and prosperous because of nineteenth- and early twentieth-century protectionism. High tariffs and other trade restrictions, they argue, kept out foreign goods and allowed America to develop its own industries. Now, they continue, we are in danger of allowing Third World competitors, using cheap labor, to compete unfairly with American businesses and pillage their domestic markets.

These arguments come from the Right as well as the Left—and both groups are contradictory in their arguments. Those who argue that the relatively weak, "developing" America of the nineteenth century couldn't compete with larger, stronger nations, now argue that twentieth-century America, the most formidable nation in the world, can't compete with the weakest of the current developing countries. They can't have it both ways. Taken alone, each argument is weak; together, they're inconsistent. In strong, free international trade, both the strongest and the weakest economies benefit.

Poor nations inevitably leads to exploitation and relegates the poorer countries to perpetual poverty. Leftist intellectuals since the fifties have dined out on horror stories about U.S. economic tyranny over Central and South America. Now we find a few of them warning that the United States will be exploited by the poorest nations of the world. The two fears are united by one common theme: they do not want America's free-market influence in the Third World, period. What they seem most to fear is the loss of the only fertile ground left in the world for their shoddy, discredited brand of socialism.

Though the United States did keep its trade barriers relatively high in the nineteenth century—a grave mistake, in my opinion—the principle of free trade was still hard at work in the American economy. Remember that during this era the nation was preoccupied with a vast expansion westward, bringing new states into the Union, and thereby creating free trade across the continent. In opening the West, America became a vast, continental free-trade zone from the Atlantic to the Pacific—the same distance as between Madrid and Moscow. We were our own Europe, with citizens of states the size of nations trading with one another without restriction. In those days, our trade outside the continent accounted for only a very modest proportion of our economy.

To put the nineteenth-century American experience in perspective, look what happened to Britain during the same period. Why did Britain, a small island of relatively few people, rise to economic dominance, frightening American protectionists into erecting trade barriers to protect the factories of the industrial North? In part, this rise occurred because Britain progressively opened its markets to imports. The British people realized that it makes little sense to waste manpower, raw materials, land, and capital to produce goods and services that could be purchased more cheaply elsewhere. It was better to allow others more efficient in producing certain goods and services to supply the British, especially the high-margin British manufacturers. The result: a higher standard of living for people living on the British Isles and the expansion of their own markets to include those selling to them.

Even nations that didn't go as far as Great Britain in liberalizing trade prospered by a more guarded embrace of the principle. Germany, for example, was united under the leadership of Prussia only in 1871. That union was the end of a process that eliminated trade barriers between the numerous small German principalities and launched one of the world's great economies.

During the 1920s by contrast the United States progressively raised its trade barriers, so that foreign firms, denied American sales, lacked the cash to buy from America in return. Despite the stock market crash in October 1929, by early 1930 the economy was on the rebound. But in that year, President Hoover transformed the recession into a depression by raising taxes twice. First, he raised taxes on personal and business income. And second, he raised taxes on purchases from overseas under the Smoot–Hawley Tariff Act.

Between 1929 and 1932 American imports dropped from $5.9 billion to $2 billion; exports fell from $7 billion to $2.4 billion.

Those preoccupied with trade surpluses should note that America ran a trade surplus during the worst economic calamity we've ever known. Yet between 1929 and 1933 America's economy was reduced by half and unemployment rose to 35 percent. I'm certain that millions of out-of-work Americans in soup lines during those times would have looked longingly at the huge trade deficits we ran during the 1980s—deficits owing to our prosperity and hence our ability to buy imported goods.

Britain followed suit with its own protectionist measures, as did Fascist Italy and Germany after the Nazi takeover. The result: worldwide depression and the beginnings of conflict in Europe.

Trade deficits as such don't matter. Most of us in America are distressed when we hear on the news that "last month the trade deficit rose." In part, this distress issues from the reporter's grim look and even grimmer tone, as if an airliner with three hundred people aboard had just crashed. The vast majority of viewers haven't the slightest idea what the trade deficit is or means—and neither does the reporter.

A trade deficit is neither inherently good nor inherently bad. The figure simply indicates that during a given period U.S. citizens have bought more goods and services than they have sold in foreign markets. The deficit may occur because the economy and purchasing power of consumers in this country are growing faster than in others. In this case, a deficit would be a sign of economic strength. On the other hand, a deficit might occur because we are inflating our currency, which would be a sign of poor economic policy and hence poor economic health.

Look at it this way. A number of families are living in a suburban neighborhood, all of them earning roughly the same income and purchasing goods and services from each other. Everybody makes about the same salary and spends about the same in the neighborhood. Then Bob Smith, a hard worker and a bright entrepreneur, is named president of his shoe company, with a huge salary increase. Suddenly, the Smith family is spending money all over the neighborhood, remodeling the house, buying a new car, entertaining the CEOs of other corporations. If you examined the checkbooks of everyone in the neighborhood, you'd find that the Smith family was spending more money in local stores than their neighbors were spending on his company's shoes. In that event, should the Smith family sit down, pale and grim-lipped, and say, "We've got to make certain the Joneses keep up with us"?

On the other hand, if, to keep up with the Joneses, the Smith family went into debt through conspicuous spending, the "trade deficit" with their neighbors would indicate deep financial problems. Obviously, Scenario #1 is nothing to worry about, while Scenario #2 indicates real trouble.

Trade deficits between two countries are even less significant than overall trade deficits. The "U.S. deficit with Japan" simply means that, in a given month or year, Americans end up with more VCRs, CD players, and camcorders than individual Japanese traders and individual Japanese traders end up with more dollars. America as a nation doesn't enter into any trading with Japan. All goods have been paid for by the individuals and private companies that engage in the transactions.

As an analogy, nearly all individuals run trade deficits with their grocery stores. The stores buy nothing from their customers. So what? The customers don't see this imbalance as a problem when they get hungry—or even after they've eaten. Meanwhile, all the customers are running large "trade surpluses" with their own employers, who buy their labor even though these employees buy nothing from them in return.

FREE TRADE AND THE FOUR-CAR GARAGE

The bottom line is that the United States remains the strongest economic power in the world and the outlook for the United States is more promising than for any other major industrialized nation. Look at the following factors:

- America still has the world's largest economy. With an estimated gross domestic product of $5.92 trillion in 1992, using "purchasing power parity," the U.S. economy is still twice the size of Japan's and four and a half times Germany's.

- America's per capita income is still the world's highest—$23,215 in 1992, compared with $20,435 for Germany, $19,689 for Japan, and $16,590 for Sweden.

- Over the past decade, more jobs have been created in the United States than in the other major industrial nations combined. Between 1982 and 1989, America added 18 million workers to the payrolls, an 18 percent increase. This employment record compares with 5.4 million, or 10 percent job growth, for Japan during the same period, and 1.1 million, or 4.2 percent job growth, in West Germany.

- Other signs confirm our higher standard of living. For example, the average Japanese consumer spends nearly 25 percent of his or her income on food, compared with 12 to 15 percent for the average American. The Japanese spend nearly twice as much for housing—and have less living space per person. Consumer prices in Japan

are around 40 percent higher than in the United States.
Nearly half of the dwellings in Japan lack indoor toilets.

Among nations, we are the family that lives in the big mansion
with a four-car garage.

Free trade got us here. We should continue to promote even
more free markets worldwide. For all the complexities of the trade
issue, the basic formula is simple: Private Property plus Free
Exchange equals Prosperity.

IMMIGRATION

If there's a danger zone that I can see in our move toward a true
Freedom agenda, it is on the subject of immigration. There are
many even in my own party, which generally accepts a fluid,
dynamic society, who are openly opposed to even our current levels of legal immigration and are quite prepared to use even the
most extreme means to halt illegal immigration. If they had their
way, every American would walk around with an electronic
national ID card, tied no doubt to a giant government computer
bank storing whatever information the government may wish to
know about its citizens. Presumably some government official
would demand, like foreign guards at checkpoints in low-budget
movies, "Let me see your papers, please."

I could make the case for a tolerant attitude toward legal immigration on moral grounds. We are all immigrants or children of
immigrants, and it does us no credit to pull up the ladder behind
us and sneer at the immigrants of the present day. But here I will
make the case for continued openness on national interest
grounds alone.

The tremendous appeal of the United States to potential immigrants around the world is an unparalleled source of national

wealth. We could pass a law tomorrow allowing any computer programmer, civil engineer, or research scientist to come here, and instantly a good portion of the smartest people on our planet would flock to our shores. You could move to Japan and never become Japanese. You could move to Germany and never become German. But any lover of Freedom can come to America and become an American. That is the mark of a great and powerful nation. Here, we generally embrace immigrants and can employ all their talents, creativity, and hard work to building a better America. To change our ways now and ban or even sharply reduce our legal immigration would be to throw away one of our greatest competitive advantages.

Immigration has periodically troubled Americans—but only periodically. It tends to trouble us when we're already troubled by other things. During most of our history, immigrants have crossed our borders uninterruptedly and have been welcomed.

Times of hostility to immigrants have usually been times of unemployment, civil unrest, or a massive influx from a single country, as happened with the Irish. To a point, this is understandable. When you're struggling yourself, it's hard to come up with much sympathy for the newcomers who rush in eager to take any job at any pay. The comfortable and secure hardly notice the new immigrants, but to the unemployed they seem to be everywhere. Thus in the early nineteenth century, the Know-Nothing movement raised the first cry to seal the borders. Their very name (which they took from detractors and wore with pride) reflected the level of their anger. The irony was that at just that moment a large influx of immigrants was helping to explore and settle the West. The idea that in 1850 the United States—mostly rural or wilderness—couldn't absorb a further influx of foreigners was absurd. Yet if you were viewing it from the steamy, packed confines of a city, the immigrants looked mighty menacing. By 1860 the fervor had faded and the Know-Nothings had disappeared into the shadow of a real crisis, the slavery issue.

Today immigration is again "a problem," and again our immigrants are more the object of fear than the source of the problem. We see foreigners pouring across our borders and begin to make the understandable, but equally unwarranted, assumptions about how it might affect us. We see them not as fellow lovers of Freedom, but as grubby rivals for employment. And to this "problem" government has added a new dimension of distrust. Since they are not only arrivals to the land of opportunity, but to a massive and overburdened welfare state, we brand our immigrants as cheats and freeloaders. In a sluggish and tax-heavy society—also the good work of government—we see the recent arrivals as nonproductive contenders for state benefits. This, and not any meaner instinct, is why in California, for instance, immigration is the issue of the day.

The mood will pass. But until it does we need to bear two things in mind. First, the problem with welfare fraud is less the fault of the immigrants who accept aid than the fault of the government system that offers it. Second, what now has the look of a burden promises, as immigration always has, to be a great burst of economic vitality.

The people we disparage today are just like earlier immigrants, differing only in the direction they traveled to get here. "Countless studies," observed scholar Stephen Moore, "have documented that immigrants to the United States tend to be more skilled, more highly educated and wealthier than the average citizen of their native countries." As for immigrants from Mexico, it's a terrible insult to greet them with our favored caricatures of their country. Would a siesta-loving layabout pick up, move to Los Angeles, and work twelve hours a day in menial labor? Studies of

Mexican immigrants reveal that 95 percent were employed when they left Mexico—a country with 15 percent unemployment. Like most immigrants of any time, ours today are adventurers, not spongers on the system. Most immigrants immigrate precisely because they carry with them the virtues that made America great.

Moreover, the vast majority of immigrants do not (1) take jobs away from natives in large numbers, (2) end up in minimum-wage positions and become a drag on the economy, or (3) go on welfare and pay no taxes. Let's sort out these familiar charges as best we can.

IMMIGRATION AND UNEMPLOYMENT

Substantial evidence indicates that immigration has hardly any impact at all on native unemployment. Thomas Muller of the Urban Institute compared employment in modern Los Angeles with conditions going back to 1900. He found that the throngs of immigrants arriving in the 1970s affected the city's employment "little, if at all."

Likewise, Muller and Thomas Espenshade of Princeton report that in West Coast cities "black unemployment rates are not increased—if anything they are lowered—by a rise in the proportion of Mexican immigrants." The same thing was noticed by Gregory DeFreitas of Hofstra University. He sifted through the 1990 census report, concluding that Hispanic immigrants, including illegals, had no "discernible negative effect" on native employment.

Two others, Joseph G. Altonji of Northwestern and David Card of Princeton, looked at the impact of immigrants on employment at low-skilled jobs in typical cities during 1979 and 1980. Their summary: "We find little evidence that inflows of immigrants are associated with large or systematic effects on the employment or unemployment rates of less-skilled natives."

Stephen Moore, Richard Sullivan, and Julian Simon studied

"the relationship between the rates of immigration and the unemployment rates among U.S. cities during all the years for which data exist—1960 to 1977," and discovered that "the effect was at most insignificant; it is likely that there was no effect at all."

And finally, in a study entitled "Do Immigrants Increase Unemployment or Reduce Economic Growth?" Richard Vedder, Lowell Gallaway, and Stephen Moore examined unemployment and economic growth over almost a hundred years—from 1890 to 1988. They then set these numbers beside immigration rates on a state-by-state basis. Their conclusions, published in a 1990 Congressional Record, lend further weight to the other studies I've cited above:

> [W]e reject outright the hypothesis that increased immigration leads to higher unemployment. We find a consistent statistically negative effect of immigration on unemployment. That is, periods of heavy immigration tended to be followed by periods of lower than normal unemployment; states with heavy concentrations of immigration in 1930 had lower unemployment between 1982 and 1985 than low-immigration states. We estimate that an increase in immigration for ten years, which is roughly an upper-bound estimate of immigration increases now under consideration by the U.S. Congress, would lead roughly to a 0.10 percent reduction in the national unemployment rate by the end of the decade than otherwise.

IMMIGRANTS AND THE ECONOMY

Now to the second charge—that immigrants end up in minimum wage jobs and do not contribute to the economy. The first thing that strikes me is that even if this were so, it should hardly be a source of bitter feelings. Somebody has to take your order at

McDonald's or sweep up the wrappers and fallen fries when you've departed. McDonald's is the largest employer in the United States. Immigrants, like teenagers, often get their first jobs in the fast-food industry—at Burger King, for example, which is the second-largest employer in America. While these immigrants work their way up the economic ladder, you get your hamburger and french fries bagged and delivered to the counter with a smile. So why complain?

The real complaint seems to be that immigrants don't stay in these jobs. But that is because the same virtues that first put them on that low rung of the ladder in the first place—a willingness to work, ambition—propel them upward, Moore found, into many of the nation's most prosperous industries: computer technology, pharmaceuticals, bioengineering, electronics, superconductivity, robotics, and aerospace engineering. Immigrants also create their own jobs. Another study reporting on one wave of recent immigrants concluded that "in Los Angeles, the propensity for self-employment is three times greater for Koreans than among the population as a whole. Grocery stores, restaurants, gas stations, liquor stores, and real estate offices are typical Korean businesses." Similarly, notes Moore, the number of Cuban-owned businesses in Miami has expanded from 919 in 1967 to 8,000 in 1976 to 28,000 in 1990. In Dallas, of the more than eight hundred businesses that operate on Jefferson Boulevard, more than six hundred are operated by first- and second-generation Hispanic immigrants—mostly Mexicans and other Central Americans.

The key point, then, is that immigrants are not merely finding jobs. They are helping to create jobs. They are providing more than their share of the ideas and ingenuity that drive our high-tech industry. Listen for example to an official at Intel Corporation, which reported earnings of $1.1 billion in 1992: "Our whole business is predicated on inventing the next generation of computer technologies. The engine that drives that quest is brain-power. And here at Intel, much of that brainpower comes from immigrants." The DuPont-Merck Pharmaceutical Company, which produces health care products and brings in $800,000 annually, reports that immigrants have come through with many of the breakthroughs in the development of new products. Robert Kelley, Jr., of SO/CAL/TEN, an association of almost two hundred high-tech companies, recently put it very plainly: "Without the influx of Asians in the 1980s, we would not have had the entre-preneurial explosion we've seen in California." And finally there is the 1988 report of the National Research Council: "A large fraction of the technological output of the United States [is] dependent upon foreign talent and... such dependency is grow-ing.... It is clear that these foreign-born engineers enrich our cul-ture and make substantial contributions to U.S. economic well-being and competitiveness."

Meanwhile, foreigners receive more than half of all doctoral degrees in science awarded by American universities. Just when high-tech industries are competing worldwide for ever-expand-ing markets, the United States is becoming increasingly depen-dent on foreign-born scientists for innovation in industry and research. In part this is the fault of our public school system, which has all but dropped science in its quest for "innovation." But we're solving the problem of supply and demand as we've often done in the past—by going to foreign markets. We're importing people, people drawn by our ideals; without them, our future would be bleak.

IMMIGRANTS AND WELFARE

Do immigrants head straight for the welfare office to sign up for the public dole, leaving us to worry about the wherewithal?

The best rebuttal to this caricature can be found right in the last U.S. Census Bureau report:

- On an average, immigrants use fewer welfare services than native families.

- Julian Simon, examining the census, reports that "for its first several decades in America, the average immigrant family pays more taxes than does the average native-born family."

- The average immigrant family pays about $2,500 more in taxes than it receives in government benefits.

- Over their lifetimes, immigrants pay about $20,000 more in taxes than they receive in benefits.

IMMIGRANTS AND FREEDOM

I'm always surprised to find conservatives who believe in free trade but adopt a protectionist attitude toward human beings. They seem to say, "We welcome your business and your ideas, but do us the favor of staying where you are." The Left takes a still more condescending view: "Live here, speak in your native language, avoid American influences, fill out this form, vote with us, and the checks will start coming next week." Both views are demeaning. Neither appreciates the immigrant for what he or she is, a friend to America and a believer in America, a person who comes here not to take but to work, earn, and give—often supporting a family back home. So many of our true problems arise from an ethic of dependency, a trust in Big Government. Here are people who for the most part represent just the opposite ethic.

The resentment of them comes from a zero-sum vision of jobs and the economy and the fixed benefits to be redistributed—a vision we owe to Big Government. Around the world that vision is dying and in its place comes the American faith in enterprise and personal achievement. Is it sheer coincidence that the new wave has arrived just as America and her ideals have prevailed?

STEPS TO TAKE ON IMMIGRATION

Do what is necessary to regain control of our borders. We must make a firm national commitment, complete with the resources required, to regain control of our borders. The current situation, in which practically anyone who wants to get into the country may do so, is plainly intolerable. Notice, however, that I said "borders." Currently, our effort to control illegal immigration is aimed at apprehending illegals after they have entered the country, effectively turning average American citizens into immigration officers, placing steep punishments on innocent businesses who may unknowingly hire an illegal immigrant, and, worst of all, prompting plans to set up a national computer registry and national ID card.

Instead, we should focus our efforts on the border and prevent illegal immigrants from entering the country in the first place. Jack Kemp and Bill Bennett have cited El Paso's "Hold the Line" program, which has reduced illegal border crossings by 75 percent, and the highly successful "Operation Gatekeeper" in California. These show that with the will and resources, we can dramatically reduce the flow of illegal immigrants to the United States. It is our duty as a sovereign nation to do so.

Encourage assimilation of new immigrants. Historically, when immigrants arrived at our shores they quickly found jobs and became integrated into our society. Unfortunately, our current welfare state tempts some of today's immigrants to delay this important step in becoming part of America. We should deny public assistance benefits to new immigrants for at least their first five years in the country. The general principle we should follow is immigration, yes; welfare, no.

Maintain or modestly increase current levels of legal immigrants. Holding to the view that legal immigrants are a benefit to our economy and society in general, we should under no circumstances reduce the current quotas for legal immigration. We can, however, reform the way visas are distributed. Some should be given to people fleeing tyranny abroad or coming from newly liberated areas such as the former Communist nations. Others can be handed out by lottery or given to family members of American citizens.

In my view, only an openness to immigrants is consistent with the legacy left by Ronald Reagan and other leaders of my party. As Jack Kemp and Bill Bennett have written, "Political parties are identified not simply by the policies they propose, but by the spirit which they embody. Ronald Reagan won 93 states in two elections. Under his leadership, the Republican party became the party of optimism, confidence and opportunity. It was a broad, embracing vision. But there is now a growing strain in the GOP—and within the conservative movement—which is pessimistic, angry and opposed. If some of the anti-immigration proponents have their way, Ronald Reagan's shining 'city on a hill' will be replaced by an isolated fortress with a moat—and a drawbridge up." This is not a vision consistent with Freedom or worthy of America.

Chapter 15

FREEDOM'S FAITH

In America today most of us stand together as we never have before on fundamentals. In Congress and most of our state capitols, the debate is about the precise extent to which Big Government should be scrapped. The accusations about "tax breaks for the rich" and "taking food from kids" are the last gasps of a passing order. And here we run into the social issues, those subtler and yet profound questions that trouble America.

To a point, I'm convinced some of these cultural issues will sort themselves out as power and money are returned to the people. One of the more perceptive bumper stickers I've ever spotted said simply, "De-fund the Left!" Whoever came up with that motto is my kind of social philosopher; he or she understands a lot about modern American culture and how we got where we are today. Along the way, "right" after "right" was declared by Big Government. Soon, each one required more and more public money and broader and broader powers of enforcement.

A few of these rights were legitimate to start with, but somehow they always ended as monumental acts of coercion that have reshaped our society for the worse. The right to economic opportunity became our massive welfare state, a system of benefits and mandates by which Big Government has corrupted so much of culture. Equal rights became quotas, undercutting our faith in the rewards of hard effort. The right of artistic expression became the taxpayer's duty to subsidize degenerate artists. The right to due process became a maze of technicalities, giving rise to the coddled criminal class that terrorizes our cities. The right to clean air and water became a bullying bureaucracy of regulators and a Washington-based cult of nature worshippers. The right to privacy, had the Clinton health plan prevailed, would have become the taxpayer's solemn duty to finance an already flourishing abortion industry. The right to religious freedom became a federal license to clear our schools and public squares of any hint of religious devotion, carried out by lawyers who see freedom in a $10 billion pornography industry but smell tyranny in a small town nativity scene.

These were all the bright ideas of liberals who pressed their own notions of freedom upon us, through the good offices of coercive bureaucrats and arrogant federal judges. Centralized government has become an artificial presence—this great big Thing occupying a place in our lives where it doesn't belong—skewing our whole outlook on American culture and our individual possibilities and responsibilities. It has gone so far that we have almost forgotten what a truly free society looks like and feels like. Clear it all away, scrap the whole apparatus of social engineering, return power to the people, and I believe our culture will awaken as if from a bad dream. Just like that, many of the social ills we quarrel over today will begin to pass away.

RELIGIOUS FREEDOM

Many of our cultural woes will pass away quickly, but not all. A lot of damage needs to be undone. I believe the Freedom Revolution offers us a chance to free religion, too—the chance truly to make our own moral choices absent the coercion of a ruling class of secularists. Before our own hyperpolitical era, a sort of cultural free market prevailed, with citizens and localities making important moral decisions for themselves. Mostly, they made wise and virtuous decisions, as free people tend to do. Even today anyone who has spent much time around flesh-and-blood cultural conservatives—say, your average Southern Baptist family in Texas—knows this to be true. Far from trying to force their opinions on others, such people have the utmost confidence that so long as government does not bring force to bear on a disputed social issue, they will win by the sheer force of example and moral persuasion.

This after all was how America has always handled social problems. A good tonic for anyone who romanticizes about our social history is the scholarship of James Q. Wilson. He notes, for example, that America in the early nineteenth century was often a violent and chaotic place, as young men migrated to cities in search of jobs. Away from their families and their churches, away from the restraints of all-seeing neighbors, they fell into vice and brought about all manner of social unrest. There were crime waves, and the era even had its own drug problem—booze. The Prohibition laws of the next century may not have been a great idea, but they came about in response to a social ill that had long troubled America.

Before our era, people on the whole operated by the adage that men can make good laws, but laws cannot make men good. True reform always went deeper, well beyond the reach of coercive state power. If other ages were able to keep social vices from getting out of hand, it was largely by the influence of religion. There were the volunteer aid societies I've already described, some of them still around, and the social ministrations of churches and private charities. Let's not discount the helpful contribution of nineteenth-century police forces, either.

But our ancestors relied ultimately—as I believe we can once again—on the spirit of simple decency that's always pervaded America, touching not only religious believers but skeptics, too. In other times it was just something there, a moral atmosphere as vital and common as the oxygen in the air. The idea of a nation of busybodies running around "imposing" their moral beliefs on others has been largely fabricated by modern liberals, who can't imagine a time when most people agreed about life's important things. There really was a simple moral consensus. Sure there were social problems. But they were seen by all as social problems. When our ancestors looked at social ills—dependency, violence, profligacy—liberal intellectuals were not around to point out that such maladies were "rights." Everyone understood that these were signs of cultural trouble, not to mention individual grief. Before government got into the business of curing social ills, that was the wholesome outlook of our entire culture—strong, self-reliant, yet truly caring. Perhaps no one described the country back then better than a foreign journalist visiting at the dawn of this century: "Americans are alarmingly optimistic, incredibly generous... it was a spiritual wind that drove them forward from the beginning."

It will be one of the challenges of the Freedom Revolution to restore that spirit in our own lives, and it won't always be easy. Big Government has attempted not only to diminish traditional religion, but in many ways to replace it. First, it attempted to assume control over all society's good works, as in the New Deal and Great Society. And today government's works border on outright evil. For the Left to accuse religious folks of trying to set up some sort of theocracy shows amazing bravado. Cultural conservatism has always been a defense against incursions by the state. In a sense Big Government has become nothing more than institutionalized moral relativism, enforcing liberalism's secular code of disbelief. Where once government defined the traditional family, now it works against it with a hostile tax code and generous benefits to the profligate.

In its more modest days, government stood aloof from churches, neither dictating to them nor taking dictation. Today Big Government is almost a church unto itself, handing down its own unforgiving commandments in such matters as abortion, school prayer, and obscenity. We are seeing the warning Theodore Roosevelt issued eighty years ago borne out in our social issues: "How foolish we should be to abandon our old ideals of duty toward God and man without better security than the radical prophets can offer us."

The resulting brand of secular spirituality is defined by what Teddy Roosevelt and his age would have called "the easy virtues"—tolerance, compassion, and a diffuse love for "humanity." The key to being a popular minister, a cleric friend once confided to me, is simple: "Talk about the sins they don't commit." We hear never-ending sermons on the themes of tolerance and compassion, which traditional faiths have taken for granted all along. They amount to the modern commandment, Be nice. But what real, day-in, day-out effort does it take to love humanity? A little harder and more meaningful to society are those quieter, domestic virtues the liberal wants to banish from public discussion: personal duty, temperance, thrift, fidelity, chastity, and so on. When reminded of these, the liberal reacts in outrage: how dare we bring morality into public matters! In truth the liberal does it all the time, only selectively. This explains how the activists can bring such an amazing moral fervor to amoral causes like abortion or pornography, indignant that we should be so "intolerant" about them. It's not that they've forgotten all virtues—just the big ones. Liberalism, when we stop to examine it, is just a morality fashioned from more venerable faiths, but stitched together in a tapestry of half-truths, easy virtues, and cheap sentimentality.

As Americans and heirs to Western culture, we enjoy the benefit of twenty centuries' worth of hard-earned moral wisdom. I suppose you could call it our spiritual trust fund, something we all naturally draw from with hardly a thought. Our belief in a personal God, just and merciful; our institution of marriage; our understanding of human freedom; our work ethic and civility; our natural law—our whole society is underwritten by that source. From it even the secular liberals receive a generous spiritual subsidy. Whatever truly decent impulses they have—helping the poor, caring for the weak—come from that fund. Often liberals speak as if they pretty much invented compassion and humanity, but they got it, as we have, from our shared Judeo-Christian trust fund. The only thing modern liberals have originated are their elaborate how to's for human betterment, which rest upon coercion and thus always turn out disastrously. Traditional religion, whether they like the thought or not, supplies the why—why we should help one another, why we should love our neighbor, why we came together as a people.

Think for instance of your typical ACLU attorney doing his work in the world. His is the great cause of civil liberties. Under this banner he charges into courtrooms to fight "religious repression"—kids praying in school, maybe, or some "threat to liberty" like setting up a manger somewhere. But where did he get this idea of human freedom, all these noble principles he takes upon himself to serve? Not all the world's systems of justice have placed the same value on individual rights. And most countries that do borrowed it from us. Just where did we learn to view our fellow man this way?

The answer—from the same Judeo-Christian heritage this ACLUer devotes his professional life to trashing. Far from being a menace to Freedom, ultimately that heritage sustains both the "civil" and the "liberties" ends of his own little world. If he woke up one morning to find that his dream of a purely secular society had been granted—no religious influence, no "value judgments" guiding our behavior—by 9:00 a.m. his brave new world would have unraveled into complete chaos, and he'd be lucky to make it to the office alive.

A similar sort of spiritual freeloading can be observed in such matters as single motherhood—affordable for the well-to-do liberal, but personal ruin for our poor—or again seen in our intellectuals sitting around discussing the "theories" of criminal rehabilitation, or the ill effects of prayer on our children, or "value-neutral" education, or New Age "spirituality." But playing the sophisticated cynic is the luxury of living in a society imbued with a Judeo-Christian morality, a society where most people can still be counted on not to live by liberalism's self-gratification gospel. Spiritually, our liberal reformers are like so many rich kids out on a wild cultural rush in the old man's car, cruising on sheer momentum with not a dime of their own to refill the tank.

As Big Government recedes from our lives, I hope its zealous devotees will ponder this humbling thought. Maybe it will make them a little more appreciative of traditional faiths and a little kinder to their fellow citizens who hold to those faiths—that "extreme fringe" the Left is always talking about.

ABORTION AND "THE FRINGE"

I am pro-life. Merely writing those three words raises in my

276 ★ THE FREEDOM REVOLUTION

mind an image of Michael Kinsley or some other liberal quivering with indignation as he berates me, "You, Dick Armey, of all people, want to bring government into people's bedrooms!"

Let's see if we can't calmly sort this out, at least for the immediate purposes of my own party. One problem is that the terms of debate are bogged down in such deep intellectual confusion that one hardly knows where to begin. The "keep out of the bedroom" line is part of a big bundle of clichés that today pass for serious social commentary.

Where does abortion, the social issue of social issues, fit in to the Freedom Revolution? Some leaders in my own party believe we should let it go. They accept the idea that abortion is a natural freedom, nothing to be too troubled about. As I write, the most audible spokesman for this view is Senator Arlen Specter of Pennsylvania. Standing in the shadow of the Lincoln Memorial to announce his presidential candidacy, Specter lashed out at "the extreme fringe" of the party. We must oppose, he said, that "radical social agenda which would end a woman's right to choose and mandate school prayer...." He went on:

> We do not need holy wars. What we need is tolerance and brotherhood and simple humanity.... I say the Republican party will not be intimidated or blackmailed by those kinds of threats. I and millions of other pro-choice Republicans will not be disenfranchised and made second-class citizens!

Reading this in the paper, two things struck me that reflect something about the spirit of this cause. I notice them a lot on the pro-choice side. First, there's that eloquent call for "brotherhood" and "humanity" in one sentence—followed a few sentences later by the accusation that tens of millions of our brothers are engaged in intimidation and blackmail. Do not sincere pro-lifers act, like the senator, by their own best lights? A similar brand of compassion could be seen in a recent op-ed piece by Hillary Clinton. In one sentence she called for "an honest debate" on children's issues. In the very next sentence she began this "honest debate" by noting that Republicans "have declared war on the children of our country." Both the senator and first lady might want to recall that lectures on tolerance are best accompanied by a demonstration of that virtue.

But the second thing I noticed about Senator Specter's defense of abortion was the odd choice of backdrop. The senator is a serious person whose able mind I have always admired. But I'm not sure why he used the Lincoln Memorial as a setting for his campaign sendoff. He may invoke Lincoln all he wants, but it seems to me he has forgotten where Lincoln stood on the great social issue of his day. Back then too a lot of people were upset about the social implications of a major Supreme Court ruling in the Dred Scott case. But I don't recall the Great Emancipator urging quiet acceptance of that opinion. Our party was founded, after all, on the conviction that no class of people can be excluded from the rights of man. No person is above the law, and no human being is beneath it either. And I've always thought that Lincoln was a great man for an even deeper reason, one that speaks to our current situation: he understood that not only did the slave have to be set free, but the slaveowner too had to be freed from his own moral blindness, from seeing his fellow humans as disposable commodities. It was a controversial position. But Lincoln believed that when the founders gathered in Philadelphia (in Specter's own constituency) and said "all men are created equal," they really did mean "created" and they really did mean "all."

We live in complex times, and it becomes more and more difficult to see that truth in all its simplicity and to accept the hardships it carries with it. Below, I want to address some of the hardships faced by the women of America. For those who would lead on the issue, I would point out that our Declaration means what it says. Complexity is no excuse for capitulation, for turning our backs on the whole tragic business. Hard decisions are no excuse for hard hearts. I am sure the first Roman citizen who expressed doubts about the common practice of letting unwanted children die by "exposure" were not very popular folks around the empire—they were "anti-exposure extremists." I suspect the first people who noticed that the West's system of human chattel and later segregation wasn't quite right also heard themselves called "zealots" and "busybodies" and the "fringe element." Indeed, for a while, they were the fringe—and thank God for that fringe.

That then is one answer to calls that we abandon our belief in the humanity of the unborn. We would cease at that moment to be the party of Lincoln. What kind of party would we become?

The great danger, as I see it, is that we will buy into a sort of free-market liberalism, protecting our salaries from Big Government but forgetting our souls. We would become little more than the Republican party of liberal caricature—concerned only about money, looking out for Number One, indifferent to matters of the heart. No party bearing that banner will ever command the votes, much less the respect, of the American people. It would be the Republican version of "It's the economy, stupid," expressing a pretty low opinion of our fellow citizens, as if we cared only about our livelihoods and not about the kind of lives we lead.

Obviously, this doesn't mean the views of liberal Republicans should be dismissed out of hand. It just means we need to think straight about what our party should stand for and what, when all the heads are counted, it does stand for. As I recall from their 1992 convention, it was the Democrats who didn't permit dissent on the subject. Already the media seeks the "social moderates" out at every sort of party gathering—"What about the abortion plank in the platform?... What about gay rights?..." They're in training for our 1996 convention, sowing discord wherever possible. The only way to avoid deadly capitulation is, as we are so often advised, to put the emotions of the debate aside and view the situation in all honesty. My own view is that on the social issues, moral principle and practical politics speak as one.

I welcome the challenge raised by my colleague Senator Specter and others like Governor Christine Todd Whitman of New Jersey and Governor Pete Wilson of California. They are in most matters comrades in the Freedom Revolution. I simply question their reading of the culture nationally, but especially in Specter's home state, Pennsylvania. (Leave aside the fact that America and Pennsylvania twice elected Ronald Reagan, who was firmly pro-life and the author of *Abortion and the Conscience of a Nation*.)

In Pennsylvania the 1990 election pitted a strongly pro-life Democrat incumbent governor, Robert P. Casey, against a pro-choice Republican woman who was endorsed by Specter. The pro-lifer won by over a million votes, the largest margin in Pennyslvania history. (The same Governor Casey nearly challenged President Clinton in their party's primaries, and who knows what might have happened?)

Casey, went on to become the defendant in *Planned Parenthood v. Casey*, an unsuccessful legal challenge to certain reasonable restraints on abortion like gender selection and parental consent. Parental consent—teenagers wanting an abortion must have the approval of their parents—is regarded by 60 to 70 percent of Americans, and at least 80 percent of parents, as a reasonable limitation on abortion. A great majority of the Pennsylvania legislature reflected that view in passing those minimal restrictions. Senator Specter favors no restrictions at all on abortion, not even in the late stages of pregnancy and not even for gender selection. So here he would seem to be in a quite narrow minority.

The revolution of November 1994 yielded the following results in Pennsylvania. A pro-choice Democrat incumbent senator, Harris Wofford, lost to Congressman Rick Santorum, a pro-life Republican. The margin of victory was about 200,000 votes. A pro-life third-party candidate, a woman, got more than 400,000 votes—most of which, according to exit polls, were Democrat votes. In other words, had incumbent Senator Wofford not waffled on the issue—he used to be pro-life—those votes would have gone to him and he'd still be a senator. And Wofford, recall, was credited in 1990 with sparking the "Clinton Revolution" of 1992. Santorum has since been replaced by a pro-life Democrat.

So the "fringe" argument doesn't hold up very well even in Specter's home state, unless he believes a majority of his own constituents are raving lunatics.

Now let's look at America generally. Of the six new United States senators, five are pro-life. Shortly after the 1994 election a pro-life Southern Democrat senator, Richard Shelby of Alabama, crossed the aisle and became a pro-life Republican (and also became a co-sponsor of my flat tax bill!). The next Supreme Court nominee can expect questioning from Judiciary Chairman Orrin Hatch, a pro-lifer.

Over in the House, a pro-life Republican is now speaker. As I mentioned earlier, we welcomed five new pro-life women to the House and bade farewell to three pro-choice women. Then there is Henry Hyde, perhaps the most eloquent pro-life leader in America. Fifteen years ago the ACLU actually rifled Hyde's trash can to find evidence of "religious influence" on the Hyde Amendment forbidding public payment for abortion. The Freedom Revolution has now made him the House Judiciary Committee chairman.

Two years ago we were assured the Freedom of Choice Act was a done deal. There was no stopping it. The bill, enshrining abortion on demand once and for all, was on the fast track to the president's desk. Where is it today? Somewhere between Inauguration Day 1993 and Election Day 1994, it just vanished, as did the health care bill, never to rise again. So we're entitled to ask, if that "narrow fringe" alone opposes abortion on demand, why weren't a Democrat president and a Democrat Congress able to pass that bill?

The answer is simple: not enough Democrats would go along. In fact, as any Southern Republican will tell you, one big reason their ranks are growing is that cultural conservatives felt the Democrat party had abandoned them. In the 1994 elections, exit polls told us, 27 percent of Americans said the abortion issue strongly shaped their vote. Of those people polled, a two to one majority were pro-life.

Whatever one's own views, then, intellectual honesty requires us to acknowledge that the pro-life position is widely held. Even if we wanted to change our party platform, most party members wouldn't let us get away with it. This is why even Bill Clinton, running in 1992, vowed to make abortion "safe, legal, and rare"— his way of soothing America's general discomfort with the practice. To dismiss pro-life America as "the fringe," or "religious zealots," or whatever is not an act of sober cultural analysis, but of cultural snobbery. It is less an attempt to measure pro-life opinion than to marginalize it—to wish the matter away. And so far the effort hasn't worked.

The reason the effort hasn't worked goes back, I believe, to abortion-on-demand's debut in American life twenty-three years ago. Liberals now insist that we revere *Roe v. Wade* in the name of judicial precedent and "consensus." But the case itself was the single boldest act of federal coercion in our history, smashing all legal precedent. Even the facts of the case were misrepresented, as the activist lawyers and "Jane Roe" now proudly boast. The consensus at the time was that abortion was a very sad thing for all parties concerned, something to be avoided at all costs. Overruling that consensus, overruling basic biology, overruling fifty legislatures, overruling twenty centuries of human experience, and overruling a Hippocratic Oath even more ancient, seven judges hearing a rigged test case suddenly decided otherwise. Having failed at moral persuasion in our legislatures and hospitals and homes and hearts, the liberals went to court and rammed their cause through, redefining humanity itself. One of those seven justices, Warren Burger, was immediately struck with deep doubts. One of the two dissenters, Byron White, called it "an act of raw judicial power." What nearly all free men and women in all times had found criminal and tragic, the Court declared a constitutional liberty—and all the little Kinsleys of liberaldom hailed the Court's brilliance and wisdom.

A generation later, as we see the unhappy fruits of that cause in, for example, four thousand daily abortions—the product of our new wisdom—we sense perhaps that life in America was better before the reformers arrived. I do not know exactly how many Americans I can speak for, but I think most us of are realizing that we cannot make a tragedy any less tragic by calling it a right. There is something about our talk of "privacy" and "terminated pregnancies" and "personally opposed, but..." that can't quite cover up the viciousness of what we're doing.

No one knows this more than the woman contemplating abortion, which is why her eager helpers at Planned Parenthood or abortion clinics don't talk of "babies" and never ever let her see the sonogram. This is why liberals react in fury to those "Life, What a Beautiful Choice" ads the DeMoss Foundation has run in recent years, which simply show mothers with their children with no polemics whatsoever. This is why they so vehemently oppose even the idea of informed consent—showing a young woman a sonogram or a likeness of the baby at that stage of pregnancy.

The enemy of the abortion industry is not intolerance, but information. In a way the industry has become a giant and lucrative racket sacrificing human beings in the name of ideology, trading on disinformation, vague euphemisms, and the vulnerabilities of young women in trouble. Even a few on the political Right miss this subtlety, shouting "murderer!" at women whose motive, at least, is not homicidal but simply to escape a hard situation none of us would envy. Often, especially in the case of our teenagers, these women are as much the victims of the abortionists as the child—"forced to be free" by a political culture exhorting them in that direction at every turn.

A few in the media, moreover, might also ask themselves why their vaunted First Amendment passion and interest in the issue has never extended to showing, even in ultrasonic images, an actual abortion. Aren't they the ones always "confronting" us with hard realities about human suffering elsewhere, from the brutality in Rwanda to bloody police beatings in Los Angeles? Why do they shy away from this particular confrontation with reality? They're all so intent that we should be for "choice." And yet, somehow, with uncharacteristic squeamishness and "good taste," they just never get around to showing us precisely what this choice involves. Pro-lifers, in fact, are treated with contempt by the media merely for distributing leaflets with those horrible images—as if they made some unforgivable breach of etiquette. There is a deep dishonesty in the media's whole glib treatment of the issue. I believe the "divisiveness" of the issue would resolve itself if the facts and details were not so carefully guarded from women in particular and America in general.

As we leave the subject, listen to Anne Stone, who presents the alternative view to this notion of human life. Mrs. Stone is the head of Republicans for Choice and pops up in the news every time the media drums up the "party of intolerance" theme. Usually she argues for a change in party principles on pragmatic terms. But a few years ago we got a glimpse of Mrs. Stone's philosophical grasp of the issue. Yes, she told an interviewer from the conservative newspaper *Human Events*, modern technology allows us to see the intricate human form in the womb at the earliest stages. And yes, these images do have "an emotional appeal." On the other hand, she reflected, "What about natural rock formations that look like people?... Just because something is formed in that shape does not necessarily mean that's what it is... and that it's there yet."

There you have, in sum, the pro-choice position. That form may look like a child, stir like a child, react to pain like a child, have the face of a child, and be born a child. But no, we must resist emotional appeals. Oddly enough, it's the pro-life side that gets accused of bringing "faith" into the abortion debate. I cannot imagine a more audacious act of faith than to look at that moving shape in his or her mother's womb and say as a society, "Not there yet."

Chapter 16

A GOVERNMENT HALF THE SIZE

Just ten years ago, even during the Reagan years, many of the proposals here would have been dismissed as wildly impractical. Something has changed in American politics beyond what even the boldest defenders of the free market imagined. A flat tax seems almost a certainty—with only the timing and exact rate in doubt. Less than a year ago Congress was debating nationalized health care; now we are debating health care freedom. For generations government has been assuming command over education; today the great issue is school choice. At the heart of all the reforms I have outlined in this book is a simple principle: the people themselves, not their government, should be trusted with spending their own money and making their own decisions.

Apologists of Big Government seem caught in a world of clichés in which "progress" is always equated with the expansion of federal power and activity. To make "progress" always means that government must do more for us—taking our money from us in order to "invest" in us. To cut spending, to eliminate any program, to reduce taxes—these are by definition to "turn back the clock." Big Government is like the guy lost on a dark, winding road who refuses to stop and ask directions or even to look at a map, angry at the suggestion he might be lost. But true progress, if you are going down the wrong road, means taking a new direction, which is what today's Freedom Revolution is about. We are turning to self-government, to a world in which free people may confidently navigate the roads for themselves. Progress today means what it has meant all along, personal freedom; it means we'll keep our own money, thank you, and handle the "investing" ourselves. At the end of a century defined by government expansion, we are yearning again for individual freedom and for modest, competent government.

If we are bold enough to see this revolution through, an American family in the next century will spend far more of their own earnings as they see fit. They may plan their lives and careers without constant supervision from what Arizona Governor Fife Symington calls "the little potentates on the Potomac." Americans' land will be their own land; their property, their own property; their earnings, their own earnings; their children, their own responsibility. Government will again be the ally of a free people, not a jealous rival for power. I heard one liberal pundit the other day saying that the first one hundred days of the Contract with America "hasn't really changed people's lives." The people, she said, didn't feel "they were getting any material benefit from their representatives." But she is one of the few people left who still associate the word "government" with "material benefit." People today are demanding from government the greatest benefit of all, the benefit of the doubt. We do not and should not trust government to manage our lives for us; we simply want government to trust us.

If we follow this spirit, there is no reason we cannot, by the time our children come of age, reduce the federal government by half as a percentage of the gross domestic product. In previous chapters I have proposed that we rid ourselves of such encumbrances as the Department of Education, cast off unnecessary programs like the National Endowment for the Arts, overhaul welfare according to the idea of personal responsibility, and end entitlements to the middle-class in favor of letting middle-class families keep more of their own money in the first place. All these reforms are good in themselves; the case for taking these measures is not just monetary but deeply moral. But if we do all this, what's left? What duties remain to government, and what will they cost? What's left is a world in which government is better able to perform the constitutional functions appropriate to it. What's left is a truly responsible government requiring relatively half the money and manpower it now claims. Reducing government's share of our economy by half sounds like a bold stroke, but really it just follows from all the lesser reforms I have described. Demanding better government, we end up with its logical result: smaller government.

Merely reducing the rate of growth is a timid goal. If we are lost, going a little lighter on the accelerator is no solution. The solution to excessive spending is not less excessive spending. The solution is less spending. What's needed is a sense of direction, a return to the map left to us by the founding fathers. Our big, intrusive state is not bad merely because we can't afford it; it would be just as bad even if we could go on forever feeding more and more money into it. It is simply not how a free country operates. It squanders not only our wealth but our creative energies; it burdens not merely our bank accounts but our belief in ourselves. It simply must be brought down to size, to constitutional proportion, to a level that reflects the spirit of Freedom instead of killing it.

Cutting Government by Half

The problem with any serious attempt to "cut" federal spending was apparent one evening shortly after we took control of the House. The Republican leadership gathered in a late night meeting to discuss exactly how we will balance the federal budget. It was, as you might expect, a somewhat tense powwow. The mood, particularly among the new freshman members, was revolutionary, but there were still members who practically broke out in hives when it came time to look at the actually budget numbers. Their attitude, as Bob Livingston, chairman of the Spending Committee, put it, was "Don't cut you, don't cut me, cut that fellow behind the tree." Such was the fear some had of going after spending programs that supposedly benefited their constituents.

Before long, though, John Kasich, our new Budget Committee chairman, and the guy charged with developing the balanced budget plan, had enough of the handwringers. He put a hat—actually, I think it was a sandwich box from the Capitol's carryout restaurant—in the middle of the table and demanded that from that moment on any member at the table who uses the three-letter word "cut" would have to put a dollar in it as a fine.

What Kasich was saying is that when we talk about "budget cuts," we are actually adopting the somewhat Orwellian language of Washington's spending interests. They have so contorted the meaning of ordinary words, that to them "cut" does not mean spending less than we had before, which is the way the typical American family understands the word. No, "cut" simply means spending less than they had planned to spend. If, for example the government spends less than the expected amount, then the Congressional Budget Office reports a "spending cut" in that program—never mind if spending actually rose. Say an urban grant program had been slated to increase by $3 billion next year, but Congress decided to trim the increase down to $2 billion. The Congressional Budget Office would then report a $1 billion spending cut.

Let me give you an analogy. Suppose I spent $100 last year on new fishing rods and reels, and this year I planned to upgrade my arsenal by spending $50 more than that, for a total of $150 in new fishing gear. But then my wife finds out. Since she doesn't entirely understand the importance of having the right fishing equipment, she insists that I prune my fishing budget back to $125. Now to any normal person, that is still a $25 increase over what I spent last year. But the way Washington looks at it, that's a $25 spending cut, since I am spending $25 less than I had hoped to spend.

In this way, over the years Congress has managed to sucker the American people into thinking they were cutting the budget, when in fact they were doing no such thing. Spending on social programs could soar by a couple hundred billion dollars in a single year, and Congress would insist that the programs had been cut simply because even this massive spending increase did not meet their fond dreams of increasing spending much further.

Now that Republicans are in charge, the Democrats use the same linguistic technique a little differently. Whenever a Republican proposes even the most modest spending restraint, Democrats cry that we are cutting aid to widows and orphans or whatever, even if all we've done is prune the projected increase of the programs a little. You saw that with school lunches. We proposed to block grant the nutrition programs to the states—that is, rather than try to run the programs from faraway Washington, we would simply give the states a lump sum on money and let them run the programs more or less as they saw fit.

Before you knew it, President Clinton and his accompanying chorus of liberal Democrats were staging photo ops in school cafeterias, serving up the baloney that the Republicans were cutting the school lunch programs. In fact, under our plan, spending on nutrition programs would still be increased by some 4.5 percent every year for the next five years.

The funny thing is, though, that once we began to follow Kasich's perfectly good advice and use that line in press conferences—"We're not cutting the budget, we're just increasing it less than the Democrats would have"—I began to get letters from some very angry people. "What's this about not cutting the budget," they said, "you should be cutting the thing. That's why we elected you."

I think they were exactly right. We should cut the budget in the literal meaning of the term, that is, spending less than we had before.

Both philosophically and practically, balancing the budget is a secondary goal. After all, if we could modestly restrain the growth of our spending, perhaps raise taxes some, then sooner or later, the budget will be brought into balance—but only after the government has grown hundreds of billions of dollars larger and is absorbing an even bigger share of our economy than it does today. Keep in mind that one of the biggest supporters of the balanced budget amendment to the constitution is Senator Paul Simon of Illinois, a paleoliberal, one of the few surviving members of Congress who still believes in the New Deal and the Great Society. When he one day noticed the importance of innovation in small business to the economy, he said, "Yes, we need a government program to encourage that." He wants to balance the budget alright, but he wants to do so, I suspect, by raising taxes to support government at its current bloated size or even larger. There's plenty of people like that in Washington.

Warnings about "the deficit crisis," without concern for the size of government itself, are a diversionary tactic. Liberals like this angle on our fiscal problems because in revolutionary times it offers just the right formula: You could favor taxing more of the people's money away and still sound like a fiscal conservative. You could loot and lecture all at once. But as it is, the federal government already spends about $1.5 trillion, which strikes most people as quite enough. It's nearly a quarter of the nation's economy. Government at all levels absorbs nearly 40 percent of our entire economy. Taxing more to cover the deficit is clearly no solution to the real crisis.

For many years "moderates" have called for a reduction in the constant increase in spending. To actually eliminate a particular program is regarded as an act of unthinkable callousness. If this is moderation, why are Americans today in extreme debt, under an extreme tax burden, extremely doubtful about the results of all that spending, and extremely worried about the future? This is not a rational person's idea of moderation.

The sheer mass of our federal government is simply inconsistent with a free society. If nearly half of what you make is spent by someone else, that means that half your work time is spent working for someone else. Call me a radical, but I think that comes dangerously close to being a form of indentured servitude. If we truly believe in the Freedom Revolution, we must throw off that yoke.

I believe we should set a goal of cutting the share of our economy the government now controls by 50 percent, from the current 22 percent of the gross national product down to 11 percent, and we should do it soon before our children come of age.

THE GREAT CATCH-22

During the recent debate on the balanced budget, ABC's "Nightline" did a show on the pain that "cutting" spending—meaning reducing the rate of increase—would create for the American family. It focused on one supposedly typical American family. The father, a construction worker, feared losing the high union wages he's receiving when he works on government construction projects. They worried that their elderly parents might lose when the Medicare program was pared back. Even their children might not be fed properly without the government school lunch program, much less eventually attend college without government grants and loans.

This is the way that government programs have always been justified. Good jobs, education, health, and nutrition are all good things, and so it is good for the government to help provide them for us. What "Nightline" left out, however, is the reason good jobs are not as plentiful as they should be and education and health care are difficult to afford is because the government itself makes us poorer through high tax rates and mountains of federal debt.

The government has thus trapped us in a catch-22. They take away a huge portion of our income by arguing that they need it to provide us with important benefits. Why can't we provide those benefits for ourselves? Because the government takes away a huge portion of our income.

In this way, to paraphrase a principle of economics, the supply of government programs creates the demand for government programs. It's a self-justifying cycle that leads inexorably to bigger and bigger government. The more benefits the government showers on us, the poorer we become as a result, and the more we need more government programs. Taken to its logical conclusion, you get Sweden.

It's time to break the cycle. The obvious solution frankly is to end many of these government programs and allow people to keep their own money, the better to provide for these benefits themselves.

Every year, I worry and fret as I try to select the right birthday gift for my wife, Susan. And every year, try as I might, I manage to choose the wrong thing. If I can't figure the needs and desires of the one person who is closest to me in the world and who I deeply love and care for, how can we expect the government to do a better job?

A TAXPAYER'S TOUR OF OUR GOVERNMENT

Of course, I don't want to give the impression that most government programs are designed, even ostensibly, to help families with the needs of everyday life. Most government programs don't even pretend to do that, and very few American families would notice their disappearance—except for the tax cuts that might result. Let's take a look at some.

The USDA

Over at the Department of Agriculture, our farm programs are among the most senseless and expensive in the budget, costing taxpayers about $17 billion annually and raising food prices about $10 billion more. Their costs are borne by the American people and their benefits go to a small number of wealthy farmers. The single largest owner of farmland in America is the Prudential Life Insurance Company.

Under the guise of promoting exports, the Department of Agriculture cuts checks to some of the largest and most profitable companies in the nation, tens of millions of dollars to a couple of dozen trade associations to "promote the sale of American agricultural products overseas." In practice, corporations simply pocket huge wads of tax dollars for doing what they'd be doing anyway—advertising and selling their own products. Dole, Sunkist, and even McDonald's have received money to underwrite their advertising budget. Even some foreign companies get money under the program.

High-tech pork barrel

Billions are spent every year on what is known as industrial policy, the government's misguided and often corrupt attempt to pick winners and losers in the marketplace. Proponents of industrial policy normally talk of "private-public partnerships to promote the industries of tomorrow," but usually industrial policy turns out to be a give-away to the industries with the most political clout—often the industries of yesterday.

Undeterred by this history of failure, the Clinton administration embarked on a host of new industrial policy ventures, one of them an agreement to write a $1 billion check to the Big Three automakers, under the auspices of the Partnership for a New Generation of Vehicles. This project is supposed to develop new technologies that would result in a "supercar" that would be cheaper, lighter, and three or four times as fuel-efficient. In other words, more profitable, which is why the Big Three have been pursuing that same goal for years at their own cost.

Then there's the Advanced Technology Program, which the Commerce Department calls "the Clinton Administration's principal civilian technology initiative to stimulate growth and job creation through the development of new industries." Price tag: $500 million a year. Who gets the money? Anderson Consulting, 3M, Unisys, AT&T, Xerox, IBM, and other such small, struggling, undercapitalized, innovative new companies.

The Commerce, Transportation, Energy, and Defense Departments are handing out billions for industrial policy programs. More and more of these programs are being funded out of the Defense Department, which is the only agency in Washington to suffer any real budget cuts over recent years. While defense readiness is progressively weakened, the Department of Defense is spending millions for "innovative commercial ship design" and dozens of other nondefense projects.

Mass transit subsidies

Over the past twenty-five years, more than $100 billion has been spent on mass transit subsidies. Yet ridership is lower today than it was in the early 1960s. In the three decades since, public transit costs have increased at a faster rate than any other sector in the economy, including health care. Costs have grown because the federal government has handed money to these inefficient systems like a busy father appeasing spoiled children. Subsidies now account for two-thirds of the operating cost of mass transit. With lower skills than the average American worker, the average transit worker is nevertheless paid 70 percent more. If laid off, many public transit workers are eligible to receive up to six years of severance pay.

Credit and insurance programs

If the national debt seems beyond comprehension at more than $4.5 trillion, consider this: the total amount of all the government's potential financial obligations is $15 trillion. We insure bank deposits, pensions, small business loans, student loans, farmer loans, home loans, and even foreign governments. Up until a few years ago, most people in Washington didn't worry about the countless guarantees of the federal government, assuming the marker would never be called in. Then came the savings and loan crisis. The taxpayer cost of this was more than $100 billion. But even with this federal commitment, the problem hasn't been fixed. Another banking or savings-and-loan crisis is a possibility. Many observers believe the Pension Benefit Guarantee Corporation will go belly up, costing perhaps tens of billions of dollars. A recent report by the CATO Institute warned that the World Bank's "irresponsible lending exposes Western taxpayers to a possible World Bank bailout on a scale comparable to the U.S. savings and loan bailout."

Don't bother to pay us back

Even when they don't go belly up and cause financial disaster, federal loaning activities bleed the government daily. Take the Farmers Home Administration (FmHA), for instance. The purpose of FmHA is to make loans to farmers who can't get private credit. To qualify for a loan, a farmer must produce two letters from separate banks stating that he has been denied credit. Here's a loan program for which you qualify by proving that no responsible financial institution will lend you money. Prove you don't merit a loan, and the government gives you one.

It gets better. A local committee made up of two individuals elected by farmers from the county and a third person appointed by the state FmHA director determine who gets loans. In other words, the potential recipients of loans decide who hands out the money. If you're a farmer whose future looks a little shaky, who will you support—Frugal Fred or Big-Spending Bob? The General Accounting Office reports that "FmHA field office lending officials [the folks the farmers choose] often failed to follow the agency's own standards for making loans, servicing loans, and managing property."

And finally, when you get the money, you don't have to pay it back. FmHA lent TexCal Land Management an incredible $51 million, not a penny of which has been paid back. George Nickel, who almost made the *Forbes* list of the four hundred wealthiest Americans, defaulted on an FmHA loan in 1985, and he still owes $17 million. Millionaire aircraft collector Bill Destefani has owed FmHA $1 million for the fifteen years now.

What does this mess cost us? Quite a bit, even by Washington standards. Over the past five years, FmHA has written off $11.5 million in bad loans. Even more astonishing, the *Washington Post* reports that "[s]eventy percent of the agency's debt in 1990 was owed by borrowers who were either behind in their payments or who are current only because the FmHA forgave some of their debt or rewrote their loans with better terms."

Small Business Administration

While it can't top FmHA, the Small Business Administration (SBA), has certainly tried. Twenty percent of all SBA loans end up in default, costing taxpayers about half a billion dollars a year. And there's more bad news on the way. The Office of Management and Budget expects nearly $4 billion more outstanding loans to end in default. Several times in the past few years, Congress has been forced to pass a "supplemental appropriation" because SBA inadvertently lends more money than Congress has provided.

But does the SBA really help small business? The 0.2 percent of businesses that do receive SBA assistance seem to fall into one of two categories: (1) businesses that could never have received a private loan and therefore don't deserve a tax-payer guaranteed loan and (2) businesses that could have gotten credit without the SBA and therefore don't deserve a taxpayer-guaranteed loan.

Supporters will argue that without SBA, many small businesses wouldn't be able to crank up their operations. This is a perfect example of Washington's single-entry bookkeeping. Rarely does anyone ask where the money comes from. It comes from higher

298 ★ THE FREEDOM REVOLUTION

taxes and from deficit spending, both of which damage the most vulnerable operations in the marketplace—small businesses. The SBA is also an example of liberal tunnel vision: they don't see anything happening in America unless they see the government doing it.

The Community Development Block Grant Program

Under this multibillion dollar program, the federal government provides aid to poor urban areas to promote "urban renewal" and economic development. In reality, this program is little more than a slush fund for big city mayors, many of whom don't represent economically distressed areas. In 1993 fifteen of the twenty wealthiest counties received fat grants. Community Development Block Grant Program funds have been used for loans to a professional hockey team and to build an off-track betting parlor.

Job training

The federal government has more than one hundred job-training programs. These cost U.S. taxpayers $17 billion each year. If they were successful, they might be worth the price tag but there is no evidence that programs produce benefits that come close to their costs. The Job Corps, for example, costs $30,000 per client with negligible results.

Less than half the money for the Job Training Partnership Act is actually used for job training: the only people who clearly benefit from these programs are the bureaucrats who run them. The American job market would not even register their disappearance.

Rural Electrification Administratration

Begun in 1935 to bring electricity to farmers and other rural dwellers, the Rural Electrification Administration's (REA's) mission is long accomplished. I climbed poles for the REA in Cando, North Dakota, and I can tell you that rural America is on line. Yet their undead agency still drains American taxpayers.

The big federal land grab

The U.S. government owns 700 billion acres of land—about a third of the land mass of the continental United States. Yet annually, the bureaucrats swallow up thousands of acres more—at a cost of billions of dollars annually. This compulsive shopping has to be stopped.

The Legal Services Corporation

The Legal Services Corporation (LSC) was started to provide legal aid for the poor. In practice, LSC is now a taxpayer-financed agency that sues state and local governments on behalf of drug dealers and violent criminals who have been evicted from public housing and on behalf of a whole host of left-wing causes. The federal government funds the LSC at the rate of about $200 million annually, but the true cost is higher. LSC lawyers spend much of their time in litigation with the government itself, costing taxpayers millions more.

Parochial and political pork

This is a brief tour of government gone wildly beyond the purposes envisioned by the founding fathers. How has it all been allowed to continue? I'd say for two reasons.

The first reason is the same liberal assumption I've explored in other chapters. Just about any problem, anywhere, requires liberals' involvement. If somewhere something isn't working quite right, there is only one solution. The full power and moral authority of the federal government must be brought to bear on that problem.

Conversely, any public good must be made a public program. Education is a good thing, so let's create a national Department of Education. Jobs are good, so let's create more public jobs. Health care is good, so let's really do things up right with an all-encompassing National Health Care Program. Art is very good too, so let's endow it. And so on in an endless digression from the defined federal powers of the Constitution.

That's the first reason for our budget of $1.5 trillion—the desire to do nice things with other people's money. The other reason is not due the same charitable interpretation.

Basically, it amounts to a job security program for members of Congress. They take your money and give it to someone else for the sole purpose of making that other person indebted to them. There's a simple calculation here: You're only dimly aware of the loss, for on the taking end, the loss is spread out across all America. But the recipient of this generosity is acutely aware of his gain; he or she gets a big chunk of money and so is correspondingly grateful.

By analogy, suppose I stole a dime from a thousand different people. I then present you with a grant of a hundred dollars. You'd say I was a great guy—your new buddy. When the time came, you would want to help me, too. The others, meanwhile, even if they noticed the missing dimes, wouldn't get too worked up because it was only a dime. The problem with the scam is that when you have almost 535 congressmen doing it at once, the dimes add up.

Around Congress, this kind of spending is called: "parochial pork"—small change like a few million here or there for roads, bridges, bike paths, and grants to constituents or local organizations. Then there's the "partisan pork." Partisan pork is "social" and "investment" spending of the sort that kept the Democrat party in power. Here the money goes not to some tangible, concrete item, but to diffuse, ideological objectives only the recipient would find meaningful—for example, a subsidized study into an issue of interest to them. Most of these programs remain in the budget not because of their contribution to the well-being of the American people, but because of the contributions their beneficiaries make to politicians.

In the modern American welfare state much of this partisan pork is out of control, literally. The entitlement programs simply set a standard of eligibility, and thereafter anyone meeting the usually minimal criteria may claim his or her due. It's automatic, relieving Congress of any further duty to vote or guard against financial ruin. A generation of congressmen have lamely answered questions about excessive spending by saying, in essence, "It's out of my hands."

Entitlement programs claimed less than a quarter of the budget thirty years ago. Today they absorb half of what we spend at the federal level. In the four years from 1989 to 1992, spending on entitlements grew $140 billion as Congress just stood there doing little or nothing. By 1998 "mandatory" spending will grow from $761 billion to over $1 trillion. In just three years, by projected estimates, entitlements will equal our total spending at present.

Besides entitlements, about $550 billion still remains "discretionary," meaning Congress has left itself a choice. This money is fought over every year in Congress' annual competition of troughsmanship: an obsolete program in one district, an obscure little subsidy or grant for another district, that new courthouse promised to another district.

Little review is ever done to see if these programs are actually serving a useful purpose. Indeed, the whole "debate" occurs in an atmosphere of warmth, congeniality, and the shared burdens of "governing." Often the committee meetings and House–Senate conferences are closed to the public, just to spare citizens the worry of how their money is being squandered. In 1992 alone one congressional reform group called the "Porkbusters" identified $2 billion in spending projects that had never once been subject to open hearings or competitive bidding.

This is how federal spending reached its current mark of more than $1.5 trillion a year—a quarter of the entire U.S. economy. And that is why I believe we will see the Balanced Budget Amendment brought again to vote and this time passed. There is hardly any alternative given the way Congress now operates. Most certain of all is that the budget cannot be balanced merely by further taxes, unless we are prepared to tax at Scandinavian levels of 70 or 80 percent. Two facts explain why.

First, even while tax rates have ranged from as high as 70 percent to as low as 28 percent in recent decades, the amount actually collected from those taxes has remained essentially at the same level. The reason is simple. When the government raises taxes, individuals shelter their funds or defer work and investment. The economy flattens, and the anticipated income is rarely collected.

Second, since World War II, the budget has been balanced in only eight of forty-eight years. But in those years, government spending averaged only 16 percent of the economy, while revenues averaged 17 percent. In other words, they have only been able to balance the budget in low-spending years. Nothing in our past experience suggests that balanced budgets can be achieved at today's high level of taxing and spending.

How to Cut Government by Half

The first step in halving the federal government in relation to gross domestic product is to get rid of the above programs and hundreds more like them in their entirety. They do no one any good except a few special interests in on the deal.

I would enact a "sunset" law within two years, covering all

domestic discretionary programs and all unearned entitlements. Social Security, Medicare, veterans benefits, and federal retirement benefits are *earned* entitlements for which the beneficiary has paid a premium or performed a service. These earned entitlements will not be affected. But unearned entitlements, such as farm subsidies and welfare benefits, as well as all programs in the discretionary budget, will be sunsetted and must be reviewed by Congress if they are to continue. This law would require Congress to take a fresh look at such spending programs and force them to decide whether (1) they're truly necessary and should be reauthorized; (2) they're necessary, but should be reformed before being resurrected; or (3) they've outlived their usefulness and should be allowed to die a natural and automatic death.

Another step, as outlined in chapter 12, is to free health care from government's artificial price controls and meddlesome regulations. After Social Security, defense, and interest payments, the biggest item in the federal budget is Medicare. Here the interests of Medicare beneficiaries and other citizens come together—the first getting a substandard product, the others paying too much for it. One possibility, as I mentioned in the health care chapter, would be to furnish senior citizens with health care vouchers: let them choose their own doctors, and let the market compete for their business. Another possibility is to convert Medicare into a managed care system, just as many private medical providers are doing. Either way we would save billions and the elderly would receive better care. Similar reforms could be directed at Medicaid, the vast government program for the poor. When we have reformed welfare, in any case, there will be far fewer chronically poor citizens and thus fewer Medicaid costs.

Toward welfare generally, our aim should be to instill the virtues of self-sufficiency. It may be true that a good society has a safety net for the truly poor, but in a truly good society tens of millions of people do not fall into that safety net. We can eliminate not just welfare but the causes of massive dependency upon the state. Indeed with the Contract with America we have already begun this.

The next step in halving the relative size of government would be to scrap entire departments like Energy, Commerce, and above all Education. If these departments do the people of America any good at all, very few of us are aware of it. First to go must be the Department of Education, which produces nothing but puffed up rhetoric, while squandering billions of dollars annually taken from the incomes of parents who could spend it better.

Next, eliminate regional subsidies. The idea of taxing people in Iowa to subsidize a project in New York City or taxing the New Yorker to subsidize the farmer in Des Moines never even entered the minds of our founders. I propose a return to their idea: All subsidies serving only regional interests should be phased out. And above all give no more handouts to big city mayors. These are just payoffs for loyal party service, and it's about time we end the whole insidious practice. Let the cities tend to their own fiscal affairs and all other regions to theirs. This is called federalism, and one of its great advantages is that it keeps local governments as well as the federal government in check. Governors, mayors, and city councils can't expand their own powers beyond what local taxpayers are willing to bear.

For the budget generally, I support the "overall limit" approach, meaning Congress sets a specific goal in spending reduction and then lives by it. If the war against spending can only be fought in a thousand battles over individual lines in the budget, much political blood will be shed, little ground will be gained, and the spending special interest will win through sheer attrition. Only if we enact spending caps and other devices impossible to evade will the spending cuts be made. If, for whatever reason, the deficit nevertheless grew beyond the preset limit, then an automatic sequester would take place—that is, certain programs would be cut automatically by a certain percentage to bring the budget into balance. The idea is to take one great vote as to the national interest and then sort the budget out accordingly.

This, after all, is how families manage their financial affairs. If a couple finds they have been living beyond their means, they don't list everything they spend money on—a vacation, a second or even third car, clothes, and entertainment—and then decide that since they're fond of all those things they simply cannot cut their family budget and must continue spending themselves into debt. Unlike the U.S. government, they don't have that option (and in fact the government won't for long, either). Instead, they decide how much they can spend and only then do they begin to decide what luxuries they can afford.

WHAT ABOUT SOCIAL SECURITY?

One of the more tiresome melodramas played out in Washington every now and then centers on Social Security. For a generation the script has never varied: Democrats want to "protect" Social Security, Republicans are out to "destroy" it, which will throw old folks out into the streets.

One problem with the script is that it was Bill Clinton who recently increased taxes on Social Security payments and it was Republicans who still more recently eliminated those taxes. President Clinton also began moving Social Security toward a means-tested system, meaning essentially a welfare program far removed from the secured pension system originally envisioned.

Politicians are forever rushing forward to assure older Americans that Social Security is "off the table," beyond question, inviolate. For the present I share this belief, but for an entirely different set of reasons. Social Security is in need of reform, but I do not believe Congress has earned the trust necessary to reform it just yet. We must first reform—meaning rethink, cut, or eliminate altogether—other programs to prove we are able to reform Social Security without doing injury to those who now rely upon it.

This is only a simple matter of keeping a promise, after all. Americans now on Social Security were assured throughout their working lives that in return for taxes taken, they would receive money enough to get by in retirement. It's the rare case when we truly do "owe" money to the recipient. I oppose any effort—such as the Clinton tax on Social Security—to prevent government from keeping up its end of the bargain.

In its defense, Social Security is also one of the few federal programs not hostile to the traditional family. As economist John Mueller points out,

> This is what now most embarrasses liberals about Social Security, no less than it offends yuppies. Social Security stands almost alone in accepting the traditional family (in which the father works to support the family and the mother raises the children) as normal. In addition to the basic retirement benefit based on each worker's lifetime of contributions, there is an extra 50 percent spouse's benefit. For most married women who work part-time, intermittently, or not at all outside the home, this spousal benefit is greater than the one to which they are entitled based on their own lifetime cash earnings. There is also a widow's benefit equal to 100 percent of the husband's basic benefit, and coverage of surviving dependents. To qualify, in general, the couple must remain married, the husband must be steadily employed, and the wife must give up a lifetime of earnings equal to at least one-half of her husband's. Thus the structure of Social Security—in sharp contrast to welfare—upholds intact marriage, a father's responsibilities, a mother's sacrifice.

This explains, as Mueller observes, why just about every liberal attempt to "reform" Social Security takes aim at spousal benefits, proposes welfare-like means-testing, and in general attempts to make the whole system less family-centered.

In practical terms the problem is that for years Democrat Congresses have been pillaging the Social Security "trust fund" even as they avowed their belief in its sanctity. Very few of us still harbor the illusion that the government has actually been setting our payments aside in a separate account from which we may one day draw, confident our money has been wisely invested for us and the earnings stored away. Social Security may be "off the table," but under the table Congress has been routinely moving these funds into all manner of other programs. It basically spends our Social Security tax money just as recklessly as it spends any other tax money, confident that when the fiscal crisis comes—well, they'll figure out something.

And then, as noted earlier, there is the further fiction that workers are paying only 7.5 percent of their salaries for Social Security. When the employer's share is counted, it's actually 15 percent. That's 15 percent of all your wages and salaries (up to $60,600) from the time you get your first job as a teenager. And with all that money the government still has not been able to keep the system solvent.

So we are left with the fact that as early as 1999, the Social Security "trust fund" will have peaked, unable to make payments to new retirees. We can face this fact in one of three ways: (1) We can go along just as we are, which will require still higher payroll taxes—certain death for our economy. (2) We can lower some benefits, raise the retirement age, and increase taxes—death for the Social Security system as we now envision it. Or (3) we can transform the system and allow younger workers to begin directing some of their money to private accounts under their own control—a sort of generational bargain whereby they agree to receive less money later, but keep more now to invest in their future.

I lean toward the latter system because it honors our pact with present recipients, offers a choice to those still working, and keeps more money in the hands of the earner. Just imagine, for example, how much better off a person would be if, instead of handing that 15 percent of lifetime earnings over to government, he had been putting it into a private required retirement account. The benefits would be far greater and more secure, and the money would remain productive in the private sector.

The building blocks of any Social Security reform must be allowing choice for today's workers and keeping our promises to the retired. But again I believe the debate must wait on other reforms. It will be the final business of the Freedom Revolution, begun only when we have first proved ourselves on other pressing issues.

Chapter 17

THE POSSIBILITIES BEFORE US

What will the nation look like when we finish the work of this Freedom Revolution? Well, first let's take a look at what our nation's capital city would look like.

Touring the Capitol itself, we would notice fewer people doing more definable tasks. No more armies of lobbyists there to lean on members for this or that special favor or appropriation. There would be no special appropriations because everyone would understand Congress served only the common national interest. It would be a place where "cuts" mean cuts, where laws are simple and regulations few, where every promise is a Contract with America. All the big city mayors would be back in their cities, all the farmers back on their farms, all the congressmen themselves back home after a brief stint in our citizen legislature, all the lobbyists back doing whatever lobbyists do without Big Government.

In their place, touring the Capitol, would be ordinary Americans just like we see now, only more of them, and for the first time in a generation truly proud to see their seat of government.

Crossing First Street, glancing off at the Library of Congress still doing its noble work of preservation, we would see the judicial branch of government hearing cases. In a free society, fewer and fewer of these would be the manufactured test cases the Supreme Court so often hears today, with one group of activist lawyers opposing another group of activist lawyers. The Court would concern itself again with true cases in controversy, with upholding instead of inventing laws, with simple justice.

Then we would move on to the White House. There, too, would be fewer staff people, but they would be doing more tangible work. The mobs of lobbyists and activists who assembled there to draw up a national health care system, producing only millions of papers and charts, would seem a distant memory. Instead the work would be clearly presidential in nature, with the chief executive and his aides safeguarding the national defense, dealing with the State Department on other foreign affairs, preparing balanced budgets with help from Treasury, seeing that crime is being prosecuted by the Justice Department, and in general carrying out the duties prescribed in the Constitution. Probably we would find fewer reporters buzzing about the pressroom, too. Our whole vision of government would have shifted away from one person or 535 people and back to the ordinary citizen and taxpayer—the governed. The visibility of our leaders would diminish, but the respect they command would grow.

Inspecting the executive departments, we would find the useful ones America has always had—State, Justice, Treasury, Defense, and a few others—performing the important duties assigned them by the Constitution. In just one modest-sized building we might find the entire Internal Revenue Service, receiving the quarterly checks and post-card size tax forms from Americans paying their 17 percent flat rate.

From there we might walk across the mall, nicely maintained by the Park Service, to visit national shrines and museums also supervised by the government. Here and there we might pass a government laboratory or hospital, where researchers are hard at work curing diseases and conceiving new technologies to relieve sickness and suffering.

And that would about cover it. That would be our federal government. Washington would become what it was always supposed to be, our federal city where the vital national business is conducted by able and modest people—all directly accountable to the citizens. Who would "manage the economy," subsidize the needy, regulate industry, and do all the things Washington does today? The people themselves, individually and through their local representatives. This is how a free country works.

This vision seems simplistic—until you imagine what's happening beyond the borders of the federal city. There, in a picture so complex no one of us can really understand it, free people are pursuing visions of their own, sacrificing, hoping, earning, producing, trading, building, cooperating—and helping each other of their own accord. It is the picture of the greatest, most generous nation on earth, the example to all nations, trusting once again in the source of her greatness.

Throughout this book I have tried to convey a sense of the possibilities before us. Tyrannies have fallen that we feared were unshakable. People we assumed would be oppressed forever rose up to freedom. Around the world and in our own country, doors opened that we thought were shut for good. And through technology and the free market, new ones open with every passing year. It's the story of our time, and yet we think of it only in episodes, not quite seeing its full implications.

All the exhortations of Big Government, all the programs, all the social "reforms" forced upon us are beginning to look like so many flailing shadows. Out there in the rest of the world, life is stirring, people are reassuming command over their own destinies. While Big Government announces its next great social mission to universal groans and outright rejection, ordinary people begin to see their personal missions more clearly. The plans for America's future are again being made in the kitchens and living rooms, from which our wisest plans and truest visions have always come. To the typical family of today, Big Government is like that towering, unsightly old tree in the front yard that may crash down on the house with the next wind unless it's cut down soon. Americans went to the polls last November with saws in hand.

As Freedom becomes more familiar again, the rhetoric of Big Government takes on a stranger and stranger sound. Two summers ago we were invited to join in the search for a New Politics of Meaning. But there were few volunteers. It was the last moral gasp of statist liberalism, and the monologue was played to an empty house. The annointed dreamers of the New Frontier and Great Society have become the annoying drones of Big Government, and our people have about had it with the whole show. We prefer the New Politics of Freedom, the deeper meaning found in private pursuits, the spiritual independence of personal responsibility.

Instead of federally-funded "Meaning," Americans are going back to church—most never left it. I read recently about an old-fashioned church in Manhattan attended largely by young professionals—in throngs, seven or eight hundred of them. The reason they go, said the article, was to get away from the "social gospel" of politicized churches and learn about the Gospel itself. The unmarried ones reportedly go partly in the hope of meeting more responsible men and women than they find elsewhere, with a view toward marriage. Here too, I suspect, is another sign of the times.

In Washington the government activists still declare their official "Year of the Child" or "Year of the Woman"—those odd new banners for abortion on demand. Meanwhile, the women of America go about the business of marrying and raising children, mostly wishing that government would tax them less and in general get out of the way. Children and the culture they grow up in are still, it turns out, the most urgent of "women's issues"—and men's, too. And so feminism's "war of the sexes" is ending just as it should, in a common concern for the children.

The politicians tell us abortion on demand is "here to stay," haranguing all who are still in doubt. Meanwhile, churches and women's groups form pregnancy crisis centers, homes for unwed mothers, and private adoption channels. And more and more young mothers, defying all the pressures of their worlds, sometimes raising children alone, children the secular world would find too burdensome, are choosing life. In darker moments we asked, "What power can overcome an arrogant court, an indifferent president, the bitterness of mobs, the police barricades, all the lobbyists and editorial boards arrayed against the innocent?" And the answer is right here, in the hearts of America's women. Abortion really is a deeply personal choice, and nothing's more personal than love.

In Washington not long ago I witnessed a huge rally of teenagers whose cause was—abstinence. Everywhere in America, even in our rotting inner cities, you can meet kids just like them. They are the true idealists of today, the true rebels, and person by person they are going to change our society for the better. They defy their own jaded teachers, who tell us how hopeless the situation is and to be "realistic" about teenagers. But more and more teenagers themselves have seen where that "realism" leads. Maybe these young people don't make the news or gossip pages in Washington, but culturally they are the day's top story. "Hopelessness," they remind us, is an adult word.

The coercive approach to social and economic improvement always carried a certain moral despair, the assumption people left to govern themselves would go wrong. Society had to be managed, social progress paid for in tax dollars, compassion made compulsory. Each day in America, in our biggest cities and smallest towns, that assumption is proved repeatedly wrong in uncounted, unheralded acts of personal courage, sacrifice, kindness, fidelity, generosity, and idealism. It was the arrogance of politics that brought about many of the divisions that trouble us. As that bitter spirit passes, we have the opportunity to come together again as a free people.

ARMEY'S AXIOMS

A selection of Dick Armey's observations on politics, the economy, and life itself.

The politics of greed always comes wrapped in the language of love. While liberals have been extraordinarily successful at convincing the public of their higher motives, these higher motives are usually used to conceal their own greed—for political power, social prestige, or just plain money.

A New Democrat is a counterfeit conservative looking for work.

There is nothing more arrogant than a self-righteous income redistributor. The arrogance of liberals as they pursue their supposed higher goods, particularly when they imagine themselves working for the poor and the downtrodden, clouds their clear-thinking and often makes them immune to common sense.

When you're weaned from the milk of sacred cows, you're bound to get heartburn.

To diagnose our problems, we must understand the full anatomy of the political economy—especially the invisible foot of the government. While the concept of the invisible hand of the marketplace is well-understood (if too often ignored), we also need to recognize and accept the visible foot of the market, which plays a necessary role in eliminating inefficient industries. Even more important, we must understand that there is an invisible foot of the government, too, which generally does unnecessary damage even as the visible hand of the government seems to do good.

If you want the government to get off your back, you've got to get your hands out of its pocket.

The market is rational and the government is dumb. There is more wisdom in millions of individuals making decisions in their own self-interest than there is in even the most enlightened bureaucrat (or congressman!) making decisions on their behalf.

Three groups spend other people's money: children, thieves, politicians. All three need parental supervision.

No one spends someone else's money as wisely as he spends his own. A key reason the market system works: When people spend their own money, they care much more deeply about its efficient and productive use than any politicians who seek to tax it away and spend it themselves.

Never trust pessimistic forecasts from people who make a living selling more government.

Never believe it when someone says, 'I'm from the government and I'm here to help.' Free people do not give up their freedom easily, and governments know that. That's why governments have become so skillful in using pretensions of altruism when they try to take a measure of our freedom away from us. We must always be on guard. (A corollary is, "A gentleman protects a lady from everyone but himself.")

Social responsibility is a euphemism for personal irresponsibility.

You can't put your finger on a problem when you've got it to the wind. Risk-evasive "yes men," forever seeking consensus, will achieve nothing but their own mediocrity. Anyone worth his salt must consult current opinion, but obey only his convictions.

It's easier (and more fun) to pass new laws than to enforce existing ones.

You don't have to belong to one of the six talking professions to cause mischief, but it helps. There is a "New Class" of opinion leaders distinguished by their ability to manipulate words. They can be grouped into the six talking professions—politicians, educators, journalists, lawyers (!), theologians, and entertainers. All have their place, but they also happen to be sheltered from the real world, rarely exposed to the consequences of their ideas, and intent on concerning themselves with other people's business. Thus, they're in a position to cause great mischief—and do.

Compassion without understanding can be cruel. Those who seek to use their power and influence for high social goods can inadvertently cause great harm if they do not understand how the world works. A parent who spoils a child, a social engineer who ruins an inner city, a politician who protects an outmoded industry—all prove the point.

A bad idea can survive only if it need not stand the test of reality. One of the many good things about the market economy is that it drives out bad ideas in the form of products and services people refuse to buy. By contrast, such industries as the education establishment and the government do not subject bad ideas to any reality test. Naturally, they become veritable fountains of them.

According to Armey's Curve, governments can eventually become so large that they imperil the very ends they were created to secure. Ours has long since passed that point. Admittedly, the government is necessary—but only to a point. We can plot the size and effectiveness of government on a graph. First, there is an upward slope, as government is not large enough to secure our liberties. But then there is a peak followed by a plunge, in which the government becomes so large that it actually endangers the liberties it was instituted to protect. We're on that downhill slope now.

If you love peace more than freedom, you lose. Without actually saying so, the government seeks to expropriate our freedom in return for greater security—from the hazards of the marketplace, the perplexity of making our own decisions, even the tribulations of life itself. It's a Faustian bargain. If you take it, you lose.

Liberals don't care what you do as long as it's mandatory.